T0183704

Lecture Notes in Computer Science   11516

Commenced Publication in 1973
Founding and Former Series Editors:
Gerhard Goos, Juris Hartmanis, and Jan van Leeuwen

Editorial Board Members

David Hutchison
Lancaster University, Lancaster, UK
Takeo Kanade
Carnegie Mellon University, Pittsburgh, PA, USA
Josef Kittler
University of Surrey, Guildford, UK
Jon M. Kleinberg
Cornell University, Ithaca, NY, USA
Friedemann Mattern
ETH Zurich, Zurich, Switzerland
John C. Mitchell
Stanford University, Stanford, CA, USA
Moni Naor
Weizmann Institute of Science, Rehovot, Israel
C. Pandu Rangan
Indian Institute of Technology Madras, Chennai, India
Bernhard Steffen
TU Dortmund University, Dortmund, Germany
Demetri Terzopoulos
University of California, Los Angeles, CA, USA
Doug Tygar
University of California, Berkeley, CA, USA

More information about this series at http://www.springer.com/series/7409

De Wang · Liang-Jie Zhang (Eds.)

Artificial Intelligence and Mobile Services – AIMS 2019

8th International Conference
Held as Part of the Services Conference Federation, SCF 2019
San Diego, CA, USA, June 25–30, 2019
Proceedings

 Springer

Editors
De Wang
Sunmi US Inc.
Pleasanton, CA, USA

Liang-Jie Zhang 🆔
Kingdee International Software
Group Co., Ltd.
Shenzhen, China

ISSN 0302-9743   ISSN 1611-3349   (electronic)
Lecture Notes in Computer Science
ISBN 978-3-030-23366-2   ISBN 978-3-030-23367-9   (eBook)
https://doi.org/10.1007/978-3-030-23367-9

LNCS Sublibrary: SL3 – Information Systems and Applications, incl. Internet/Web, and HCI

© Springer Nature Switzerland AG 2019
This work is subject to copyright. All rights are reserved by the Publisher, whether the whole or part of the material is concerned, specifically the rights of translation, reprinting, reuse of illustrations, recitation, broadcasting, reproduction on microfilms or in any other physical way, and transmission or information storage and retrieval, electronic adaptation, computer software, or by similar or dissimilar methodology now known or hereafter developed.
The use of general descriptive names, registered names, trademarks, service marks, etc. in this publication does not imply, even in the absence of a specific statement, that such names are exempt from the relevant protective laws and regulations and therefore free for general use.
The publisher, the authors and the editors are safe to assume that the advice and information in this book are believed to be true and accurate at the date of publication. Neither the publisher nor the authors or the editors give a warranty, expressed or implied, with respect to the material contained herein or for any errors or omissions that may have been made. The publisher remains neutral with regard to jurisdictional claims in published maps and institutional affiliations.

This Springer imprint is published by the registered company Springer Nature Switzerland AG
The registered company address is: Gewerbestrasse 11, 6330 Cham, Switzerland

Preface

The 2019 International Conference on AI and Mobile Services (AIMS 2019) aims at providing an international forum that is dedicated to exploring different aspects of AI (from technologies to approaches and algorithms) and mobile services (from business management to computing systems, algorithms, and applications) to promoting technological innovations in research and development of mobile services, including, but not limited to, wireless and sensor networks, mobile and wearable computing, mobile enterprise and e-commerce, ubiquitous collaborative and social services, machine-to-machine and Internet-of-Things clouds, cyber-physical integration, and big data analytics for mobility-enabled services.

AIMS 2019 was part of the Services Conference Federation (SCF). SCF 2019 had the following ten collocated service-oriented sister conferences: 2019 International Conference on Web Services (ICWS 2019), 2019 International Conference on Cloud Computing (CLOUD 2019), 2019 International Conference on Services Computing (SCC 2019), 2019 International Congress on Big Data (BigData 2019), 2019 International Conference on AI and Mobile Services (AIMS 2019), 2019 World Congress on Services (SERVICES 2019), 2019 International Congress on Internet of Things (ICIOT 2019), 2019 International Conference on Cognitive Computing (ICCC 2019), 2019 International Conference on Edge Computing (EDGE 2019), and 2019 International Conference on Blockchain (ICBC 2019). As the founding member of SCF, the First International Conference on Web Services (ICWS) was held in June 2003 in Las Vegas, USA. The First International Conference on Web Services—Europe 2003 (ICWS-Europe 2003) was held in Germany in October 2003. ICWS-Europe 2003 was an extended event of the 2003 International Conference on Web Services (ICWS 2003) in Europe. In 2004, ICWS-Europe was changed to the European Conference on Web Services (ECOWS), which was held in Erfurt, Germany. To celebrate its 16th birthday, SCF 2018 was held successfully in Seattle, USA.

This volume presents the accepted papers for AIMS 2019, held in San Diego, USA, during June 25–30, 2019. The major topics of AIMS 2019 included but were not limited to: AI modeling, AI analysis, AI and mobile applications, AI architecture, AI management, AI engineering, mobile backend as a service (MBaaS), user experience of AI and mobile services.

We accepted 13 papers, including 12 full papers and one short paper. Each was reviewed and selected by three independent members of the AIMS 2019 international Program Committee. We are pleased to thank the authors, whose submissions and participation made this conference possible. We also want to express our thanks to the Program Committee members, for their dedication in helping to organize the conference and in reviewing the submissions. We look forward to your great contributions as a volunteer, author, and conference participant for the fast-growing worldwide services innovations community.

May 2019

De Wang
Liang-Jie Zhang

Organization

Program Chair

De Wang   Sunmi US Inc., USA

Services Conference Federation (SCF 2019)

SCF 2019 General Chairs

Calton Pu	Georgia Tech, USA
Wu Chou	Essenlix Corporation, USA
Ali Arsanjani	8x8 Cloud Communications, USA

SCF 2019 Program Chair

Liang-Jie Zhang   Kingdee International Software Group Co., Ltd., China

SCF 2019 Finance Chair

Min Luo   Services Society, USA

SCF 2019 Industry Exhibit and International Affairs Chair

Zhixiong Chen   Mercy College, USA

SCF 2019 Operations Committee

Huan Chen	Kingdee International Software Group Co., Ltd., China
Jing Zeng	Kingdee International Software Group Co., Ltd., China
Yishuang Ning	Tsinghua University, China
Sheng He	Tsinghua University, China
Liping Deng	Kingdee International Software Group Co., Ltd., China

SCF 2019 Steering Committee

Calton Pu (Co-chair)	Georgia Tech, USA
Liang-Jie Zhang (Co-chair)	Kingdee International Software Group Co., Ltd., China

AIMS 2019 Program Committee

Onur Altintas	Toyota Info Technology Center, USA
Cheng Cai	Northwest A&F University, China
Hao He	Thumbtack, Inc., USA
Shiyin Kang	Tencent AI Lab, China
Fabrizio Lamberti	Politecnico di Torino, Italy
Jialin Liu	Lawrence Berkeley National Lab, USA

Yi Liu	Shenzhen Raisound Technology, China
Shang-Pin Ma	National Taiwan Ocean University, Taiwan
Zakaria Maamar	Zayed University, United Arab Emirates
Rong Shi	The Ohio State University, USA
Weifeng Su	Beijing Normal University, Hong Kong, SAR China
Xiaohui Wang	University of Science and Technology Beijing, China
Ruifeng Xu	Harbin Institute of Technology, Shenzhen, China
Zhen Xu	Google, USA
Yuchao Zhang	Beijing University of Posts and Telecommunications, China
Hongbo Zou	Petuum Inc., USA

Contents

Population-Based Variable Neighborhood Descent for Discrete Optimization

Petar Afric(✉), Adrian Satja Kurdija, Lucija Sikic, Marin Silic, Goran Delac,
Klemo Vladimir, and Sinisa Srbljic

Faculty of Electrical Engineering and Computing,
University of Zagreb, Unska 3, Zagreb, Croatia
{petar.afric,adrian.kurdija,lucija.sikic,marin.silic,
goran.delac,klemo.vladimir,sinisa.srbljic}@fer.hr

Abstract. Many problems in smart solution development make use of discrete optimization techniques. It is expected that smart cities will have a constant need for parcel delivery and vehicle routing which is heavily reliant on discrete optimization. In this paper we present an improvement to the *Variable neighborhood descent* (VND) algorithm for discrete optimization. Our method makes the search procedure more exhaustive at the expense of time performance. Instead of keeping track of a single solution which is being improved, we allow branching of the solution into at most M promising solutions and keep track of them. Our experiments show that the proposed method produces results superior to VND. We analyze the impact on time complexity and give general usage guidelines for our method.

Keywords: Variable neighborhood descent · Population ·
Discrete optimization · Capacitated vehicle routing problem

1 Introduction

Discrete optimization often occurs in AI and smart solution development. It interacts with AI development whenever there is a need to optimize on discrete sets. Examples of smart solution development include vehicle routing problem and its variances [1,2], bin packing problem and its variances [3,4], network planning [5], knapsack problem [6], assignment problem [7], transportation problem [8], and many other problems which are becoming increasingly relevant in the context of smart cities.

In the last decades there has been a huge advancement in hardware technology. This has allowed for massively parallel systems. The algorithm presented in this work is motivated by exploiting this fact in order to improve the existing optimization techniques. A massive parallelization allows exploration of a much larger search space, which is done by branching the search into promising search directions and then investigating each of them concurrently.

© Springer Nature Switzerland AG 2019
D. Wang and L.-J. Zhang (Eds.): AIMS 2019, LNCS 11516, pp. 1–12, 2019.
https://doi.org/10.1007/978-3-030-23367-9_1

Variable neighborhood descent (VND) is a meta-heuristic method described by Duarte, Sanchez-Oro, Mladenovic and Todosijevic in [9] for solving combinatorial optimization problems. The algorithm is shown in Algorithm 1. It explores the neighborhoods of the incumbent solution and iterates as long as it can find an improving solution. Namely, it keeps a list of neighborhood generation strategies (ways of modifying a candidate solution) and applies them to the current solution one at a time. If an improving solution is found among neighbors generated from a certain strategy, then the current solution is set to the improving solution and the next iteration is started from the first strategy. If a neighborhood generation strategy cannot produce an improving solution, the next strategy is examined. If no strategy can produce an improving solution, the algorithm stops and the current solution is returned as the search result. Notice that this ensures that the solution returned is a local optimum with respect to the defined neighborhood generation strategies.

Algorithm 1. Variable neighborhood descent

$x \leftarrow startingSolution$
$k \leftarrow 0$ (neighborhood strategy index)
while $k < neighborhoodGenerationStrategies.size()$ **do**
    $strategy \leftarrow neighborhoodGenerationStrategies[k]$
    $neighbors \leftarrow strategy.generateNeighborsOf(x)$
    $y \leftarrow neighbors.selectBetterThan(x)$
    if y *is not None* **then**
        $x \leftarrow y$
        $k \leftarrow 0$
    else
        $k \leftarrow k + 1$
    end if
end while
return x

VND is often used as a local search procedure for the VNS (Variable neighborhood search) algorithm [10]. Also, it has been heavily used in various applications such as routing problems [1,2], packing problems [3,4], scheduling problems [11,12] and many others.

We point out that in VND, only one improving solution is being selected. Although [9] specifies that the best improving solution in the neighborhood is selected, this is not necessary and can be changed to a different strategy. One can select the first improving, best improving, random improving or some other improving solution. If there are multiple improving solutions, only one of them will be selected. This can result in a convergence towards a local optimum instead of a global optimum. In order to alleviate this effect, we propose branching into a population of solutions. We call this variation of the VND algorithm the *Population-based variable neighborhood descent* and describe it in the following sections.

The rest of the paper is organized as follows. The proposed algorithm is described in Sect. 2. Section 3 describes the experimental results achieved using the proposed algorithm in relation to the base algorithm. It also discusses the time complexity and gives usage advice for the proposed algorithm. Conclusions are given in Sect. 4.

2 Proposed Algorithm

By introducing a population of current solutions, we are expanding the search, making it less likely to get stuck in local optima. The population is limited to M units to prevent an explosion of solutions whose neighborhoods are searched. The proposed algorithm is shown in Algorithm 2. *Improving neighbors* are those better than the best solution in the current population. The next population is formed by selecting at most M units from the set of improving neighbors of all current solutions. If there are none, the next neighborhood generation strategy is examined. When the algorithm cannot find any improving solution for any strategy, the best solution in the last population is returned as the result.

Although the members of the population seem independent at first they share information through the fact that their neighbors can only become candidates for the next population if they are better then the best solution in the current population.

If the maximum population size M is set to 1, the algorithm becomes the VND algorithm. Therefore, the proposed algorithm can be seen as a generalization of VND.

Algorithm 2. Population based variable neighborhood descent

```
population[0] ← startingSolution
k ← 0    (neighborhood strategy index)
while k < neighborhoodGenerationStrategies.size() do
    strategy ← neighborhoodGenerationStrategies[k]
    neighbors ← ∅
    x ← BestIn(population)
    for solution in population do
        neighbors ← neighbors ∪
            strategy.generateNeighborsOf(solution, betterThan=x)
    end for
    y ← neighbors.select(M)
    if y is not None then
        population ← y
        k ← 0
    else
        k ← k + 1
    end if
end while
return BestIn(population)
```

Selecting the next population among the improving neighbors of all current solutions can be done in various ways. There are three main selection strategies:

- *Randomly* select M among all improving neighbors.
- Select the *best* M among all improving neighbors. — This selection strategy leads to a quicker convergence; however, the result might be only a local optimum.
- Select the *first* M improving neighbors. — This selection strategy speeds up the iteration, but can result in inferior quality or a higher number of iterations.

3   Evaluation

We performed experiments comparing VND and our algorithm on capacity vehicle routing problem (CVRP), using several similar search strategies. The aim of the experiment was not to produce the best possible results on the given dataset, but to show that a population-based variable neighborhood descent will on average outperform the VND algorithm in solution quality. Therefore, we do not present the absolute achieved results, but only the relative improvement (*reduction*) in the quality of the obtained solution. The evaluation code is available at[1].

Section 3.1 presents the evaluation results on CVRP instances. Section 3.2 provides complexity analysis of the proposed approach compared to the base VND approach. Finally, Sect. 3.3 provides useful tips and advices while using the approach.

3.1   Capacity Vehicle Routing Problem

Capacity vehicle routing problem is a well known problem in combinatorial optimization.

The capacity vehicle routing problem is defined as follows:

- There are N customers.
- Customer nodes are indexed from $i \in \{1, ..., N\}$.
- The commodity should be delivered using K independent delivery vehicles of identical capacity C.
- Each customer $i \in \{1, ..., N\}$ requires a quantity q_i of a commodity being delivered. $q_i \in \{1, ..., C\} \forall i \in \{1, ..., N\}$.
- All deliveries start from node 0 which marks the central depot.
- For each transit from node i to node j there is an associated cost c_{ij}. The cost structure is assumed to be symmetric $c_{ij} = c_{ji}, \forall i, j \in \{0, 1, ..., N\}$. And the cost of transit from a node to itself is always 0, $c_{ii} = 0, \forall i \in \{0, 1, ..., N\}$
- If a devicer vehicle $k \in 1, ..., K$ travels from node i to node j then $x_{kij} = 1$ otherwise $x_{kij} = 0$.

---

[1] https://github.com/pa1511/CVRP-POP_VND.

- Each customer node can only be visited by a single delivery vehicle. It is not possible to split a delivery among multiple delivery vehicles.
- The aim is to minimize the total travel distance of all delivery trucks.

This can formally be defined as follows:

$$\text{minimize} \quad \sum_{i,j \in \{0,...,N\}, \, k \in \{1,...,K\}} x_{i,j,k} \cdot c_{ij} \quad \text{subject to:} \tag{1}$$

$$\sum_{j \in \{0,...,N\}, \, k \in \{1,...,K\}} x_{i,j,k} = 1, \quad \forall i \in \{1,...,N\} \tag{2}$$

$$\sum_{i \in \{0,...,N\}, \, k \in \{1,...,K\}} x_{i,j,k} = 1, \quad \forall j \in \{1,...,N\} \tag{3}$$

$$\sum_{j \in \{1,...,N\}, \, k \in \{1,...,K\}} x_{0,j,k} = k \tag{4}$$

$$\sum_{i \in \{1,...,N\}, \, k \in \{1,...,K\}} x_{i,0,k} = k \tag{5}$$

$$\sum_{i \in \{1,...,N\}, \, j \in \{0,...,N\}} x_{i,j,k} \cdot q_i \leq C, \quad \forall k \in \{1,...,K\} \tag{6}$$

We used the Augerat 1995 dataset from the CVRPLIB dataset [13]. We defined three different neighborhood generation strategies: one merges two routes into one, one swaps stations between two routes, and one moves the station from one route to another. For each change, the route is re-optimized using a simple TSP solver. In the starting solution, the number of routes is equal to the number of stations and each route contains a single station.

We solved the dataset using VND with three different selection strategies. One strategy selects the best improving neighbor, one selects the first improving neighbor, and one selects a random improving neighbor. The dataset was solved 100 times per strategy. The average solution length for all instances of VND is:

- 679 for RANDOM strategy,
- 686 for FIRST strategy and
- 687 for BEST strategy.

This information is provided in the hopes it will help readers get a better feeling for the performance improvement of the proposed algorithm.

We solved the same dataset with our proposed algorithm using the same neighborhood generation strategies, with and without strategy shuffling (permuting the list of neighborhood generation strategies from iteration to iteration), using the same starting solution, and using three similar selection strategies: one selects M *best* improving solutions, where M is the maximum population size; one selects M *first* improving solutions, and one selects M *random* improving solutions. We use population sizes ranging from $M = 5$ to $M = 15$. The dataset was solved 100 times per strategy per population size. Parallelization was not used in Population based VND in these experiments. The achieved results by similar strategies are presented in Figs. 1, 2 and 3. These figures help visualize the relationship between the population size and the route length reduction, as well as the effect of strategy shuffling. We filtered out outlier results which deviated more then one standard deviation from the average result per strategy per population size. The results show that, on average, shorter routes were produced by our proposed algorithm: *length reduction* is a relative difference of the proposed solution from the VND solution.

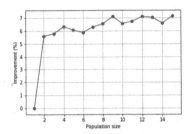

(a) Avg. route length reduction

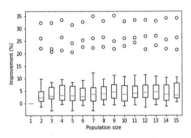

(b) Route length reduction

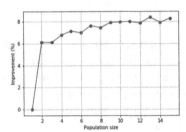

(c) Avg. route length reduction with shuffling

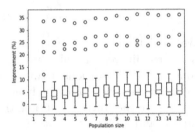

(d) Route length reduction with shuffling

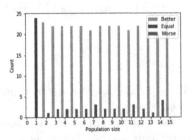

(e) Number of instances solved better/equal/worse than VND

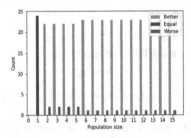

(f) Number of instances solved (using shuffling) better/equal/worse than VND

Fig. 1. Route length reduction for RANDOM selection strategy

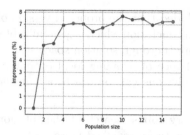

(a) Avg. route length reduction

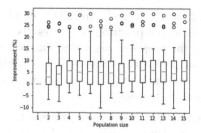

(b) Route length reduction

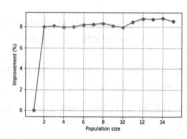

(c) Avg. route length reduction with shuffling

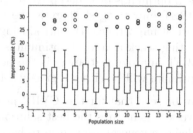

(d) Route length reduction with shuffling

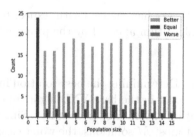

(e) Number of instances solved better/equal/worse than VND

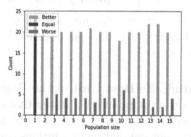

(f) Number of instances solved (using shuffling) better/equal/worse than VND

Fig. 2. Route length reduction for FIRST selection strategy

Figure 4 shows the relationship between the population size and execution time of the algorithm for different strategies. It is important to note that the figure shows an execution time comparison between a Population-based VND and a VND using the same strategy. The execution time is presented as a time increase factor. For example, factor of 1 corresponds to the time which is equal to the execution time of the VND algorithm. Factor of 2 corresponds to the time which is twice the time of the original algorithm etc. From the presented data we can see a linear correlation between the time increase and the population size.

From the presented results it can be concluded that the proposed version of the algorithm produces better results. This is a conclusion which is generalizable. Since the proposed algorithm allows for a more thorough solution space search, in non deceptive problems it has a higher chance of avoiding local optimums and reaching the global optimum. Also, conclusions can be drawn about the presented strategies:

- RANDOM improving strategy makes a very robust search of the solution space. By allowing a population of solutions to be searched more paths are being investigated. This is a good strategy to use if a problem has a lot of local optimums or is deceptive in nature.
- FIRST improving strategy is the best candidate when execution time is of critical importance. By introducing a population of solutions the chance of getting stuck in a local optimum is reduced.
- BEST improving strategy is the best candidate when we suspect the global optimum will be either a greedy solution or very similar to it.

It can be seen that for this CVRP problem the RANDOM improving strategy, on average, generates the best solutions. This is an expected result, since VRP problems in general are known to have local optimums.

3.2   Time Complexity Analysis

In this section we examine how the time performance has changed with respect to VND and discuss three sections of the VND algorithm affected by the proposed changes.

Finding the Best Unit in the Population. Determining the best solution in the current population is a step that does not exist in the base VND algorithm. In this step, the best out of the current population of solutions is identified. Since the current population of solutions can have at most M solutions, the worst case complexity of this step is $O(M)$.

Item Neighborhood Generation. In the base version of VND, one neighborhood per iteration is generated. Here we are generating between 1 and M neighborhoods per iteration. Under the assumption that neighborhood generation generates approximately the same size neighborhood for each solution given the fact that we are generating upto M neighborhoods if both algorithms are run sequentially (without parallelization), our algorithm will be M times slower if the population size is maximal in each iteration, which is the worst case. If neighborhood generation can generate neighborhoods of significantly different sizes for different solutions then it is possible for our algorithm to be more then M times slower if it is generating M neighborhoods in each iteration. If the neighborhoods are generated concurrently, where a separate thread generates the neighborhood of each solution in the population, this factor is reduced. The complexity of generating a single neighborhood depends on the problem at hand and the generation strategy.

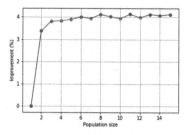

(a) Avg. route length reduction

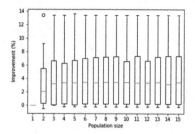

(b) Route length reduction

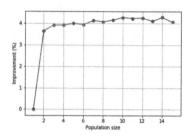

(c) Avg. route length reduction with shuffling

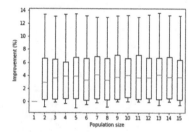

(d) Route length reduction with shuffling

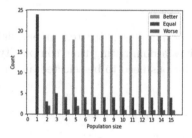

(e) Number of instances solved better/equal/worse than VND

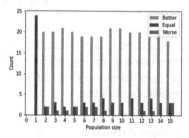

(f) Number of instances solved (using shuffling) better/equal/worse than VND

Fig. 3. Route length reduction for BEST selection strategy

Selecting the Next Population. In this step only selecting the next population out of candidate neighbours is considered. If less then M improving neighbors are found then regardless of strategy all improving are set as the next population and this has time complexity $O(1)$. If more then M improving neighbors are found then the time required to select the next population (M units out of all improving neighbors) depends on the selection strategy, the amount of available improving neighbors, and whether parallelization is utilized. If *first* M improving neighbors are immediately received from the threads and selected, the effect of this step is $O(1)$. On the other hand, if *best* M or *random* M improving neighbors are selected, receiving (at most) M neighbors from each of (at most)

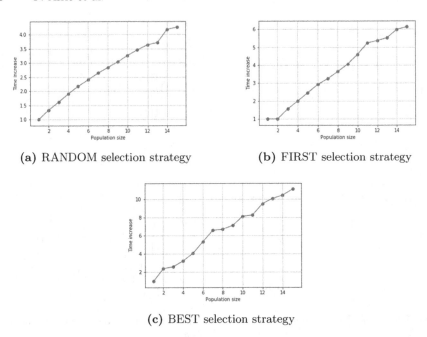

(a) RANDOM selection strategy   **(b)** FIRST selection strategy

(c) BEST selection strategy

Fig. 4. Time increase

M neighborhoods, assuming that each neighborhood is generated in parallel and keeps track of its improving solutions, gives a dominating time complexity of $O(M^2)$ per iteration since M improving solutions need to be selected among M^2 possible candidates.

3.3   Usage Advice

In order to get the most out of the proposed algorithm, we give some guidelines to improve quality and/or time performance of the implementation. We divide the guidelines into suggestions for quality and suggestions for time performance, noting that sometimes there is a trade-off between these two properties.

Suggestions for Quality. *Find a starting solution as good as possible.* A better starting solution should reduce the average population size per iteration and the number of algorithm iterations. This will reduce the overall execution time of the algorithm. The proposed algorithm is best used for the *intensification* phase of the optimization procedure, after a reasonable starting solution has already been found.

Permute the strategies between iterations. Permuting the list of neighborhood generation strategies from iteration to iteration adds to the randomness of the search procedure and can often help produce better solutions. This claim is supported by our experimental results which are presented in Figs. 1, 2 and 3.

Select a larger population when possible. Selecting a larger population will add to the execution time of the algorithm, but will make the search procedure more exhaustive and thus increase the chance of producing better solutions. This claim is supported by our experimental results which are presented in Figs. 1, 2 and 3.

Suggestions for Time Performance. *Sort the strategies in ascending order by size.* If the neighborhood generation strategies are not being permuted between iterations (see Subsect. 3.3), sorting them in ascending order by the number of generated neighbors could help reduce the overall execution time, because then the faster strategies are used more often. This, however, depends on the assumption that different strategies have a similar chance of producing an improving neighbor, which is sometimes not the case.

Parallelize the neighborhood generation step. If the resources are available, the neighborhood of each solution in the population can be generated concurrently, in a separate thread, since the generated neighborhoods are mutually independent. This will often be a very significant reduction in the overall execution time. Each thread can send every improving neighbor (as soon as found) to the main thread. Using a *first M* selection strategy, when a total of M improving neighbors are received by the main thread, the neighborhood generation can be aborted. Note that, when neighbors of a single solution are examined, if more than M improving solutions are found, only M of them can be returned to the main procedure because at most M will ultimately be selected. This implies that a list of improving solutions can be pre-filtered in a neighborhood-generating thread, depending on the selection strategy.

4   Conclusion

We have presented a new variation of the VND algorithm for discrete optimization, applicable to many combinatorial problems in smart solution development such as capacity vehicle routing problem. By introducing a population of current solutions, we have made the algorithm more exhaustive and thus able to produce better solutions. The algorithm should be used for the intensification phase of solving the optimization problem. The increase in execution time is alleviated by parallelization and justified by the production of better search results. For the capacity vehicle routing problem, we have showed the superiority of the proposed algorithm over VND. Future work in this area will explore ways of determining improving solutions, hybrid algorithms, and other applications in the context of intelligent services.

Acknowledgment. This research has been partly supported by the European Regional Development Fund under the grant KK.01.1.1.01.0009 (DATACROSS).

The authors acknowledge the support of the **Croatian Science Foundation** through the *Reliable Composite Applications Based on Web Services* (**IP-01-2018-6423**) research project.

The Titan X Pascal used for this research was donated by the NVIDIA Corporation.

References

1. Schittekat, P., Kinable, J., Sörensen, K., Sevaux, M., Spieksma, F., Springael, J.: A metaheuristic for the school bus routing problem with bus stop selection. Eur. J. Oper. Res. **229**(2), 518–528 (2013)
2. Harzi, M., Krichen, S.: Variable neighborhood descent for solving the vehicle routing problem with time windows. Electron. Notes Discrete Math. **58**, 175–182 (2017)
3. Dahmani, N., Krichen, S., Ghazouani, D.: A variable neighborhood descent approach for the two-dimensional bin packing problem. Electron. Notes Discrete Math. **47**, 117–124 (2015)
4. Zudio, A., da Silva Costa, D.H., Masquio, B.P., Coelho, I.M., Pinto, P.E.D.: Brkga/vnd hybrid algorithm for the classic three-dimensional bin packing problem. Electron Notes Discrete Math. **66**, 175–182 (2018)
5. Oliveira, G.C., Costa, A.P.C., Binato, S.: Large scale transmission network planning using optimization and heuristic techniques. IEEE Trans. Power Syst. **10**(4), 1828–1834 (1995)
6. Feng, Y., Wang, G.G., Deb, S., Lu, M., Zhao, X.J.: Solving 0–1 Knapsack problem by a novel binary Monarch butterfly optimization. Neural Comput. Appl. **28**(7), 1619–1634 (2017)
7. Taha, H.A.: Operations Research: An Introduction, 8th edn. Prentice-Hall Inc., Upper Saddle River (2006)
8. Reinfeld, N., Vogel, W.: Mathematical Programming. Prentice-Hall, Upper Saddle River (1958)
9. Gendreau, M., Potvin, J.Y. (eds.): Handbook of Metaheuristics, vol. 2. Springer, Cham (2010). https://doi.org/10.1007/978-3-319-91086-4
10. Mladenović, N., Hansen, P.: Variable neighborhood search. Comput. Oper. Res. **24**(11), 1097–1100 (1997)
11. Lamghari, A., Dimitrakopoulos, R., Ferland, J.A.: A hybrid method based on linear programming and variable neighborhood descent for scheduling production in open-pit mines. J. Glob. Optim. **63**(3), 555–582 (2015)
12. Gao, J., Sun, L., Gen, M.: A hybrid genetic and variable neighborhood descent algorithm for flexible job shop scheduling problems. Comput. Oper. Res. **35**(9), 2892–2907 (2008)
13. Uchoa, E., Pecin, D., Pessoa, A., Poggi, M., Vidal, T., Subramanian, A.: New benchmark instances for the capacitated vehicle routing problem. Eur. J. Oper. Res. **257**(3), 845–858 (2017)

The Constrained GAN with Hybrid Encoding in Predicting Financial Behavior

Yuhang Zhang[1,2], Wensi Yang[1,2], Wanlin Sun[1,3], Kejiang Ye[1(✉)], Ming Chen[1], and Cheng-Zhong Xu[4]

[1] Shenzhen Institutes of Advanced Technology, Chinese Academy of Sciences, Shenzhen 518055, China
kj.ye@siat.ac.cn
[2] University of Chinese Academy of Sciences, Beijing 100049, China
[3] Northeast Normal University, Changchun 130024, China
[4] Department of Computer and Information Science, Faculty of Science and Technology, State Key Laboratory of IoT for Smart City, University of Macau, Macau SAR, China

Abstract. Financial data are often used in predicting users' behaviors in business fields. The previous work usually focuses on the positive samples which means those specific persons can bring the profit to companies. However, in most cases, the proportion of positive samples is very small. The traditional algorithms do not perform well when the positive and negative samples are extremely unbalanced. To solve this problem, we propose an integrated network. Meanwhile, the original dataset includes both objective and index data, our method integrates the one-hot encoding and float encoding together to uniform the data which named hybrid encoding. Then, the article uses GAN framework to overcome the shortcoming of unbalanced dataset. Finally, voting rules put both data sensitive and data insensitive classifiers together to make a strong classifier. We evaluated the performance of our framework on a real world dataset and experimental results show that our method is effective, with 5%($\pm$0.5%) to 87% improvement in accuracy as compared with other methods mentioned in this paper.

Keywords: Hybrid encoding · GAN · Mahalanobis distance · Financial data

1 Introduction

Bigdata is the foundation of the machine learning. A lot of financial companies including most of the banks value the power of the data. In 2015, the global card fraud rate was 7.76BP[1](The amount of fraud per 10,000 dollars.). The report of UK antifraud agency CIFAS[2] said that their own agency and affiliates

---

[1] http://tenlearning.cn/.
[2] https://www.cifas.org.uk/.

© Springer Nature Switzerland AG 2019
D. Wang and L.-J. Zhang (Eds.): AIMS 2019, LNCS 11516, pp. 13–27, 2019.
https://doi.org/10.1007/978-3-030-23367-9_2

had prevented a total loss about 1 billion pounds by using 325,000 records and related algorithms. In China, many banks and financial enterprises lose more than billions of Yuan per year because of financial fraud. Those are few examples happened in predicting financial fraud, but it can be concluded that can prevent enormous economic losses if financial behaviors forecasts can be deployed to more institutions.

According to the previous data, fraud detection is an important application in predicting financial behaviors [1]. The fraud events are detected from the real huge datasets which record different information about clients and their transaction data. Researchers usually sort those behaviors [2] into different categories and then to solve corresponding problems. There are some common applications in financial fraud detection, such as outlier detection [3,4], clustering and regression. With the increase of the fraud behaviors, people use more approaches to identify the fraud events. Data mining [5] is a necessary technology in fraud detection. In the early stage, data mining with PCA [6], SVM [7] and other methods have made progress in this field. Meanwhile, statistical models such as Naive Bayes [8–10], belief stage [11] and logistic model [12] are appeared in real applications. Starting from 2000, with the rapid development of computer technology and blowout of data volume, some unsupervised [13,14] algorithms and neural networks [15,16] have attracted people's attention, fuzzy neural network [17] is also included in it.

Especially in recent years, deep learning [18,19] is widely used for forecasting and has made a lot of research achievements in academic field. At the same time, industry and academia also combine [20] statistical model and deep learning to achieve a better result.

We compare some main methods in the following figure in order to show a clearer illustration (Fig. 1).

Comparison of main approaches		
Classifiers	Strengthens	Weaknesses
Neural Networks	This algorithm can get accurate results based on complex features.	This algorithm relies on network structure and easily causes over-fitting.
Naïve Bayes	It has strong theoretical feasibility.	Artificial analysis causes subjective influence
Logistic Regression	It is robust and its results are reliable.	Low accuracy rate when classifications over two
Statistical Models	It is easy to understand the model behavior and to assess the model's ability.	Decreased performance as features increase.
AdaBoost	Simple design structure.	High consumption of computer resources.

Fig. 1. Algorithms summary

In this study, we are motivated by the fact that citizens' deposits in banks are usually used for centralized investment by financial institutions. It is necessary for banks to predict those potential customers. We design an efficient algorithm for deposit prediction based on an existing real dataset[3] (Fig. 2).

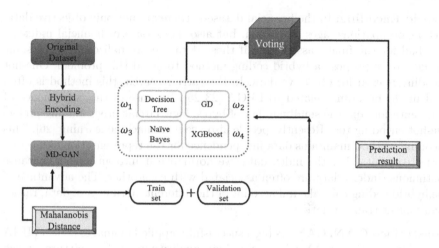

Fig. 2. Integrated network

Our contributions are as follows:
(1) Compared with other studies, different data attributes were taken into account in the algorithm of this paper and then different coding methods were adopted. (2) We restrict the GAN and make it more robust, especially under the condition that the data distributions are approximate.

2   Related Work

Comparing with earlier data volume, today's data are always huge. So, people can not label data like before, and the useful positive samples with labels are very few in the whole dataset. The network has to learn more nonsense information instead of useful features. Meanwhile, the study of Generative Adversarial Nets (GAN) [21] provides us a new idea to exploit the power of data, according to the application of image processing [22], we can further use it in other fields.

Data attributes influence a lot in the following procedure, it can decide which classifier you will use and also indicate the method that used in learning features. This problem pushes us to think twice how to process the original data before it passed to classifiers and do not influence the data attributes at the same time. Data encoding is a normal method to represent raw data, one-hot encoding [23] has been proved that is an efficient way in machine learning to keep data

---

[3] The dataset source: https://archive.ics.uci.edu/ml/datasets/Bank+Marketing.

attributes. We notice that it is unreliable when relying on only one encoding method. Inspired by some popular algorithms [24] in deep learning. Through observation, we find that the data always can be divided into two categories, one is no correlation between data, we call it objective data. Another part of the data is index data, and we need to consider its numerical attributes.

Hybrid Encoding: In the financial datasets, there are not only objective data, such as occupations, ages and so on, but also index data of financial industry. It is bad for the final classification if those data are normalized into the same format, so we propose a hybrid coding method to avoid this problem. One-hot encoding is used for objective data. In the early research, this method is often used in the encoding related to FPGA [23,25]. Because of the convenience of representation and the small number of bytes, logic circuit programming prefers one-hot encoding too. Recently, people also use it in machine learning [26]. This encoding method maintains data independence for the representation of discrete (objective) data. For the index data, we normalize it into an integer, because continuous (index) data are often associated with each other. The advantage of the hybrid coding can take full account of the different attributes of data, rather than violent transformation.

Constrained GAN: GAN has been successfully applied in images [27]. NVIDIA group [28] used the GAN to generate high quality human face pictures which are very similar to real face. This technology has developed quiet well and is constantly applied to various applications, fake pictures made by GAN are hard to be distinguished by human eyes today. Actually, GAN uses the KL divergence to do the optimization. However, we find that the distribution of positive and negative samples in dataset are very similar, so we introduce the MD [29] as the constraint in the GAN. With the help of MD, the new generated positive samples are closer to the original data.

Integrated Classifiers: The successful application of AdaBoost [30] tells us that the combination of weak classifiers can become a strong classifier. In fact, the idea of model fusion comes from industry more. Industry often uses the different advantages of multiple models to integrate a better performance model [31]. This method can often achieve better experimental results. But in practical application, we find that is not so simple to apply, it still need to select the better performanced classifiers, and combine them according by the voting rules. In this process, the important thing is to drop those classifiers with the worst results.

3   Designed Method

3.1   Hybrid Encoding

STEP 1: Our work distinguishes the data which is discrete (objective) or continuous (index). For discrete data, we encode it by the one-hot encoding. Two-bit binary numbers can represent four different combinations. There are no more than nine sub-categories in our dataset, so 4-bit binary digits can meet the requirement. Every main feature is encoded by four-bit binary, even though some contain only a few categories. We process data like this because that can prevent the difference of binary digits between different categories from affecting the result of classification. Experiments show that the uniform representation of digits can ultimately improve the accuracy by $1\% - 2\%$, and it won't bring the dimension disaster.

STEP 2: The continuous data are unified into numerical data within 10. The maxi-mum occurrence is assigned 10, and the minimum occurrence is 0.

STEP 3: After forming the data according to the above encoding methods, one-hot encoding are put in the high position and continuous data are put in the low position to form such a data sequence. As shown in the Table 1.

Table 1. The format of hybrid encoding

One-hot Encoding 1	One-hot Encoding 2	One-hot Encoding N	Continous data 1	Continous data 2	Continous data N
1101	...	0010	9	...	6

3.2 Constrained GAN

GAN often used in the field of image classification and video tracking, but in the application scenario of financial data, we can still turn the data into corresponding pixel values. Even if every data is meaningless pixel values, the corresponding pictures are statistically significant. In this case, positive samples are changed into corresponding pixel [22] values to form a picture. These pictures are sent into the new network for training to produce new pictures, then the pictures are converted into corresponding data. This process can complete the whole enrichment of positive samples.

The objective of optimization can be written as:

$$MinMax[V(G,D)] = \mathbb{E}_{x \in P_{data}}[logD(x)] + \mathbb{E}_{z \in P_z}[log(1 - D(Z))] \tag{1}$$

To optimiz the discriminator, we need to train the discriminator continuously so that it can identify the probability from the real data to the largest. We can rewrite the Eq. (1) as:

$$V(G,D) = P_{data}(x)logD(x) + P_z(Z)log(1 - D(Z)) \tag{2}$$

Then, the solution D' is:

$$D' = \frac{P_{data}(x)}{P_{data}(x) + P_z(Z)} \tag{3}$$

Bringing (3) back to (2):

$$V(G,D') = \mathbb{E}_{x \in P_{data}} \left[log \frac{P_{data}(x)}{P_{data}(x) + P_z(Z)} \right]$$
$$+ P_z \left[log \left(1 - D \left(\frac{P_z(Z)}{P_{data}(x) + P_z(Z)} \right) \right) \right] \tag{4}$$

K-L [32] is used to measure the similarity between two probabilities, it can be defined as:

$$D_{KL}(P\|Q) = \sum_{i=1}^{N} P(x_i) log \frac{P(x_i)}{Q(x_i)} \tag{5}$$

With the K-L, we can further rewrite (4) in:

$$V(G, D') = -2log2 + KL(P_{data}(x)\|A) + KL(P_z(Z)\|A) \tag{6}$$

$$A = \frac{P_{data}(x) + P_z(Z)}{2} \tag{7}$$

Now, our next goal is to minimize $P_z(Z)log(1 - D(Z))$. According to the method of gradient descent, we can get the following results by using D', the P'_Z is the solution of G:

$$P_z' \leftarrow (P_z - \eta \partial V(G, D^*)) \tag{8}$$

The MD is defined as:

$$D_{MD}^2 = (x - m)^T C^{-1}(x - m) \tag{9}$$

$$C = (x - m)(x - m)^T \tag{10}$$

x represents the whole pattern vectors, m means one of specific vector in the whole. In this paper, we use $data(x)$ replaces x, z means m. The constrained GAN is:

$$f_{goal} = V(G^*, D^*) + \lambda(P_{data}(x) - P_z(Z))^T C^{-1}(P_{data}(x) - P_z(Z)) \tag{11}$$

This formula (11) is introduced into GAN as a new objective function, from which some newly generated data can be obtained.

3.3   Integrated Classifiers

In the experiment, we found that the positive and negative sample distributions of some attributes are very similar. It is the reason why we choose different methods to integrate a stronger classifier. According to the latest paper [33], if the distributions of the two kinds of data are similar, it is hard to find a way to separate the two kinds of data away clearly. The practical approach is to integrate different classifiers, and the different features can be used effectively by different classifiers.

Firstly, we tested some common classification algorithms. For example, Decision tree model and Random Forest model. Due to the simplification of algorithm and flexibility in handling the multiple data attribute types, Decision tree [34, 35] are widely used in classification problem. Random Forest [36] is a combination of multiple tree predictors such that each tree depends on a random independent dataset and all trees in the forest are the same distribution.

Then, in order to further understand the performance of weak classifiers are integrated into strong classifiers, this paper further tested the performance of some classifiers, such as AdaBoost, XGBoost and Gradient Boosting. Adaboost is the original edition of weak classifier integrated into the strong classifier. However, unlike AdaBoost, Gradient Boosting [37] chooses the direction of gradient descent in iteration to ensure that the final result is the best, Gradient Boosting can achieve highly accurate. XGBoost [38] implements machine learning algorithms under the Gradient Boosting framework. It is an optimized distributed gradient boosting library which is used by data scientists to achieve state-of-the-art results on many machine learning challenges. Compared with the Gradient Boosting, the advantage of XGBoost is a regular term added to it first. Then, the error of XGBoost loss function is second-order Taylor expansion and Gradient Boosting is first-order Taylor expansion, so the loss function approximation is more accurate.

Last, due to the outstanding performance of Multi-layer Perceptron (MLP) [39] and Naive Bayes in classification tasks, these two algorithms are also included in our candidate list. As the initial model of neural network, MLP has been used in a variety of applications. Performances in some statistical models can be improved in the neural networks. The Naive Bayes [40] method is a set of supervised learning algorithms. It is based on Bayes theory and assumes that each pair of features is independent. Although the assumption is simple, Naïve Bayes classifier works well on many real classification problems, such as document classification and spam filtering. It only needs a small amount of training data to estimate the necessary parameters. Linear Regression (LR) [41] [42] and Stochastic Gradient Descent (SGD) [43] added to this framework, however, the performances are not satisfied.

Table 2. Recall of different classifiers in predicting positive samples. The ratio in Table. 2 represents the ratio of positive samples to negative samples. In practice, we found such an interesting phenomenon: not the more joint cascaded classifiers mean the better result. Because some classifiers have the negative impact on the results, we have to discard some of them which has poor result, that is why we chose 4 form 9 classifiers finally.

Recall of positive samples				
Classifiers	1 : 1	1 : 10	1 : 20	1 : 30
LR	0.60	0.04	0.02	0.01
Decision tree	0.68	0.28	0.11	**0.21**
AdaBoost	0.75	0.29	0.09	0.02
Random Forest	0.72	0.28	0.07	0.04
Gradient Boosting	0.78	0.24	0.18	0.14
XGBoost	**0.79**	0.25	0.09	0.03
SGD	0.67	0.02	0.01	0.01
MLP	0.65	0.14	0.07	0.01
Naive Bayes	0.68	**0.37**	**0.33**	0.20

After comprehensive measurement, we chose the final four classifiers: Decision Tree, Gradient Boosting (GB), XGBoost and Naive Bayes[4]. The voting rules are defined as:

$$\mathbb{P}(x) = \omega_1 * P_{Decisiontree} + \omega_2 * P_{NaiveBayes} + \omega_3 * P_{GB} + \omega_4 * P_{XGBoost} \quad (12)$$

In Eq. (12), ω means the weight of final training within $[0, 1]$, and P represents the possibility of current prediction.

Here, we need to explain a question. GB and XGBoost are very similar, why we keep both two methods? In fact, after our experiments, the comprehensive experimental results of deleting GB are not better than preserve it, so we chose to retain them both.

3.4   Algorithm Framework

Algorithm 1. The Constrained GAN with Hybrid Encoding Network. The original data is represented as an array by original_data[m][n], the function Transform() means transform data to specific type.

Input: The dataset with 20 features.
Output: A binary-classification result in probabilistic form.
  Hybrid_Encoding()
    // *Picking the objetive data from dataset and encoding them in one-hot way.*
    one-hot_encoding[p][n'] = Transform(original_data[p]);
    // *Using the rest of dataset to encode in integer data.*
    index_data[p][n-n'] = Transform(original_data[p]);
    Hybrid_Encoding[m][n] = index_data + one-hot_encoding;
  Constrained_GAN()
    // *Transforming all the original data to integer data.*
    processed_data[m][n] = Transform(original_data[m][n]);
    picture_format[ ] ⟵ processed_data[x];
    Split(picture_format[])
    $f_{goal} = V(G^*, D^*) + \lambda(P_{data}(x) - P_z(Z))^T C^{-1}(P_{data}(x) - P_z(Z));$
    new_positive_samples[][] = Inverse_transformation[][];
    new_data[][] = new_positive_samples + original_data;
  main()
    Hybrid_Encoding();
    X = Constrained_GAN();
    For each iteration i=1,2,...N do:
      train(X);

---

[4] We used Gaussian distribution in this model. Well, people can implement other distribution functions.

4 Experiments

4.1 Data Analysis

This dataset contains some basic information about customers. It includes ages, occupations, education and some macroeconomic indicators of the current time. A total of 20 features data, including about 40,000 customer information, of which more than 4,000 persons are marked as positive samples. The statistical results show that the distribution of positive and negative samples with many feature components are very similar (Fig. 3). Considering that, we introduce a constrained GAN naturally. Another point should to know is that we found that some features have no correlation with the result, which are discarded as noise value in our subsequent processing.

Finally, we chose the item 1, 2, 3, 4, 6, 7, 8, 9, 10, 12, 14, 15, 16 from the original dataset as the final feature components.

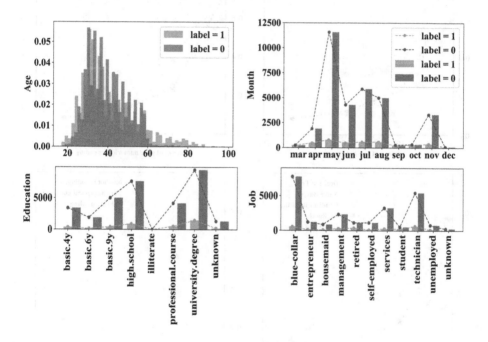

Fig. 3. Part of the data distributions

4.2 The Result of Different Encoding Methods

In machine learning, recall and precision are contradictory indicators. In this problem, we focus on how many customers that institutes want to pick correctly by our algorithm, and we use the recall to evaluate models.

$$Recall = \frac{TP}{TP + FN} \tag{13}$$

where TP represents True Positive, FN means False Negative. Four data sets are divided into positive and negative samples with ratios of $1 : 1(4k : 4k)$, $10 : 1(10k : 1k)$, $20 : 1(20k : 1k)$ and $30 : 1(30k : 1k)$. The $X - axis$ represents the result of the division of this proportion. The validation set consists of 200 positive samples and 800 negative samples.

We evaluated the performance of different encodings. They are: pure binary coding (All data are encoded in one-hot encoding mode.), pure numerical coding (Data are encoded in integer mode.), and hybrid encoding mode proposed by us. This experiment concentrate on the samples with labeled 1.

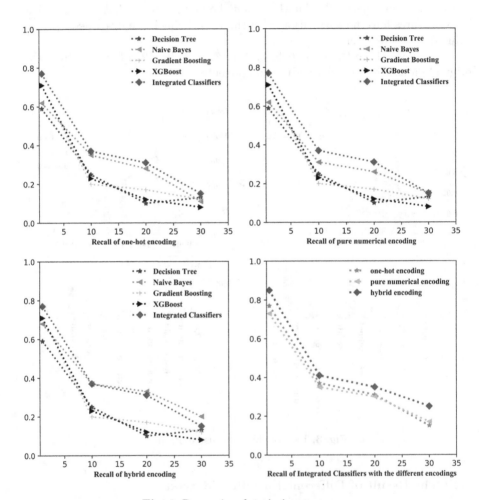

Fig. 4. Processing data in image way.

We can see that different coding methods have different effects on classification recognition. The hybrid encoding method is obviously superior to other methods. At the same time, with the increase of the proportion of negative samples and positive samples, the accuracy decreases rapidly.

4.3   Generating Positive Samples

(a) Firstly, the dataset of positive and negative samples are divided into two data sets. Then, according to the way in Sect. 3, the objective data and the index data are both converted into integer values. All numerical constraints are in the range of 0 to 255, then the data are stored as a matrix. In this way, two matrix graphs are obtained.

(b) Cutting two matrix graphs into several pictures with size 20 * 13.

(c) Sending the pictures which processed in (2) to the constrained GAN to produce images.

(d) All pictures are inversely transformed according to the process in step 1 to obtain new data (Fig. 5).

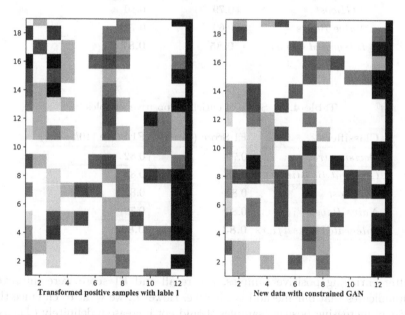

Fig. 5. Processing data in image way. We show the result about transformed data and a new generating picture in Fig. 4. This paper used the size of 20 * 13 to show the data. 20 represents training with 20 users in once, and 13 means thirteen feature components. The last column represents label.

4.4   The Constrained GAN

Previous experiment shows:

(a) Unbalanced samples have a negative impact on the final recognition. An order of magnitude difference between positive and negative samples can cause a rapid decline in accuracy. Integrated classifiers do improve classification performance.
(b) The encoding method influences the final classification results.

Next, in order to test the performance of enriching positive samples with constrained GAN, we increased the number of positive samples from 4,000 to 10,000, and keep the ratio of positive and negative in 1:1 ($10k : 10k$) (Tables 3 and 4).

Table 3. Result of enriching positive samples

Classifiers	Recall ($4k : 4k$)	Recall ($10k : 10k$)
Decision tree	0.68	0.66
Gradient Boosting	0.78	0.79
XGBoost	0.79	0.80
Naive Bayes	0.69	0.72
Integrated Classifiers	**0.85**	**0.87**

Table 4. F1 Score of enriching positive samples

Classifiers	F1 Score ($4k : 4k$)	F1 Score ($10k : 10k$)
Decision tree	0.79	0.82
Gradient Boosting	0.78	0.83
XGBoost	0.81	0.82
Naive Bayes	0.80	0.79
Integrated Classifiers	**0.83**	**0.86**

After enriching positive samples, the recall and F1 score were improved, which indicates that our method is effective. However, we want to enhance that the way of increasing positive samples should not increase indefinitely (The correct proportion of positive and negative samples should be consistent with real situation, this article also keep the positive and negative ratio in 1:4.). Enriching positive samples can make the recall higher when the proportion of positive and negative samples are extremely unbalanced. but if the number of positive samples lose restriction to increase, it will only lead to inadequate learning of negative samples, even the accuracy of positive samples are improved, it becomes a meaningless digital game.

5   Conclusion

In this article, we proposed a hybrid encoding and sample enrichment method. Experiments show the proposed methods achieve an obvious performance improvement. Firstly, data with different attributes are transformed into different codes, and then positive samples are enriched by using constrained GAN. Constrained GAN can avoid producing false data when the distribution of positive and negative are similar. Finally, we select some stable and reliable classifiers with good performance through experiments, and use these classifiers to integrate a soft classifier. Our method works well on dataset mentioned in this paper.

Acknowledgment. This work is supported by China National Basic Research Program (973 Program, No. 2015CB352400), National Natural Science Foundation of China (No. 61572488,61572487), Shenzhen Basic Research Program (No. JCYJ201803021457 31531,JCYJ20170818163026031), and Shenzhen Discipline Construction Project for Urban Computing and Data Intelligence.

References

1. Phua, C., Lee, V., Smith, K., Gayler, R.: A comprehensive survey of data mining-based fraud detection research, arXiv preprint arXiv:1009.6119 (2010)
2. Kou, Y., Lu, C.-T., Sirwongwattana, S., Huang, Y.-P.: Survey of fraud detection techniques. In: IEEE International Conference on Networking, Sensing and Control, 2004, vol. 2, pp. 749–754. IEEE (2004)
3. Hung, E., Cheung, D.W.: Parallel mining of outliers in large database. Distrib. Parallel Databases **12**(1), 5–26 (2002)
4. Williams, G., Baxter, R., He, H., Hawkins, S., Gu, L.: A comparative study of RNN for outlier detection in data mining. In: Proceedings of the 2002 IEEE International Conference on Data Mining, ICDM 2003, pp. 709–712. IEEE (2002)
5. Ngai, E.W., Hu, Y., Wong, Y., Chen, Y., Sun, X.: The application of data mining techniques in financial fraud detection: a classification framework and an academic review of literature. Decis. Support Syst. **50**(3), 559–569 (2011)
6. Brockett, P.L., Derrig, R.A., Golden, L.L., Levine, A., Alpert, M.: Fraud classification using principal component analysis of ridits. J. Risk Insur. **69**(3), 341–371 (2002)
7. Zanetti, M., Jamhour, E., Pellenz, M., Penna, M.: A new SVM-based fraud detection model for AMI. In: Skavhaug, A., Guiochet, J., Bitsch, F. (eds.) SAFECOMP 2016. LNCS, vol. 9922, pp. 226–237. Springer, Cham (2016). https://doi.org/10. 1007/978-3-319-45477-1_18
8. Ezawa, K.J., Norton, S.W.: Constructing bayesian networks to predict uncollectible telecommunications accounts. IEEE Expert **11**(5), 45–51 (1996)
9. Viaene, S., Dedene, G., Derrig, R.A.: Auto claim fraud detection using bayesian learning neural networks. Expert Syst. Appl. **29**(3), 653–666 (2005)
10. Viaene, S., Derrig, R.A., Dedene, G.: A case study of applying boosting naive bayes to claim fraud diagnosis. IEEE Trans. Knowl. Data Eng. **16**(5), 612–620 (2004)
11. Das, K., Moore, A., Schneider, J.: Belief state approaches to signaling alarms in surveillance systems. In: Proceedings of the Tenth ACM SIGKDD International Conference on Knowledge Discovery and Data Mining, pp. 539–544. ACM (2004)

12. Sharma, A., Panigrahi, P.K.: A review of financial accounting fraud detection based on data mining techniques. arXiv preprint arXiv:1309.3944 (2013)

13. Bolton, R.J., Hand, D.J., et al.: Unsupervised profiling methods for fraud detection, Credit Scoring and Credit Control VII, pp. 235–255 (2001)

14. Lepoivre, M.R., Avanzini, C.O., Bignon, G., Legendre, L., Piwele, A.K.: Credit card fraud detection with unsupervised algorithms. J. Adv. Inf. Technol. **7**(1), 34–38 (2016)

15. Cerullo, M.J., Cerullo, V.: Using neural networks to predict financial reporting fraud: Part 1. Comput. Fraud Secur. **1999**(5), 14–17 (1999)

16. Dorronsoro, J.R., Ginel, F., Sánchez, C.R., Santa Cruz, C.: Neural fraud detection in credit card operations. IEEE Trans. Neural Networks **8**(4), 827–834 (1997)

17. Lin, J.W., Hwang, M.I., Becker, J.D.: A fuzzy neural network for assessing the risk of fraudulent financial reporting. Manag. Auditing J. **18**(8), 657–665 (2003)

18. Roy, A., Sun, J., Mahoney, R., Alonzi, L., Adams, S., Beling, P.: Deep learning detecting fraud in credit card transactions. In: 2018 Systems and Information Engineering Design Symposium (SIEDS), pp. 129–134. IEEE (2018)

19. Wang, Y., Xu, W.: Leveraging deep learning with lda-based text analytics to detect automobile insurance fraud. Decis. Support Syst. **105**, 87–95 (2018)

20. Zhou, Z.-H.: Ensemble Methods: Foundations and Algorithms. Chapman and Hall/CRC, New York (2012)

21. Goodfellow, I., et al.: Generative adversarial nets. In: Advances in neural information processing systems, pp. 2672–2680 (2014)

22. Lin, D., Fu, K., Wang, Y., Xu, G., Sun, X.: Marta gans: unsupervised representation learning for remote sensing image classification. IEEE Geosci. Remote Sens. Lett. **14**(11), 2092–2096 (2017)

23. Cassel, M., Lima, F.: Evaluating one-hot encoding finite state machines for SEU reliability in SRAM-based FPGAs. In: 12th IEEE International On-Line Testing Symposium, IOLTS 2006, pp. 6-pp. IEEE (2006)

24. Sikora, R., et al.: A modified stacking ensemble machine learning algorithm using genetic algorithms. In Handbook of Research on Organizational Transformations Through Big Data Analytics, pp. 43–53. IGi Global (2015)

25. Golson, S.: One-hot state machine design for FPGAs. In Proceedings 3rd Annual PLD Design Conference & Exhibit, vol. 1, no. 3 (1993)

26. Duvenaud, D.K., et al.: Convolutional networks on graphs for learning molecular fingerprints. In: Advances in Neural Information Processing Systems, pp. 2224–2232 (2015)

27. Song, Y., et al.: Vital: Visual tracking via adversarial learning. In: Proceedings of the IEEE Conference on Computer Vision and Pattern Recognition, pp. 8990–8999 (2018)

28. Karras, T., Laine, S., Aila, T.: A style-based generator architecture for generative adversarial networks. arXiv preprint arXiv:1812.04948 (2018)

29. Mahalanobis, P.C.: On the generalized distance in statistics. National Institute of Science of India (1936)

30. Rojas, R.: Adaboost and the super bowl of classifiers a tutorial introduction to adaptive boosting. Freie University, Berlin, Technical report (2009)

31. Vincent, P., Larochelle, H., Lajoie, I., Bengio, Y., Manzagol, P.-A.: Stacked denoising autoencoders: learning useful representations in a deep network with a local denoising criterion. J. Mach. Learn. Res. **11**, 3371–3408 (2010)

32. Yu, D., Yao, K., Su, H., Li, G., Seide, F.: Kl-divergence regularized deep neural network adaptation for improved large vocabulary speech recognition. In: 2013 IEEE International Conference on Acoustics, Speech and Signal Processing (ICASSP), pp. 7893–7897. IEEE (2013)
33. Xiong, H., Cheng, W., Fu, Y., Hu, W., Bian, J., Guo, Z.: De-biasing covariance-regularized discriminant analysis. In: IJCAI, pp. 2889–2897 (2018)
34. Safavian, S.R., Landgrebe, D.: A survey of decision tree classifier methodology. IEEE Trans. Syst. Man Cybern. 21(3), 660–674 (1991)
35. Kamiński, B., Jakubczyk, M., Szufel, P.: A framework for sensitivity analysis of decision trees. CEJOR 26(1), 135–159 (2018)
36. Liaw, A., Wiener, M., et al.: Classification and regression by randomforest. R News 2(3), 18–22 (2002)
37. Natekin, A., Knoll, A.: Gradient boosting machines, a tutorial. Front. Neurorobotics 7, 21 (2013)
38. Chen, T., Guestrin, C.: Xgboost: A scalable tree boosting system. In: Proceedings of the 22nd ACM SIGKDD International Conference on Knowledge Discovery and Data Mining, pp. 785–794. ACM (2016)
39. West, J., Bhattacharya, M.: Intelligent financial fraud detection: a comprehensive review. Comput. Secur. 57, 47–66 (2016)
40. Patil, T.R., Sherekar, S.: Performance analysis of naive bayes and j48 classification algorithm for data classification. Int. J. Comput. Sci. Appl. 6(2), 256–261 (2013)
41. Yan, X., Su, X.: Linear Regression Analysis: Theory and Computing. World Scientific, Singapore (2009)
42. Mercer, L.C.: Fraud detection via regression analysis. Comput. Secur. 9(4), 331–338 (1990)
43. Bottou, L.: Large-scale machine learning with stochastic gradient descent. In: Lechevallier, Y., Saporta G. (eds) Proceedings of COMPSTAT 2010, pp. 176–186. Physica, Heidelberg (2010). https://doi.org/10.1007/978-3-7908-2604-3_16

ECGAN: Image Translation with Multi-scale Relativistic Average Discriminator

Weihao Xia[1]([✉]), Yujiu Yang[1], and Xian-yu Bao[2]

[1] Graduate School at Shenzhen, Tsinghua University,
Shenzhen, People's Republic of China
`xiawh16@mails.tsinghua.edu.cn`
[2] Shenzhen Academy of Inspection and Quarantine,
Shenzhen, Guangdong, People's Republic of China

Abstract. Image-to-image translation aims to transform an image of one source domain to another target domain, which can be applied to many specific tasks, such as image restoration and style transfer. As one of the most popular frameworks, CycleGAN with cycle consistency loss can transform between different domains with unpaired training data, which greatly expands its application efficiency. However, due to its under-constrained mapping and dissatisfactory network design, the results of CycleGAN are sometimes unnatural and unreal. In some cases, there are visible artifacts in the synthetic images. In this paper, we propose an **E**nhanced **C**ycle**GAN** (ECGAN) framework with multi-scale relativistic average discriminator, which integrates the loss function design and network structure optimization to make the generated images have more natural textures and fewer unwanted artifacts. In the evaluation, besides using quantitative full reference image quality assessment metrics (such as PSNR, SSIM), we also conduct an evaluation on the Frechet Inception distance (FID), which are more consistent with human subjective assessment according to natural, realistic and diverse. Experiments on two benchmark datasets, including CMP facades and CUHK face datasets, show that the proposed ECGAN framework outperforms the state-of-the-art methods in both quantitative and qualitative evaluation.

1 Introduction

With the development of deep learning technology, image-to-image translation has received great attention in recent years. Many computer vision tasks can be handled under the framework of image-to-image translation framework, such as image restoration and image enhancement. As we all know, the Generative Adversarial Network (GAN) framework is one of the most popular frameworks in this application field, and it has very powerful functions and vigorous vitality.

© Springer Nature Switzerland AG 2019
D. Wang and L.-J. Zhang (Eds.): AIMS 2019, LNCS 11516, pp. 28–38, 2019.
https://doi.org/10.1007/978-3-030-23367-9_3

And it has been significantly improved in some special image processing tasks, such as image super-resolution [1–3], semantic segmentation [4], image inpainting [5–7], etc.

In Generative Adversarial Network (GAN), the generator G is trained to increase the probability that fake data is real and the discriminator D tries to distinguish if one input image x is natural and realistic. Different from the standard discriminator D, Alexia et al. [8,9] argues that it should also simultaneously increase the probability that fake data is real and decrease the probability that real data is real. They introduced this property by changing the discriminator into a relativistic form, which calculates the probability that a real image is relatively more natural and realistic than a fake one.

However, this discriminator is in the relativistic form of a single scale, which can still lead to artifacts in the generated image. To solve this problem, we propose an **Enhanced CycleGAN** (ECGAN) framework with multi-scale relativistic average discriminator. To sum it up, we improve the key components of original CycleGAN model in three aspects:

- We improve the discriminator by introducing Multi-Scale Relativistic average Discriminator (MS-RaD), which tries to distinguish on different scales whether one image is more realistic than the other, rather than whether one image is real or fake.
- We add a complementary loss item calculating between the synthesized images and real images while the cycle-consistency loss calculating between the cycled images and real images. The final complementary cycle-consistent loss is able to increases the quality and reduce artifacts of the results.
- We introduce the Residual-in-Residual Dense Block (RDDB) to generator G as its basic module. This makes the network be of higher capacity and easier to train. We don't apply Batch Normalization (BN)[10] or Instance Normalization (IN)[11] layers in generator as in [1].

Experiments show that those improvements help the generator create more realistic texture and details. Extensive experiments display that the $ECGAN$, outperforms the state-of-the-art methods on both similarity metrics and perceptual scores.

2   Related Works

For convenience of description, we define the task of image-to-image translation as follows: given a series of images $\{I_X^i\}_{i=1}^N$ from source domain X and $\{I_Y^j\}_{j=1}^M$ from target domain Y, we find the mapping relationship between the same image from a source domain X to a target domain Y, denoted by $\mathcal{T}: I_X \to I_Y$. Many methods [12–15] have been proposed to solve this problem. Among them, the most famous framework is the pix2pix generalized framework (proposed by Isola et al. [16]) based on Conditional GANs (cGANs).

Zhu et al. [17] presented CycleGAN using Cycle-Consistent Loss to handle the paired training data limitation of pix2pix. While converting an image from a source domain X to a target domain Y referred to as $\mathcal{T}: I_X \to I_Y$, cycle consistency loss manages to enforce $\mathcal{F}(\mathcal{T}(I_X)) \approx I_X$ by introducing an inverse mapping $\mathcal{F}: I_Y \to I_X$ (and vice versa). Except for original adversarial losses and cycle consistency loss, perceptual loss [18] or L_1 loss is also used to improve the quality of synthesised images in many works afterwards [19].

Isola et al. [16] applies the U-Net [20] architecture generator and patch-based discriminator. Besides U-Net [20], ResNet [21] is another popular architecture for generator. It use Residual block as basic module. Wang et al. [14] made it possible for pix2pix to synthesize 2048×1024 high-resolution photo-realistic images from semantic label maps [22,23]. They improved original pix2pix framework by using a coarse-to-fine generator and a multi-scale discriminator. Coarse-to-fine generator can be decomposed into a global generator network and a local enhancer network. Multi-scale discriminator [14] are composed of three discriminators that share identical structure but operate at three different scales. Those discriminators are respectively trained with real and synthesized images at different scales. The discriminator at the coarsest scale can generate globally consistent images, while the finest one produces finer details.

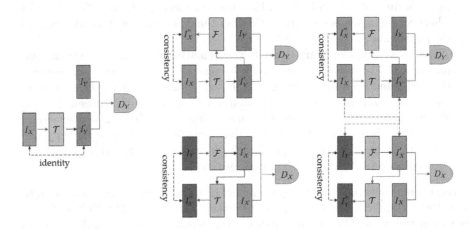

Fig. 1. complementary cycle-consistent loss. **Left**: loss with paired samples. **Middle**: original cycle-consistent coss. **Right**: complementary cycle-consistentcoss. The complementary loss item is shown as the red dash line and is calculated as L_1 loss between the synthesized images and real images. (Color figure online)

3   ECGAN with Multi-Scale Relativistic Average Discriminator

Similar to the aforementioned definition, given a series of images $\{I_X^i\}_{i=1}^N$ from source domain X and $\{I_Y^j\}_{j=1}^M$ from target domain Y, our goal is to learn a mapping $\mathcal{T}: I_X \to I_Y$ from the source domain X to the target domain Y

such that the distribution of images from $T(I_X)$ is indistinguishable from the distribution I_Y.

There are mainly three modifications at the structure of network: (1) use Multi-Scale Relativistic average Discriminator (MS-RaD); (2) add a complementary loss item to the original cycle-consistent loss; (3) replace the original basic residual blocks with the Residual-in-Residual Dense Block (RRDB) and remove all BN or IN layers in generator G. The following will be described in detail one by one.

3.1   Multi-Scale Relativistic Average Discriminator

In standard GAN, the discriminator usually be defined as $D(x) = \sigma(C(x))$, where σ means activation function and $C(x)$ represents the output of the discriminator. The simplest way to make it relativistic [8], i.e, making the output of D on both real and fake data, is to define it as $D(x) = \sigma(C(x_r) - C(x_f))$ with samples from real and fake pairs $\hat{x}(x_r, x_f)$, where, subscripts r and f denote real image and fake image, respectively.

Rather than judging the probability that the input data is real, relativistic discriminators measure the probability that the input data is relatively more realistic than a randomly sampled data of its counterpart. To make it more globally, we can focus on the average of the relativistic discriminator: $D(x) = \sigma(C(x_r) - E(C(x_f)))$, as shown in Fig. 2.

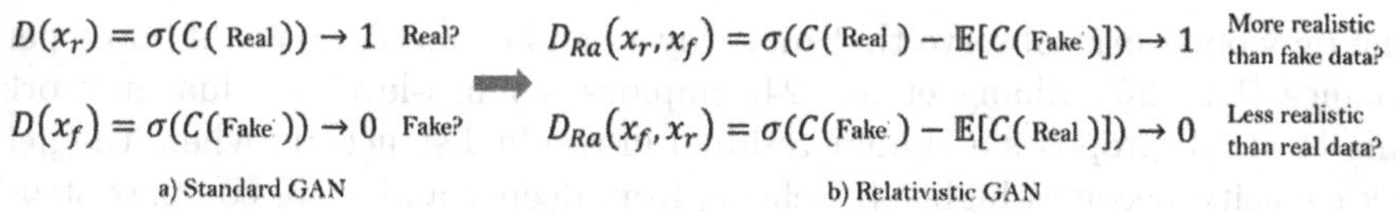

$$D(x_r) = \sigma(C(\text{Real})) \to 1 \quad \text{Real?}$$
$$D(x_f) = \sigma(C(\text{Fake})) \to 0 \quad \text{Fake?}$$
a) Standard GAN

$$D_{Ra}(x_r, x_f) = \sigma(C(\text{Real}) - \mathbb{E}[C(\text{Fake})]) \to 1 \quad \text{More realistic than fake data?}$$
$$D_{Ra}(x_f, x_r) = \sigma(C(\text{Fake}) - \mathbb{E}[C(\text{Real})]) \to 0 \quad \text{Less realistic than real data?}$$
b) Relativistic GAN

Fig. 2. The different between standard discriminator and relativistic average discriminator [3]. **Left:** Standard discriminator judges the probability that the input data is real or fake. **Right:** Relativistic average discriminator judges the probability that a real (or fake) image is relatively more realistic than a fake (or real) one.

Here we extend the relativistic design of discriminators into multiple different scales,

$$\min_G \max_{\{D_k\}_{k=1}^N} \sum_k L_D(G, D_k),\tag{1}$$

L_D can be formulated as:

$$\begin{aligned} L_D(G, D_k) =& E_{x_r^k \sim \mathbb{P}}[\sigma(C(x_r^k)) - E_{x_f^k \sim \mathbb{Q}} C(x_f^k)] \\ &+ E_{x_f^k \sim \mathbb{Q}}[\sigma(C(x_f^k)) - E_{x_r^k \sim \mathbb{P}} C(x_r^k)], \end{aligned}\tag{2}$$

where $\mathbb{P}$ represents the distribution of real data, $\mathbb{Q}$ represents the distribution of fake data and $D(x)$ is the discriminator evaluated at x.

3.2   Complementary Cycle-Consistent Loss

Our goal is to learn a mapping $\mathcal{T} : I_X \rightarrow I_Y$ such that the distribution of images from $\mathcal{T}(I_X)$ is indistinguishable from the distribution I_Y using an adversarial loss. Because this mapping is highly under-constrained, we couple it with an inverse mapping $\mathcal{F} : I_Y \rightarrow I_X$ and introduce a cycle consistency loss to enforce $\mathcal{F}(\mathcal{T}(I_X)) \approx I_X$ (and vice versa).

Cycle-consistent loss helps learn the translation mapping $\mathcal{T} : I_X \rightarrow I_Y$ coupled with an inverse mapping $\mathcal{F} : I_Y \rightarrow I_X$, but it's still highly under-constrained. As depicted in Fig. 1, cycle-consistent loss is calculated as L_1 loss between real images I_X and cycled images $I_X'' \triangleq \mathcal{F}(\mathcal{T}(I_X))$ in domain I_X , real image I_Y and cycled image $I_Y'' \triangleq \mathcal{T}(\mathcal{F}(I_Y))$ in domain Y. We observe that the relationship between real images I_X, I_Y and the synthesized image $I_X' \triangleq \mathcal{F}(I_Y)$, $I_Y' \triangleq \mathcal{T}(I_X)$ is missing. The translation $I_X' \triangleq \mathcal{F}(I_Y)$ and $I_Y' \triangleq \mathcal{T}(I_X)$ are not specifically constrained. So we add this term to the original loss and name the final loss as complementary cycle-consistent loss.

The final complementary cycle-consistent loss is defined as follows:

$$L_{CCCL_X} = \underbrace{||I_X - I_X''||_1}_{\text{cycle-consistent loss}} + \lambda_1 ||I_X - I_X'||_1,$$

$$L_{CCCL_Y} = \underbrace{||I_Y - I_Y''||_1}_{\text{cycle-consistent loss}} + \lambda_2 ||I_Y - I_Y'||_1 \tag{3}$$

3.3   Residual-in-Residual Dense Block

Some previous works observe that more layers and connections could boost performance [1,24,25]. Zhang et al. [24] employs a multi-level residual network. Wang et al. [3] proposes a similar residual-in-residual structure, where the network capacity becomes higher benefiting from deeper and more complex structure. We replace original residual block with this Residual Block with Residual-in-Residual Dense Block (RRDB). The basic structure of RRDB are depicted in Fig. 3.

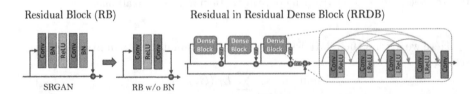

Fig. 3. The different between RB and RRDB [3]. **Left:** Residual Block with or without Batch Normalization (BN) layers. **Right:** RRDB block (β is the residual scaling parameter).

We empirically observe that Batch Normalization layers [10] tend to bring artifacts also in image translation processing as Wang et al. [3] found in super-resolution, which they called BN artifacts. Removing all Batch Normalization layers achieves stable and consistent performance without artifacts, but reduces memory usage and computational resources dramatically.

The Generator and Discriminator architectures in our work are adapted from CycleGAN [17]. We replace Residual Block with Residual-in-Residual Dense Block using no Batch Normalization Layers.

4   Experiment

4.1   Datasets

To appraise the efficiency of the proposed method, we conducted some experiments on two benchmark datasets, namely CUHK and Facades. First, we describe the datasets in brief here.

(1) CUHK Face Sketch Database [26]: The CUHK dataset consists of 188 face image pairs of sketch and corresponding face of students. We use its $256 \times 256 \times 3$ resized and cropped version in our experiment. 100 images are used for the training and rest for the testing.
(2) CMP Facade Database [27]: The Facade Database present facade images from different cities around the world and diverse styles. It includes 606 rectified images pairs of labels and corresponding facades with dimensions of $256 \times 256 \times 3$. 400 pairs are used for the training while the others remaining for the testing.

4.2   Evaluation Metrics

The quantitative and qualitative results are computed to evaluate the performance of the proposed method. The Structural Similarity Index (SSIM)[28], Peak Signal to Noise Ratio (PSNR) and the Frechet Inception distance (FID)[29] are adapted to assess the results.

PSNR and SSIM are Full Reference Image Quality Assessment (FR-IQA)[30, 31] metrics, usually applied to judge the similarity between the generated image and ground truth image in many tasks such as image enhancement [32,33], image de-raining [34–36] and super-resolution [1–3,37].

FID [29] calculates the Wasserstein distance between the synthesized and real images in the feature space of an Inception-v3 network [38]. Lower FID score means the distance between synthetic and real image distributions are closer. It's has been shown to be more principled, comprehensive and consistent with human evaluation in diversity and realism of the synthesized images. The qualitative comparison results of SSIM, PSNR and FID are shown in Figs. 4 and 5.

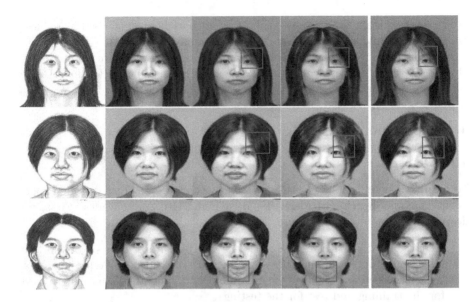

Fig. 4. Qualitative comparison on CUFS dataset. From left to right: Input, Ground truth, CycleGAN, CSGAN and ours. Our method generates the realistic and natural images with less artifacts.

Fig. 5. Qualitative comparison on Facades dataset. From left to right: Input, Ground truth, CycleGAN, CSGAN and ours. Our method generates the realistic and natural images with less artifacts.

Table 1. The average scores of the SSIM, MSE, PSNR, FID on CUHK and Facedes Dataset. The values in bold highlights the best values.

Methods	CUHK			Facades		
	PSNR	SSIM	FID	PSNR	SSIM	FID
CycleGAN	27.63	0.65	40.34	27.9489	0.0678	67.96
CSGAN	27.87	0.66	21.17	27.9715	0.2183	20.34
the proposed ECGAN	**28.97**	**0.67**	**17.14**	**28.1583**	**0.2254**	**16.39**

4.3 Training Information

We train with ADAM [39] optimizer by setting $\beta_1 = 0.9$, $\beta_2 = 0.999$ and a learning rate of 0.0002. The joint training of generator and discriminator networks are performed. We perform the training for 200 epochs with batch size 1, which took roughly 5 hours on an i7 with 8 GB of memory and a GeForce GTX 1080 Ti GPU.

4.4 Experimental Results and Analysis

4.5 Quantitative Evaluation

Table 1 lists the comparative results of CycleGAN [17], CSGAN [40] and the proposed method over the CUHK sketch-to-face and Facede labels-to-buildings datasets, respectively. In terms of the average scores given by SSIM and PSNR metrics, the proposed method clearly shows improved results over the others. The highest scores of SSIM and PSNR metrics show that the proposed method generates more structurally similar faces for a given sketch. The lowest FID score means it also achieves the most perceptual results.

4.6 Qualitative Evaluation

Figures 4 and 5 show the qualitative comparison of the proposed results on CUHK and Facades dataset, respectively. The results generated by CycleGAN contain different type of artifacts such as face distortion, color inconsistencies, BN artifacts [3], etc. The results of CSGAN is better, but still suffers with the BN artifacts for different images. Those unwanted side effects are significantly reduced by our method. The results of proposed method are more natural, realistic and diverse with reduced artifacts.

4.7 Ablation Experiments

We also conduct ablation study on each part. The results are shown at Table 2. Multi-RaD, CCCL, and RRDB represent Multi-Scale Relativistic average Discriminator, Complementary Cycle-Consistent Loss and the Residual-in-Residual Dense Block, respectively. It can be seen from the Table 2 that with those three components helps achieve better results than without.

Table 2. Ablation experiments on CHUK dataset.

Methods	PSNR	SSIM	FID
CycleGAN(baseline)	27.63	0.65	40.34
+CCCL	27.87	0.66	21.17
+RRDB	28.35	0.67	20.34
+Multi-RaD	**28.97**	**0.67**	**17.14**

5   Conclusion

We present an ECGAN model that achieves both structurally similar and better perceptual quality results. We firstly expend the Relativistic average Discriminator into a multi-scale form, which learns to judge on different scales whether one image is more realistic than another, leading the generator G to create more natural textures and details. A Complementary Cycle-Consistent Loss is introduced to the original CycleGAN objective function to guide the translation to the desired direction and minimize unwanted artifacts. We have also introduced the structure containing several RDDB blocks without batch normalization layers into the field of image-to-image translation. The experiment shows that the proposed method is better or comparable with the recent state-of-art methods on two benchmark image translation datasets.

Acknowledgement. This work was supported in part by the National Key Research and Development Program of China (No. 2018YFB1601102 and No. 2017YFC1601004), and Shenzhen special fund for the strategic development of emerging industries (No. JCYJ20170412170118573).

References

1. Lim, B., Son, S., Kim, H., Nah, S., Lee, K.M.: Enhanced deep residual networks for single image super-resolution. In: The IEEE Conference on Computer Vision and Pattern Recognition (CVPR) Workshops, July 2017
2. Wang, X., Yu, K., Dong, C., Loy, C.C.: Recovering realistic texture in image super-resolution by deep spatial feature transform. In: IEEE Conference on Computer Vision and Pattern Recognition (CVPR) (2018)
3. Wang, X., et al.: Esrgan: enhanced super-resolution generative adversarial networks. In: The European Conference on Computer Vision Workshops (ECCVW), September 2018
4. Lin, G., Milan, A., Shen, C., Reid, I.: Refinenet: multi-path refinement networks for high-resolution semantic segmentation. In: Proceedings of the IEEE Conference on Computer Vision and Pattern Recognition, pp. 1925–1934 (2017)
5. Jo, Y., Park, J.: Sc-fegan: face editing generative adversarial network with user's sketch and color. arXiv preprint arXiv:1902.06838 (2019)
6. Yu, J., Lin, Z., Yang, J., Shen, X., Lu, X., Huang, T.S.: Generative image inpainting with contextual attention. arXiv preprint arXiv:1801.07892 (2018)

7. Nazeri, K., Ng, E., Joseph, T., Qureshi, F., Ebrahimi, M.: Edgeconnect: generative image inpainting with adversarial edge learning (2019)
8. Jolicoeur-Martineau, A.: The relativistic discriminator: a key element missing from standard gan. arXiv preprint arXiv:1807.00734 (2018)
9. Jolicoeur-Martineau, A.: On relativistic f-divergences. arXiv preprint arXiv:1901.02474 (2019)
10. Ioffe, S., Szegedy, C.: Batch normalization: accelerating deep network training by reducing internal covariate shift. arXiv preprint arXiv:1502.03167 (2015)
11. Ulyanov, D., Vedaldi, A., Lempitsky, V.: Instance normalization: the missing ingredient for fast stylization. arXiv preprint arXiv:1607.08022 (2016)
12. Pumarola, A., Agudo, A., Martinez, A., Sanfeliu, A., Moreno-Noguer, F.: Ganimation: anatomically-aware facial animation from a single image. In: Proceedings of the European Conference on Computer Vision (ECCV) (2018)
13. Choi, Y., Choi, M., Kim, M., Ha, J.W., Kim, S., Choo, J.: Stargan: unified generative adversarial networks for multi-domain image-to-image translation. In: The IEEE Conference on Computer Vision and Pattern Recognition (CVPR), June 2018
14. Wang, T.C., Liu, M.Y., Zhu, J.Y., Tao, A., Kautz, J., Catanzaro, B.: High-resolution image synthesis and semantic manipulation with conditional gans. In: Proceedings of the IEEE Conference on Computer Vision and Pattern Recognition (2018)
15. Xian, W., et al.: Texturegan: Controlling deep image synthesis with texture patches. arXiv preprint arXiv:1706.02823 (2017)
16. Isola, P., Zhu, J.Y., Zhou, T., Efros, A.A.: Image-to-image translation with conditional adversarial networks. In: 2017 IEEE Conference on Computer Vision and Pattern Recognition (CVPR) (2017)
17. Zhu, J.Y., Park, T., Isola, P., Efros, A.A.: Unpaired image-to-image translation using cycle-consistent adversarial networkss. In: 2017 IEEE International Conference on Computer Vision (ICCV) (2017)
18. Johnson, J., Alahi, A., Fei-Fei, L.: Perceptual losses for real-time style transfer and super-resolution. In: Leibe, B., Matas, J., Sebe, N., Welling, M. (eds.) ECCV 2016. LNCS, vol. 9906, pp. 694–711. Springer, Cham (2016). https://doi.org/10.1007/978-3-319-46475-6_43
19. Nah, S., Kim, T.H., Lee, K.M.: Deep multi-scale convolutional neural network for dynamic scene deblurring, pp. 257–265 (2016)
20. Ronneberger, O., Fischer, P., Brox, T.: U-net: convolutional networks for biomedical image segmentation. In: Navab, N., Hornegger, J., Wells, W.M., Frangi, A.F. (eds.) MICCAI 2015. LNCS, vol. 9351, pp. 234–241. Springer, Cham (2015). https://doi.org/10.1007/978-3-319-24574-4_28
21. He, K., Zhang, X., Ren, S., Sun, J.: Deep residual learning for image recognition. In: Computer Vision and Pattern Recognition, pp. 770–778 (2016)
22. Cordts, M., et al.: The cityscapes dataset for semantic urban scene understanding. In: Proceedings of the IEEE Conference on Computer Vision and Pattern Recognition (CVPR) (2016)
23. Cordts, M., et al.: The cityscapes dataset. In: CVPR Workshop on The Future of Datasets in Vision (2015)
24. Zhang, K., Sun, M., Han, T.X., Yuan, X., Guo, L., Liu, T.: Residual networks of residual networks: multilevel residual networks. IEEE Trans. Circuits Syst. Video Technol. **28**(6), 1303–1314 (2018)

25. Zhang, Y., Li, K., Li, K., Wang, L., Zhong, B., Fu, Y.: Image super-resolution using very deep residual channel attention networks. In: Proceedings of the European Conference on Computer Vision (ECCV), pp. 286–301 (2018)
26. Wang, X., Tang, X.: Face photo-sketch synthesis and recognition. IEEE Trans. Pattern Anal. Mach. Intell. **31**(11), 1955–1967 (2009)
27. Tyleček, R., Šára, R.: Spatial pattern templates for recognition of objects with regular structure. In: Weickert, J., Hein, M., Schiele, B. (eds.) GCPR 2013. LNCS, vol. 8142, pp. 364–374. Springer, Heidelberg (2013). https://doi.org/10.1007/978-3-642-40602-7_39
28. Wang, Z., Bovik, A.C., Sheikh, H.R., Simoncelli, E.P., et al.: Image quality assessment: from error visibility to structural similarity. IEEE Trans. Image process. **13**(4), 600–612 (2004)
29. Heusel, M., Ramsauer, H., Unterthiner, T., Nessler, B., Hochreiter, S.: Gans trained by a two time-scale update rule converge to a local nash equilibrium. In: Advances in Neural Information Processing Systems, pp. 6626–6637 (2017)
30. Sheikh, H.R., Sabir, M.F., Bovik, A.C.: A statistical evaluation of recent full reference image quality assessment algorithms. IEEE Trans. Image Process. **15**(11), 3440–3451 (2006)
31. Zhang, L., Zhang, L., Mou, X., Zhang, D.: A comprehensive evaluation of full reference image quality assessment algorithms. In: 2012 19th IEEE International Conference on Image Processing, pp. 1477–1480. IEEE (2012)
32. Chen, Y.S., Wang, Y.C., Kao, M.H., Chuang, Y.Y.: Deep photo enhancer: unpaired learning for image enhancement from photographs with gans. In: Proceedings of the IEEE Conference on Computer Vision and Pattern Recognition, pp. 6306–6314 (2018)
33. Liu, R., Ma, L., Wang, Y., Zhang, L.: Learning converged propagations with deep prior ensemble for image enhancement. IEEE Trans. Image Process. **28**(3), 1528–1543 (2019)
34. Zhang, H., Sindagi, V., Patel, V.M.: Image de-raining using a conditional generative adversarial network. arXiv preprint arXiv:1701.05957 (2017)
35. Fu, X., Huang, J., Ding, X., Liao, Y., Paisley, J.: Clearing the skies: a deep network architecture for single-image rain removal. IEEE Trans. Image Process. **26**(6), 2944–2956 (2017)
36. Kim, J.H., Lee, C., Sim, J.Y., Kim, C.S.: Single-image deraining using an adaptive nonlocal means filter. In: 2013 IEEE International Conference on Image Processing, pp. 914–917. IEEE (2013)
37. Dong, C., Loy, C.C., He, K., Tang, X.: Learning a deep convolutional network for image super-resolution. In: Fleet, D., Pajdla, T., Schiele, B., Tuytelaars, T. (eds.) ECCV 2014. LNCS, vol. 8692, pp. 184–199. Springer, Cham (2014). https://doi.org/10.1007/978-3-319-10593-2_13
38. Szegedy, C., Vanhoucke, V., Ioffe, S., Shlens, J., Wojna, Z.: Rethinking the inception architecture for computer vision. In: Proceedings of the IEEE Conference on Computer Vision and Pattern Recognition, pp. 2818–2826 (2016)
39. Kingma, D., Ba, J.: Adam: a method for stochastic optimization. Computer Science (2014)
40. Kancharagunta, K.B., Dubey, S.R.: Csgan: cyclic-synthesized generative adversarial networks for image-to-image transformation. arXiv preprint arXiv:1901.03554 (2019)

Pork Registration Using Skin Image with Deep Neural Network Features

Daohang Song, Cheng Cai$^{(\boxtimes)}$, and Zeng Peng

College of Information Engineering, Northwest A&F University,
Yangling 712100, China
cheneychengcai@163.com

Abstract. Pork food safety is not optimistic in China. Some pork carrying viruses can damage the liver and kidneys of consumers. At present, the pork traceability system in China mainly relies on the information of the stamp on the pork skin. However, there is no unified stamp standard in China to regulate pork market, and information on the stamp is likely to be destroyed during the circulation process. In this study, deep convolutional neural network (DCNN) was used to extract the features of pork skin, and dynamic inlier selection was used to register pork skin images to achieve accurate traceability of pork. The data set consists of 810 images, which containing images captured from three angles and nine position. The results show that features extracted using DCNN are better than SIFT features, and the average matching rate is 92.59%. Compared with KNN (K-Nearest Neighbor), CPD (Coherent Point Drift), ICP (Iterative Closest Point), our dynamic inlier selection has better registration effect. In our pork skin dataset, the success rate of registration reached 86.67%, which provided a reference for subsequent pork traceability research.

Keywords: Food safety · Pork skin · Image registration · CNN · Scale invariant feature transformation

1 Introduction

Building a reliable pork information tracking system is an important way to ensure that residents can buy reliable pork [1]. First, the public can confirm the safety of the purchased pork with the pork traceability system. Secondly, once the pork in the market has food safety problems, relevant inspection and quarantine personnel can quickly get access to pork production and circulation information with the pork food safety information traceability system to find out which part has gone wrong. The development of pork traceability technology is not only conducive to enhancing the safety of residents' daily diet, but also regulates the pork production and sales industry, which brings benefits to related companies [2].

At present, many countries use the stamp on pig skin as a method of traceability which is shown in Fig. 1, but this method has many limitations. First, the label of the stamp may not be the same in different regions or companies. Secondly, the clarity of the stamp cannot be guaranteed when pork is stamped. In addition, during the circulation of pork, the stamp may be worn and unclear. Due to these problems, the

© Springer Nature Switzerland AG 2019
D. Wang and L.-J. Zhang (Eds.): AIMS 2019, LNCS 11516, pp. 39–53, 2019.
https://doi.org/10.1007/978-3-030-23367-9_4

information carried by the stamp is sometimes not effective to exchange information, and the traditional method of traceability is not reliable. This study will use the image registration technology to record the images using the features of the pork skin and overcome the above problems and achieve effective and reliable traceability of pork.

Fig. 1. Stamps on the pork skin

Image registration is the transformation that finds the best alignment between two images, that is, converting different datasets to the same spatial location. These data may come from different perspectives with all kinds of sensors. This algorithm is widely applied to many computer vision fields, such as plant leaves detection [3, 4], medical images analysis [5, 6], image repair [7], and satellite images [8].

There are two kinds of methods to match images. The first are the methods based on neighborhood information, such as Mutual Information [9], Cross Correlation [10], and FFT-based phase correlation method [11]. The optimal mutual information method is often used for the registration of medical images and remote sensing images because of its high precision. However, its computational speed deficiency makes it impossible to have further development in the field of high-precision image registration. The FFT-based phase correlation method has good scale and rotation invariance, but this method is sensitive to noise, and there must be a significant linear relationship between the registered images [12]. The second are the methods based on feature extraction, where the most common method is to extract point features in the image, such as Scale Invariant Feature Transform [13]. In addition to point feature, line features and surface features could also be extracted from edge detection algorithms [14] and image segmentation algorithms [15] respectively.

The method based on neighborhood image information (area-based) uses image intensity for registration. The feature-based approach can represent more advanced information; therefore, its descriptors are preferable in applications where the image intensity varies greatly. Because the algorithm proposed in this paper is an image registration method based on feature extraction, we will focus on the method of discussion (ii).

SIFT and its developed algorithms are always chosen in most feature-based image registration methods. SURF [16] uses image integration instead of convolution operation because its descriptor is 64-dimensional, its calculation speed is faster than that of SIFT, but its performance is not good in running on images with large scale changes. To overcome this problem, Morel et al. presented the Affine-independent ASIFT algorithm [17]. For the problem that the SIFT feature is too large due to the excessive number of dimensions. Liu drew on the idea of PCA-SIFT [18] proposed by He, and proposed the use of Kernel Independent Component Analysis [19] to reduce dimensionality, which is called KICA-SIFT [20]. However, in some multi-time or multi-sensor registration processes with visual differences, the feature points selected by the methods above might include some outliers. In more extreme cases, enough points cannot be selected by SIFT-like algorithms [21]. These problems have led to the limitations of the SIFT in registration process. We also found many different point set registration methods. The classic method is to estimate the degree of registration by using the idea of probability optimization, that is, using the Gaussian mixture model (GMM) like Coherent Point Drift [22].

In this paper, we have adopted a dynamic pork skin image registration algorithm. We demonstrate our method in Fig. 2. This method has the following two prominent features: (i) The pre-trained (on ImageNet [23]) VGG network [24] is used to generate multi-scale feature descriptors, and the extracted features can be obtained by convolution operations while obtaining more stable high-dimensional information of the image. (ii) A feature point set matching method with preference is used. This method uses the idea of gradually increasing the number of inliers in the matching process rather than the idea of distinguishing between inliers and redundant points. In the first stage of registration, Pre-matching is done by finding confidence points. Then, we found that the more feature points, the better optimization of the registration results. Also we can reduce the impact of mismatches. The registration is assessed by convolutional features and neighborhood information.

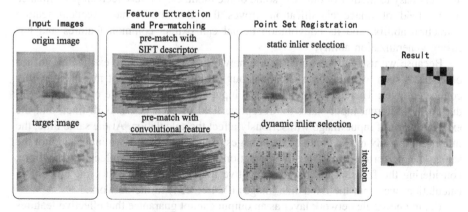

Fig. 2. The flow of our algorithm

We compared the above feature detection methods with SIFT and tested them on a multi-angle pork skin dataset and compared dynamic inlier selection with other three registration methods.

In the following sections, we will first demonstrate our registration algorithm based on convolutional architecture, including how to use the convolutional neural network as a feature extractor to extract high-dimensional features in the pig skin dataset, and the specific implementation of dynamic inlier selection. Later, we will compare these methods and analyze our experimental results. Finally, we will present the conclusions and future works.

2   Method

In this study, a remote sensing image registration algorithm based on image collection is used to analyze the pig skin image collection. We firstly use the VGG-16 pre-train model to extract image features without any screening. In order to get a rough registration parameter, we choose relatively reliable points to do the pre-match process. In the registration stage, we propose a point-to-point registration algorithm based on Gaussian mixture model to achieve accurate registration. Finally, the TPS (thin plate spline [25]) method is introduced.

2.1   Feature Extraction Using the VGG-16 Pretrain Model

Our feature descriptors are obtained by processing the VGG-16 pre-training model, which is a 1000 class image classification network. Compared with other models, the VGG-16 pre-training model has these advantages: (a). Except for very few convolution kernels, the size of other convolution kernels is 3 × 3 so that the receptive field of each convolution kernel is smaller. It is more suitable for images with more obvious local features such as pig skin images. (b). The structure of this model is relatively simple and very easy to modify or only use some of the modules. (c). Its excellent performance in the field of image classification proves that this model has excellent feature extraction ability, and its convolution kernel can extract common features and has strong generalization ability.

Because we use convolutional neural networks only for feature extraction, not for other tasks such as image classification, our use of CNN does not include the fully connected layer. Therefore, the size of the input can be any multiple of 32. However, due to the different input sizes, the receptive field of each kernel is distinct, and the excessive size of input image will seriously affect the calculation. At the same time, the input of our CNN model contains two images, if the sizes of the two inputs are not the same, the performance of feature extraction will be seriously affected. Therefore, considering the fact that the unified receptive field can greatly reduce the amount of calculation, we input the fixed size images (224 × 224) to the network.

Using one single network layer as an output cannot guarantee that effective features could be extracted from images under various conditions. In order to solve this problem, our feature descriptor is obtained through multiple layers. After placing an image generated using random values into VGG-16, the convolution kernel of each network layer can be visualized by a gradient rise. The shallow network layer pays attention to the detailed features, and the deep network layer outputs are influenced by the specific category, which is not suitable as the only feature descriptor. So, we choose $pool_3$, $pool_4$ layer output to build our feature descriptors (Fig. 3).

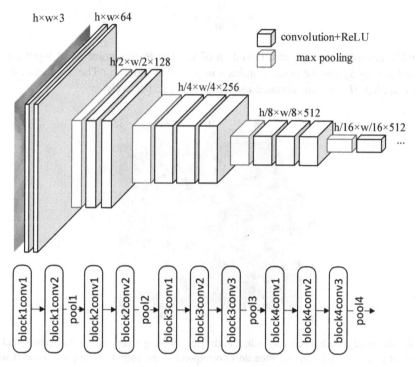

Fig. 3. Part of the VGG-16 network structure

VGG-16 has 5 convolutional blocks. Each convolutional layer contains multiple convolution operations. We use pooling layers after the third and fourth convolutional layers for feature extraction. The $pool_3$ layer output is of the size $28 \times 28 \times 256$. We divide the input image into 28×28 cells, each with 8×8 pixels. Each 8×8 square maps a 256-dimensional vector of the $pool_3$ layer, so each square center serves as one feature point whose descriptor is a 256-dimensional vector, and the $pool_3$ feature map M_1 is the output of $pool_3$ itself.

The size of the $pool_4$ layer output is $14 \times 14 \times 512$. Each 16×16 pixels of the input image map a 512-dimensional vector. The $pool_4$ layer output cannot directly form features because the 16×16 pixels of the input image include 4 feature points, so the 512-dimensional vector generated in the square is shared by 4 feature points. The $pool_4$ layer output after the Kronecker product (see Eq. 1) forms the M_2. The method of feature extraction is shown in Fig. 4.

$$M_2 = O_{pool_4} \otimes I_{2 \times 2 \times 1} \tag{1}$$

The obtained feature maps M_1, M_2 should be normalized before proceeding to the next step as shown in Eq. 2.

$$M_i \leftarrow \frac{M_i}{\sigma(M_i)}, i = 1, 2 \tag{2}$$

$\sigma(M_i)$ calculates the standard deviation of M_i. The feature point set of input image I_a is donated as S_a and the point at index x in S_a is donated as a_x. The features of point a_x in mapping M_1, M_2 are donated as $F_1(x)$, $F_2(x)$ respectively.

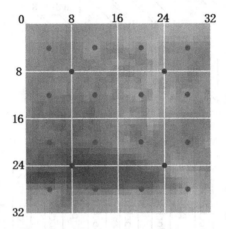

Fig. 4. The perception field corresponding to different pooling layers. Green dots correspond to the output of the pool$_3$ layer, and blue dots correspond to the output of the pool$_4$ layer (Color figure online)

2.2   Feature Pre-Matching

In order to reduce the computation and compare our feature descriptors with other feature extraction algorithms, pre-matching is introduced. As shown in Eq. 3, the weighted sum of the features extracted from pool$_3$ and pool$_4$ means the feature distance of the feature points a_x and b_y

$$d(x,y) = \lambda d_1(x,y) + d_2(x,y) \tag{3}$$

The coefficient λ is taken here as $\sqrt{2}$, because the pool$_3$ feature is a 256-dimensional vector, and the pool$_4$ layer is characterized by a 512-dimensional vector. The Euclidean distance is used to measure the similarity between features as shown in Eq. 4.

$$d_i(x,y) = \|F_i(x) - F_i(y)\|, i = 1, 2 \tag{4}$$

We assume that the feature point a_x matches b_y if they satisfy the following condition:

$$\forall a_{x_0} \in S_a, \nexists d(x_0, y) > d(x, y) \land \forall a_{x_1} \in S_a, \nexists d(x_1, y) < \theta \cdot d(x, y) \tag{5}$$

The role of the parameter θ is to control the fault tolerance of the pre-match stage. When θ is larger, the match between a_x and b_y is more reliable. However, in this pre-matching stage, we need a large number of feature points to make a rough registration, so a smaller threshold θ_0 is chosen, which can select the most robust 128 pairs of feature points for pre-matching.

2.3 Dynamic Inlier Selection

After rough processing, we perform a fine registration of images. However, the feature points we extracted are evenly distributed at the center of 8×8 pixels instead of the randomly occurring points obtained by other feature extraction algorithms such as SIFT. The similarity between pixel patches varies. Therefore, we have designed a dynamic inlier selection method. For pixel blocks with a large degree of overlap, we believe that the matching of their corresponding feature points is more reliable and should play a greater role in the overall matching. For pixel blocks with lower overlapping, their effect on the registration process should be smaller because they may be errors or outliers. Even if they are not errors or outliers, their corresponding pixel patches are less overlapping, which means these features are not obvious, so their presence in the registration process should be reduced.

Convolution feature values and spatial neighborhood information are considered simultaneously when judging whether a pair of feature points match with each other. The probability that a_x matches b_y is donated as $P_R[x, y]$. The posterior probability matrix P_R derived from convolutional and spatial features can be obtained by the following steps:

Calculate the Convolution Feature Distance. As shown in the pre-matching stage, when the point a_x matches b_y, their Euclidean distances of eigenvalues should be small, while the Euclidean distance is larger when they do not match. In order to compare the distance and future processing, the distance needs to be normalized, and the resulting convolution cost matrix is shown in Eq. 6.

$$C_\theta^{conv}[x, y] = \begin{cases} \frac{d(x,y)}{d_\theta^{max}}, & condition\ 1 \\ 1, & otherwise \end{cases} \tag{6}$$

d_θ^{max} is the maximum value of all feature distance in the feature pair selected by θ. Condition 1 means that a_x and b_y satisfy Eq. 5.

Calculate Neighborhood Information. Unlike the pre-matching phase, which only uses convolutional feature distance to select feature points, in the fine matching stage, we also consider the influence of neighborhood information. The shape context algorithm [26] can describe the neighborhood information of a point and form a histogram-based feature descriptor. Taking each feature point as the center point, then the polar coordinate system is established. After the polar coordinates are divided into several different arc-shaped regions, feature descriptors of each point are derived from the distribution of the surrounding points, and the resulting neighborhood cost matrix is shown in Eq. 7.

$$C_\theta^{geo}[x,y] = \frac{1}{2}\sum_{b=1}^{B} \frac{[h_a^x(t) - h_b^y(t)]^2}{h_a^x(t) + h_b^y(t)} \tag{7}$$

$h_a^x(t)$ means the number of points fell in the tth region centered on a_x.

Calculate the Overall Cost Matrix. Combine C_θ^{conv} and C_θ^{geo} using Hadamard product, which is shown in Eq. 8.

$$C = C_\theta^{conv} \odot C_\theta^{geo} \tag{8}$$

Calculate the Prior Probability Matrix. The purpose of dynamic interior point selection is to select more reliable parts among the large number of feature points obtained by feature extraction. The LAPJV algorithm [27] can be used to determine whether a_x and b_y match. Finally, the prior probability matrix is given in Eq. 9.

$$P_R[x,y] = \begin{cases} 1, & a_x \ matches \ b_y \\ \frac{1-\in}{N}, & otherwise \end{cases} \tag{9}$$

$\in$, whose value is between 0 and 1, represents the degree of trust we have in the inliers selected by the above steps. The larger the value of $\in$, the more we trust the selected feature points. N represents the number of point set S_a.

At the beginning of the selection, we choose a larger initial threshold θ_1 to select the most reliable 64 points. In the future registration iteration process, inliers are reselected in every k iteration. After each selection, the value of θ is subtracted by the step δ, which is shown in Eq. 10, so that more points are used for registration each time. Since the more credible points are used in the earlier process, errors or outliers cannot have a fatal effect on the registration process. At the same time, the most reliable points affect the overall registration, while other points will optimize the registration effects.

$$\delta = \frac{\theta_1 - \theta_0}{10} \tag{10}$$

2.4   Gaussian Mixture Model

GMM is a method of describing the sample probability density distribution by weighting the Gaussian model and effectively expressing the sample distribution. Let the point in the point set P_a be the observation data generated by the GMM, and the center of the GMM is related to the point in the P_b, and then the GMM probability density function is shown in Eq. 11.

$$p(a_x) = \sum_{m=1}^{M+1} p(a_x|m)p(m) \tag{11}$$

$p(m)$, which values 1/M, is the proportion of the mth Gaussian model in GMM and $p(a_x|m)$ is the mth Gaussian model. Also we add a uniform distribution of $p(a_x|M+1)$ to the mixture model to handle noise and outliers. Let the weight of uniform distribution be ω. The equation can be rewritten as Eq. 12.

$$p(x) = \omega \frac{1}{N} + (1 - \omega) \sum_{m=1}^{M} \frac{1}{2\pi\sigma^2} e^{-\frac{\|x-z\|^2}{2\sigma^2}} \tag{12}$$

Unlike the traditional GMM, the center z of our Gaussian model $p(a_x|m)$ is determined by P_b, Gaussian radial basis function G and the parameter matrix W. The transformation formula can be defined as Eq. 13.

$$Z = P_b + GW \tag{13}$$

The parameters (σ^2, ω, W) of the GMM can be obtained from the maximum likelihood estimation, and the equivalent minimization of the negative log-likelihood function is shown as Eq. 14.

$$L(\sigma^2, \omega, W) = -\sum_{n=1}^{N} \log \sum_{m=1}^{M+1} P_R[x, y]p(a_x|m) \tag{14}$$

2.5 Registration Using the EM Algorithm

We apply the EM algorithm [28] to the parameters (σ^2, ω, W) in the negative log-likelihood function. The main idea of the EM algorithm is to calculate the posterior probability of each Gaussian model by using the Bayesian theory and the initial values of the parameters. After expanding and simplifying redundant items, Eq. 14 can be written as Eq. 15.

$$Q(\sigma^2, \omega, W) = -\frac{1}{2\sigma^2} \sum_{n=1}^{N} \sum_{m=1}^{M+1} N_p - N_p \log\left(\frac{\sigma^2 \omega}{1 - \omega}\right) - N \log \omega \tag{15}$$

where $N_p = \sum_{n=1}^{N} \sum_{m=1}^{M} p^{old}(m|a_x)$. Equation 15 is the lower bound of the likelihood function as shown in Eq. 14. The EM algorithm alternately executes E step and M step so that the Eq. 15 continually approximates the minimum value of Eq. 14.

E Step. Calculate the posterior probability using the Bayesian formula and parameters obtained from previous iterations.

$$P_O[x, y] = p^{old}(m|a_x) = \frac{P_R[x, y]p(a_x|m)}{p(a_x)} \tag{16}$$

M Step. Update the parameters for next iteration.

$$\sigma^2 := \frac{1}{2N_P} \sum_{n=1}^{N} \sum_{m=1}^{M} p(m|a_x) \left\| a_x - z_y^2 \right\| \tag{17}$$

$$\omega := 1 - \frac{1}{N} \sum_{n=1}^{N} \sum_{m=1}^{M} p(m|a_x) \tag{18}$$

$$W := \left(G + \lambda \sigma^2 P_d^{-1} \right)^{-1} \cdot \left(P_d^{-1} P_O X - Y \right) \tag{19}$$

where $P_d = diag(P_O \cdot \alpha)$, α is an N dimension column vector as $[1, 1, \ldots, 1]^T$.

3   Experiment and Result Analysis

Our work has been verified on the pork skin dataset. We used SIFT to compare the proposed feature extraction algorithm and CPD [22], ICP [29] and KNN [30] to compare our registration algorithm respectively.

3.1   Experiment Design

Feature Pre-Matching Test. Since feature pre-matching is the most important intermediate process of this method, we compare the convolution features used in this method with the traditional SIFT features. We test those two methods by extracting features from the same dataset and matching them. After that, we select the most reliable 100 pairs of pre-matched results and use them to calculate the accuracy rate Precision = TP/(TP + FP). The number of pre-matched results can be controlled by controlling the value of the parameter θ.

Image Registration Accuracy Test. In this test, we mark 15 coordinate points in each pair of corresponding images. The test compares the coordinate of the original image with the coordinate of the image after registration, and measures the error of the

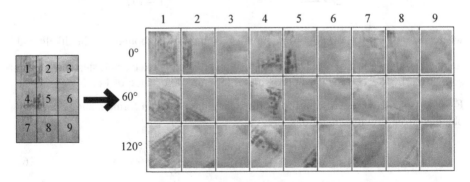

Fig. 5. Local pig skin image collection method and example.

distance between these coordinate point pairs. We used the median of the distance (MoD), the standard deviation of the distance (SDoD), the root mean square distance (RMSD), and the mean absolute distance (MAD) to measure our error (Fig. 5).

Dataset. The experimental place was in the room under natural light, and the fresh pork skin images were collected. Each pig skin was about 28 cm long and 21 cm wide. The illumination condition was fluorescent light scattering, the light intensity was about 100 lx, and the sensor was about 10 cm from the center of the pork skin. The sensor is Sony IMX 298. For each piece of fresh pork skin, it is divided into 9 areas of 3 $\times$ 3, and 0°, 60°, 120° rotations respectively based on the center of each area. Through the above operation, the data collection was carried out on different 30 pieces of fresh skinned pork, and a total of 810 pieces of pork skin images were collected for the experiment.

3.2 Results Analysis

Pre-Matching Test Results. The accuracy of the feature pre-matching results on existing datasets using CNN features and traditional SIFT features is shown in Table 1. At the same time, in order to explain the position of the feature points in the pre-matching phase and the assignment of correct and erroneous points, a representative representation of the three of matching results is shown in Fig. 6. In addition, the proposed algorithm guarantees that each square region has only one feature point (because they have only one center) so that the distribution of feature points is more even in the overlap patch.

Table 1. Feature pre-matching precision test result

Index	CNN feature/%	SIFT feature/%
avg.	92.59	71.60
min.	61.72	37.03
max.	100.00	94.44

Registration Accuracy Test Results. The values and comparisons of the registration accuracy are shown in Table 2. The experimental results show that the proposed method performs best, especially when the image displacement or rotation is small, our algorithm can accurately register each key point. Although KNN is not sensitive to outliers, this method consumes too much computation and takes a long time. When the scale of the image changes greatly, the accuracy of the CPD method will decrease. In addition, as shown in Fig. 8, our algorithm performs best when we rotate the image with a step of 10° (Fig. 7).

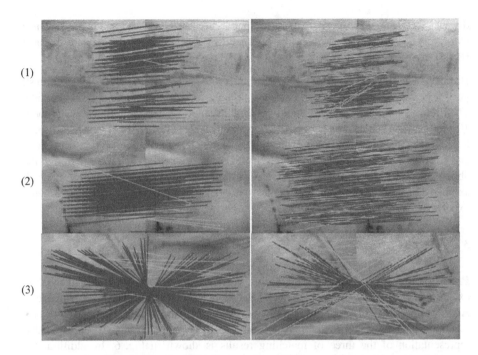

Fig. 6. Results of the feature pre-matching precision test

Table 2. Registration accuracy test result

Method	RMSD/pixel	MAD/pixel	MoD/pixel	SDoD/pixel
ICP	9.35	10.62	7.48	6.35
KNN	20.36	28.92	8.07	11.68
CPD	12.84	15.40	5.46	7.48
Ours	**10.64**	**14.57**	5.52	**5.37**

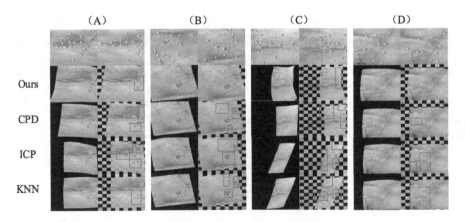

Fig. 7. Results of registration test

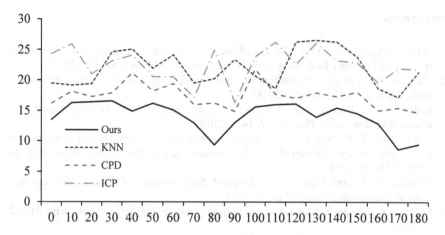

Fig. 8. The effects of rotation on the accuracy of four registration algorithms

4 Conclusion and Future Work

In view of the current pork food safety in our country and the shortcomings of the current domestic pork traceability technology, this paper proposed a pork traceability technique based on the feature analysis of convolutional neural networks. We proposed an image registration method based on the convolutional feature: (i) A feature extraction method is constructed using convolutional neural network with the pre-trained VGG. In order to effectively utilize the deep convolutional neural architecture in pork skin image registration applications, our feature descriptors utilize the advanced convolutional information while preserving some local information. (ii) A non-rigid feature point registration method is proposed which uses a gradual expansion of the inlier selection method to quickly determine the coarse transformation through the most reliable feature points in the first stages, and then we have found that the increased feature points can directly improve the registration performance while reducing the impact of outliers. Compared with SIFT, the considerable accuracy is raised from feature pre-matching tests on pork skin image datasets, and image registration tests show that our approach is superior to common methods in most cases.

So far, no similar deep learning solutions have been found in the traceability of pork. By now the tracing success rate of local pigskin images needs to be improved. According to the current research and the samples of the pig skin images held, the registration success rate of the local pig skin image is 86.67%, and there will be a small number of skinned pork that cannot be registered successfully. Experiments show that the proposed algorithm cannot describe the features of pig skin with very low resolution. Also the pork traceability technology can only apply to skinned pork. Some pork sold in the market today does not have pig skin, so future research in this area can explore the pork itself to achieve the traceability of various types of pork. Therefore, in the future development of the algorithm, we will consider the features of pork itself instead of pig skin and try to trace the unmarked pork.

References

1. Ortega, D.L., Wang, H.H., Wu, L., Olynk, N.J.: Modeling heterogeneity in consumer preferences for select food safety attributes in China. Food Policy **36**, 318 (2011)
2. Channon, H.A., et al.: Guaranteeing the quality and integrity of pork–an Australian case study. Meat Sci. **144**, 186–192 (2018)
3. Mohanty, S.P., Hughes, D.P., Salathé, M.: Using deep learning for image-based plant disease detection. Front. Plant Sci. **7**, 1419 (2016)
4. Arivazhagan, S., Shebiah, R.N., Ananthi, S., Varthini, S.V.: Detection of unhealthy region of plant leaves and classification of plant leaf diseases using texture features. Agric. Eng. Int. CIGR J. **15**, 211 (2013)
5. Duindam, V., Chopra, P.: Systems and methods for registration of a medical device using a reduced search space. Google Patents (2018)
6. Maintz, J.A., Viergever, M.A.: A survey of medical image registration. Med. Image Anal. **2**, 1 (1998)
7. Schulz, C.J., Schmitt, M., Böckler, D., Geisbüsch, P.: Fusion imaging to support endovascular aneurysm repair using 3D-3D registration. J. Endovasc. Ther. **23**, 791 (2016)
8. Ma, J., Zhou, H., Zhao, J., Gao, Y., Jiang, J., Tian, J.: Robust feature matching for remote sensing image registration via locally linear transforming. IEEE Trans. Geosci. Remote Sens. **53**, 6469 (2015)
9. Shen, L., Huang, X., Fan, C., Li, Y.: Enhanced mutual information-based medical image registration using a hybrid optimisation technique. Electron. Lett. **54**, 926 (2018)
10. Nasihatkon, B., Fejne, F., Kahl, F.: Globally optimal rigid intensity based registration: a fast fourier domain approach. In: Proceedings of the IEEE Conference on Computer Vision and Pattern Recognition, vol. 5936 (2016)
11. Ordonez, A., Arguello, F., Heras, D.B.: GPU accelerated FFT-based registration of hyperspectral scenes. IEEE J. Sel. Top. Appl. Earth Obs. Remote Sens. **10**, 4869 (2017)
12. Yu, X., Lu, Z., Hu, D.: Review of remote sensing image registration techniques. Opt. Precis. Eng. **21**, 2960 (2015)
13. Lowe, D.G.: Object recognition from local scale-invariant features, vol. 2, pp. 1150. IEEE (1999)
14. Aggarwal, V., Gupta, A.: Integrating morphological edge detection and mutual information for nonrigid registration of medical images. Curr. Med. Imaging Rev. **15**, 292 (2019)
15. Zhu, X., Cao, H., Zhang, Y., Tan, K., Ling, X.: Fine registration for VHR images based on superpixel registration-noise estimation. IEEE Geosci. Remote Sens. Lett. **99**, 1 (2018)
16. Bay, H., Ess, A., Tuytelaars, T., Van Gool, L.: Speeded-up robust features (SURF). Comput. Vis. Image Underst. **110**, 346 (2008)
17. Morel, J., Yu, G.: ASIFT: a new framework for fully affine invariant image comparison. SIAM J. Imaging Sci. **2**, 438 (2009)
18. Ke, Y., Sukthankar, R.: PCA-SIFT: a more distinctive representation for local image descriptors, vol. 2, pp. II. IEEE (2004)
19. Bach, F.R., Jordan, M.I.: Kernel independent component analysis. J. Mach. Learn. Res. **3**, 1 (2002)
20. Liu, X., Tian, Z., Leng, C., Duan, X.: Remote sensing image registration based on KICA-SIFT descriptors. In: 2010 Seventh International Conference on Fuzzy Systems and Knowledge Discovery, vol. 1, pp. 278. IEEE (2010)
21. Wu, W., Zhao, W., Liu, H.: Overview of remote sensing digital image registration technology. Infrared **10**, 14 (2009)

22. Saval-Calvo, M., Azorin-Lopez, J., Fuster-Guillo, A., Villena-Martinez, V., Fisher, R.B.: 3D non-rigid registration using color: color coherent point drift. Comput. Vis. Image Underst. **169**, 119 (2018)

23. Deng, J., Dong, W., Socher, R., Li, L., Li, K., Fei-Fei, L.: ImageNet: a large-scale hierarchical image database. In: 2009 IEEE Conference on Computer Vision and Pattern Recognition, vol. 248. IEEE (2009)

24. Simonyan, K., Zisserman, A.: Very deep convolutional networks for large-scale image recognition. arXiv preprint arXiv:1409.1556 (2014)

25. Bookstein, F.L.: Principal warps: thin-plate splines and the decomposition of deformations. IEEE Trans. Pattern Anal. Mach. Intell. **11**, 567 (1989)

26. Zheng, M., Zhou, J., Cao, Z., Dong, X.: PPOIM: privacy-preserving shape context based image denoising and matching with efficient outsourcing. In: Naccache, D., et al. (eds.) ICICS 2018. LNCS, vol. 11149, pp. 215–231. Springer, Cham (2018). https://doi.org/10.1007/978-3-030-01950-1_13

27. Jones, W., Chawdhary, A., King, A.: Optimising the Volgenant-Jonker algorithm for approximating graph edit distance. Pattern Recogn. Lett. **87**, 47 (2017)

28. Ma, J., Jiang, J., Liu, C., Li, Y.: Feature guided Gaussian mixture model with semi-supervised EM and local geometric constraint for retinal image registration. Inf. Sci. **417**, 128 (2017)

29. Lin, C., Tai, Y., Lee, J., Chen, Y.: A novel point cloud registration using 2D image features. EURASIP J. Adv. Sig. Process. **1**, 5 (2017)

30. Bhavani, R.R., Wiselin Jiji, G.: Image registration for varicose ulcer classification using KNN classifier. Int. J. Comput. Appl. **40**, 88 (2018)

ORB-Based Multiple Fixed Resolution Approach for On-Board Visual Recognition

Daniel Phillips[1]([✉]), Akash Pooransingh[1], and Sinem Guven[2]

[1] The University of the West Indies, St. Augustine Campus,
St. Augustine, Trinidad and Tobago
{daniel.phillips,apooransingh}@my.uwi.edu
[2] IBM Research, TJ Watson Research Center, Yorktown Heights, New York, USA
sguven@us.ibm.com

Abstract. Maintenance and troubleshooting of hardware on a large scale pose a challenge in deploying expert technicians at multiple sites. Augmented Reality-based technology support equips the technicians with the skills they need to solve hardware problems even without expert level training, thereby reducing training time and cost to the vendor. Enabling Augmented Reality for technology support requires the ability to visually recognize the hardware in real time using mobile devices, and train the underlying algorithms at scale. This paper proposes a novel approach to address these issues. Our ORB-based fixed multi-resolution recognition algorithm achieves over 95% accuracy at a resolution scale of 0.2, and an approximately 60% faster recognition time than the next best comparable method. We also demonstrate the real-world applicability of our algorithm through an implementation of an Augmented Reality application.

Keywords: Oriented FAST rotated BRIEF (ORB) ·
Scale Invariant Feature Transform (SIFT) ·
Speeded Up Robust Features (SURF)

1 Introduction

Technical support services for the maintenance of hardware (servers, computers, printers, mobile devices, etc.) is becoming a core service offered by companies responsible for system maintenance of hundreds of components around the globe. They employ tens of thousands of support specialist that maintain equipment made by various vendors. These technicians must be fully trained to troubleshoot various components, which requires substantial training time and incurs cost to the vendor. Conventionally, paper-based manuals or videos have been used to receive technical guidance during repair sessions. As hardware becomes more and more complex, ways of reducing the cost and time of a repair has become a topic of interest. Augmented Reality (AR), which overlays graphics or media

© Springer Nature Switzerland AG 2019
D. Wang and L.-J. Zhang (Eds.): AIMS 2019, LNCS 11516, pp. 54–71, 2019.
https://doi.org/10.1007/978-3-030-23367-9_5

on top of what we see in the real world, is increasingly becoming popular as a new way to visually guide the technicians through the repair process. Object detection and recognition form the fundamental processes toward an AR system, as shown in Fig. 1. Feature point detection based methods are used for both object recognition and object localization. These methods are used for image classification [1], image matching [2], localization [3] and object detection [4] with success. Three common feature point descriptors are the Oriented FAST rotated BRIEF (ORB), Speeded Up Robust Features (SURF) and Scale Invariant Feature Transform (SIFT). These feature point methods have been combined with the methods such as the Bag of Features [5] to yield an accuracy of up to 90% [6]. Feature point methods have been successful, but they are not always the most efficient or the fastest method. Alternative methods, such as Histogram Intersection and Local Binary Patterns, have also yielded success in various applications. Using Local Binary Patters (LBP) combined with Support Vector Machines, accuracy of up to 97% have been achieved [7]. The Histogram Intersection methods have the added advantage of being able to detect objects based on color, which can be useful in various applications. This method can also be combined with a support vector machine to improve its classification of images. However, the accuracy of this method is typically low as reported in [9] of about 58%.

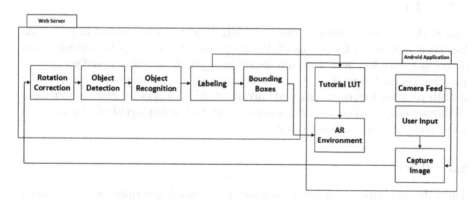

Fig. 1. A typical augmented reality system

2   Feature Point Detection Techniques

Feature Point detection methods contribute significantly toward object recognition applications. In [4], object recognition implementation, which utilized SURF feature points, was able to achieve high recognition accuracy. This method was successful even though background noise was introduced into the images containing the objects. Piccinini [3], also used feature point detection techniques in applications where occlusion occurred. During these applications, the SIFT technique also yielded a high recognition accuracy. Even though these feature point techniques yield a high accuracy, they are still computationally intensive causing them to perform slowly. The ORB technique is much faster and is able to yield a result in a fraction of the time. It is also able to yield an accurate result especially when combined with other methods as shown in [14]. From these implementations, it can be seen that feature point detection has performed well in various applications despite being exposed to varying environments. This paper proposes the use of the ORB feature point technique as part of our approach and compare it to the traditional feature point methods: SIFT and SURF.

2.1 ORB

ORB has been recognized for its speed as it is easily one of the fastest and light weight feature descriptors currently in existence [7]. This detector is both scale invariant and rotation invariant making it very useful for a wide array of applications. ORB was built by merging in the Features from Accelerated Segment Test (FAST) key point detector with the Binary Robust Independent Elementary Features (BREIF) descriptor. Since neither FAST nor BRIEF are inherently rotation invariant, an intensity centroid was assessed to measure the corner orientation [8].

2.2 SIFT

The Scale Invariant Feature Transform (SIFT) was first presented in [15]. This has been recognized to be one of the more robust feature point detector and descriptor. This has been proven to be robust against the affine transform, intensity changes and even certain view point changes. Just like ORB, this detector is both rotation invariant and scale invariant. SIFT works by first computing a Difference of Gaussians to get a similar effect to the Laplacian of Gaussians in a less computational intensive way [16].

2.3 SURF

The SIFT descriptor can be considered a successful descriptor as it has been used in a wide array of applications. One major problem that arises during its implementation is that, it is computationally intensive and not suitable for low powered devices. Therefore, more development was done to find a less computationally intensive, but still robust detector and descriptor [17]. In [2], produced the Speeded Up Robust Features (SURF) descriptor and detector. This was developed to be both rotation and scale invariant, just as SIFT was. Instead of approximating the Laplacian of Gaussians (LoG) using a Difference of Gaussians (DoG) as was done with the SIFT detector, SURF uses a box filter. The box filter was chosen since the integral of the image can be used, which makes the algorithm much more efficient. Also, the approximation can be more easily calculated and done in parallel, reducing the computational time requirements.

3 Non-Feature Point Techniques

Non-feature point methods have also been very successful in the areas of object recognition. Unlike feature point methods, they seek to recognize objects based on physical features, such as color and texture. These methods in some cases are less affected by rotation, scaling, background noise and even occlusion [10]. These methods have been successfully tested in areas, such as facial recognition, yielding good results [11].

3.1 Local Binary Patterns

Introduced in 1996, [12], Local Binary Patterns (LBP) have been used to extract features from images using thresholding. This method has been used to tackle difficult recognition problems, such as facial recognition with success [13]. This is accomplished by using a 3×3 pixel block of an image and thresholding the outer pixels of an image block using the blocks center pixel value multiplied by a power of 2. The resulting values are then summed together to produce the value or label for that center pixel [18]. This can be defined as follows:

$$LBP(x_c, y_c) = \sum_{n=0}^{7} 2^n g(I_n - I(x_c, y_c))$$

where (x_c, y_c) is the LBP centre pixel value, I_n represents the neighbor pixel value. $I(x_c, y_c)$ represents the centre pixel value and n represents the index of the neighbor pixels. The function is designed to function as follows:

$$g(x) = \begin{cases} 0, x < 0 \\ 1, x \geq 0 \end{cases}$$

Therefore, during the thresholding, if the current block pixel value is larger than the center pixel value, it is assigned a value of 1, if not, it is assigned a value of 0. An 8-bit number is used giving the center pixels 256 possible values [12]. This method was improved in [3] to make the method more customizable improving its performance in a wider array of applications. These improvements removed the restrictions on size of the sampling operator and number of sampling points used. Also, it allowed for variable block size [18]. Linear Binary patterns have also been paired with Support Vector Machines for improved image classification. The LBP-SVM was tested in [7], with the Indian pines data set, Pavia Data set and the Salinas Data Set, which contained hyperspectral imagery taken by satellites and airborne vehicles. The percentage accuracy achieved from these datasets were between 89.47% to 97.53% for this method.

3.2 Histogram Intersection

The Histogram Intersection method was introduced by Swain and Ballard [10]. This method was developed as a technique for comparing the similarity between two histograms. This method has been useful in many recognition tasks such as identifying species of trees in Malaysia [19]. The match between the histograms are computed and the result yields a number. For this method, the greater the number the better the match. If the histograms are normalized, the result provided would be a number between 0 and 1. This method is robust against many changes such as resolution, occlusion, view point changes, background changes and even rotational changes. This makes this method useful for the recognition of the same objects in different environments. If the histograms are normalized, this improves the robustness of this method against the distraction of background pixels in the image. The intersection between the two histograms is described as follows:

$$\cap(I, M) = \sum^{n} min(I, M)$$

The histograms are normalized by using the number of pixels in the model histogram. The normalized histogram can be defined as follows:

$$H(I, M) = \frac{\sum_{j=1}^{n} min(I_i, M_j)}{\sum_{j=1}^{n} M_j}$$

Histogram intersection is not the only method of histogram comparison, but was found to be one of the most robust methods [19]. Histogram intersection can be used with many different color schemes. The most common schemes are the HSV (Hue, Saturation, Value) scheme and the RGB (Red, Green, Blue) color scheme. RGB has been used in many applications with a good result despite being very sensitive to light changes and noise. It is also composed of components that are highly correlated with each other and not intuitive to human perception. Also the chrominance and luminance values cannot be separated easily making images difficult to process in this scheme [20]. Using the HSV scheme can, however, be used to remove the luminance information from the image so that this method would be invariant to light changes improving the accuracy of the method.

4   Classification Techniques

4.1   Bag of Features

The bag of Features model was introduced in 2004 as a way of classifying images [5]. This method can be broken down into four main parts. This includes detection and description, the assignment of descriptors to predetermined clusters, constructing a bag of key points and the application of a multi-class classifier. The first step, detection and description, can be accomplished with a feature point detector and descriptor. The more invariant and robust the descriptor, the more suited it would be for this process. Since it would be used to train an image classifier, the descriptor should be also invariant to illumination and the affine transform. For the next stage, the construction of the visual vocabulary is accomplished. The visual vocabulary is used to relate descriptors from a test image back to previously collected descriptors in the training images. To improve the efficiency of the comparison of the training descriptors to the test descriptors, clustering is used. K means clustering is used to accomplish this in an efficient manner. The categorization is then completed on the clusters produced. During the supervised training of the model, the labels of the images are sent to the categorizer to develop a statistical method for distinguishing categories. This categorization step can be completed using a support vector machine. Since this is a multiclass classification problem, the support vector machine is trained using a one-against-all approach. For this stage, a Naive Bayes method can also be used. During testing however, the Support Vector Machine method outperformed the Naive Bayes method [21].

5 Multiple Fixed Resolution Based On-Board Component Recognition Algorithm

This paper proposes a simple multiple fixed resolution method for recognition. This approach is a two staged process as shown in Fig. 2.

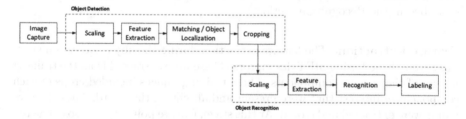

Fig. 2. Recognition algorithm steps

5.1 Algorithm

Detection

1. Convert image to greyscale
2. Scale image
3. Extract SIFT feature points
4. Complete brute force matching

Recognition

1. Convert to grayscale
2. Scale image
3. Compute local descriptors using ORB features
4. Load bag of features model
5. Image prediction using bag of features model
6. Label component

5.2   Image Capture

The images were captured from the mobile device using an appropriate resolution. During the implementation of this algorithm, we used the Wikitude Camera API extension along with a camera plug in to capture images. This allowed for direct access to the camera feed at the resolution specified. The captured Image was then stored to internal storage of the device in the PNG format since it was lossless compression scheme. Next, this image was sent to the web server to process the image. During this stage, the image was also converted to gray-scale using the following equation:

$$Y \leftarrow 0.299R + 0.587G + 0.114B$$

5.3   Object Detection

Scaling. The images are scaled on two different occasions. The first scaling occurs after image capture to allow the image to be at the optimal resolution, where the object detection would operate at its peak accuracy. Each image at this stage was scaled equally in the x and y plane at a fixed scale. (The second scaling occurs after cropping of the localized components in the image, as later described in the Recognition section.)

Feature Extraction. The feature extraction during the object detection stage was accomplished using SIFT descriptors. These were extracted from the training images of the various components. These training images included crops of each component of interest that were present and absent on the board. These feature points were extracted and stored. At this stage, feature points were also extracted from the full motherboard image, which was the testing image and these feature points were also stored for use in the localization step.

Matching - Object Localization. At this stage, the previously extracted feature points of the components were matched with the feature points in the testing image. For this stage, a knn Brute-Force Matcher was used. The matches were calculated using the L^2 distance. This distance can be expressed using the following equation.

$$d(f_a, f_b) \sum (f_a - f_b)^2$$

where f_a and f_b represent the feature points descriptors from the query and test image respectively. Once the feature matching was completed, outlying points were detected and removed using the RANSAC algorithm. This step was done to remove the false matches allowing for a more accurate localization of the components. Next, the in-lying points were used to calculate a homography matrix so that a bounding box can be calculated and placed over the components found.

Given a set of feature point matches that contains both true positive matches and false positive matches, it would be difficult to determine which matches are the true positives. Using the distance ratio proposed by Lowe [21] alone may cause many points that are true positives to be also removed. To solve this problem the Random Sample Consensus (RANSAC) method can be used. RANSAC is used to first estimate a global relation that fits the dataset using the hypothesize and verify framework. This is achieved by first sampling the subsets of data at random enough intervals so that a solution can be computed. This allows for the global relation to be found while simultaneously dividing the data into outlying and inlying points. Using the data that was sampled, a hypothesis for the model is determined and then all the points are compared against the hypothesis to verify it. To make this method more robust, this step is repeated until some pre-defined termination criteria is met based on a confidence criterion. This confidence criteria is usually satisfied when one of the subsets are outlier free [22]. This termination criteria can be calculated using the following equation:

$$N = \frac{log(1 - p)}{log(1 - (1 - v)^m)}$$

where N is the number of iterations, p is the probability that at least of the sets have no outliers and m is the minimum number of points required.

Cropping. Cropping was accomplished using the bounding boxes produced in in the matching and localization stage. The locations, where the bounding boxes were placed, were cropped by extracting the pixels within the range of the bounding boxes.

5.4   Object Recognition

Scaling. The second scaling occurs after cropping of the localized components in the image, as per Fig. 2. This scaling was done so that the object recognition algorithm can operate at its maximum recognition accuracy. Each image at this stage was scaled equally in the x and y plane at a fixed scale.

Feature Extraction. The feature extraction at this stage was accomplished for the methods that required features to be extracted from the images. These included ORB, SIFT, SURF and the Local Binary Patterns (LBP) method. For the Histogram Intersection method, this step was ignored. During this stage, the images were converted to grey-scale before the features were extracted. These feature points once extracted were stored for use in the subsequent step.

Recognition. The recognition module was done with the Bag of Features Model. This model was trained using the orb features extracted from the training images. A support vector machine was also used to assist with making predictions from the collection of feature points in the model. The support vector machine was used to find the best hyperplane to separate data usually of two classes. The best hyperplane is defined as the hyperplane with the largest margin between the two classes of data. The support vectors are the data points closest to the hyperplane. The general equation for a hyperplane can be written as follows:

$$f(x) = x^{'}\beta + b = 0$$

where $\beta \epsilon R^d$ and b is a real number. Support vector machine seek to find a solution for β and b that minimize $\| \beta \|$ such that for all the data point (x_j, y_j).

Labeling. Once the prediction was completed, the components were labeled using the output of the recognition step. These labels were used to determine which components were present so that the user can be prompted in the Augmented Reality application.

6   Results

The image processing algorithms and code were executed on a computer which ran Ubuntu 16.04 using Intel Core i7-2620M operating at 2.70 GHz with 16 GB of RAM operating at 1333 MHz. During testing, Open-CV 3.1.0 was used along with python 2.7.

6.1   Web Server Processing

Since the feature point matching and extraction steps were heavily CPU and memory intensive processes, they could not be accomplished on a mobile device. Therefore they were done on a remote server and results were sent back to the mobile device. The camera feed on the mobile Android device was used to acquire the images of the scene and then the images were scaled and sent to the sever for processing. Upon the completion of processing, the co-ordinates and labels were sent back to the mobile device for plotting and displaying in the AR application. This allowed the object recognition to also run at faster speeds as it did not have to share resources with the AR application.

6.2   Augmented Reality Application

The AR application was designed to provide visual guidance to technicians during repair sessions. It is implemented using the Wikitude Android Native API. After the bounding box location was calculated, the relevant bounding boxes were placed in the AR scene to be viewed by the user. The boxes were tracked with 6DOF and anchored to the recognized components in the camera feed so that even if the mobile device was moved, the bounding boxes would remain in same position over the components. The current component relevant to the tutorial instruction was also highlighted in this environment. The bounding box visualization was implemented using the instant tracking module, as shown in Fig. 3.

Fig. 3. (a) Showing the feature points, bounding boxes and labels placed during the recognition stage with (b) Showing the bounding boxes placed in the augmented reality application.

7   Training

Some methods, such as the Bag of Words Method and Local Binary Patterns Method, required a much larger training set than the Histogram Intersection method. Therefore a different training dataset was used for this implementation. The breakdown of this dataset is described in Table 1.

Table 1. Showing the image breakdown for the training dataset

	Heatsink	Memory	PCIE	Heatsink	Memory	PCIE
Component present	Yes	Yes	Yes	No	No	No
Image count	56	56	56	56	56	56

8   Testing

8.1   Motherboard Image Dataset

A dataset was compiled for testing the performance of various algorithms of interest. This dataset comprised of images of a Dell Optiplex g × 260 motherboard still in the case. The images were taken with a Samsung S7 (SM-G930A)

camera, had a height of 3024 pixels and a width of 4032 pixels, and were saved to a JPEG format. Different images were taken with the motherboard containing different components while varying the proximity of the camera to the motherboard. Also, the dataset contained slight changes in lighting conditions, but all of the photos were taken indoors. All images were taken parallel to the motherboard to reduce errors caused by changing the pitch of the camera. The breakdown of the dataset can be seen in Table 2.

Table 2. Showing the image breakdown for the training dataset

Heatsink	Memory	PCIE	Image count
Yes	Yes	Yes	14
Yes	Yes	No	14
Yes	No	Yes	14
Yes	No	No	14
No	Yes	Yes	14
No	Yes	No	14
No	No	Yes	14
No	No	No	14
Total			113

8.2   Motherboard Component Dataset

Another dataset was created to test the recognition of the mother board components. To create this dataset, the images from the Motherboard image dataset were used and the individual components of interest were cropped out and saved. These images were stored in the same JPEG format as the original images. The dimensions of the images varied depending on the component. The breakdown of this dataset can be seen in Table 3 below.

Table 3. Showing the image breakdown for the component dataset

	Heatsink	Memory	PCIE	Heatsink	Memory	PCIE
Component present	Yes	Yes	Yes	No	No	No
Image count	56	56	56	56	56	56

8.3   Object Detection Testing

Feature Point Method Testing. The feature point object detection algorithm was also tested against the Motherboard Image Dataset. To test the algorithm, three different feature point detectors were tested against the dataset. These detectors included ORB, SURF and SIFT detectors and descriptors. For each descriptor tested, the feature point matches detected were drawn on the images so that false matches can be easily detected. Each feature point method was assigned a different color so that the results can be easily detected. For binary string descriptors, such as ORB, the hamming distance was used as the measurement, but for descriptors, such as SIFT and SURF, euclidean distance was used. This distance was used as a threshold for the point matches so that matches that were far off were not plotted. To assist with evaluating the performance of the algorithm, many parameters were recorded. The algorithms were tested at different image scaling to see how re-sizing the images impacted the performance of the algorithm. The size of the image was varied by increments of 10%. The number of feature points in the training image and the number of feature points matched in the test image was recorded. The percentage of matches was calculated using this value. The processing time taken for each iteration was also recorded. The results from this testing are seen in Table 4.

Table 4. Showing the object detection accuracy

	SIFT	SURF	ORB	SIFT	SURF	ORB	SIFT	SURF	ORB
	True positives			False positives			Accuracy		
0.1	122	13	0	217	326	339	35.99	3.83	0.00
0.2	209	150	0	130	189	339	61.65	44.25	0.00
0.3	273	201	0	66	138	339	80.53	59.29	0.00
0.4	285	241	0	54	98	339	84.07	71.09	0.00
0.5	285	221	0	54	118	339	84.07	65.19	0.00
0.6	279	215	0	60	124	339	82.03	63.42	0.00
0.7	258	217	0	81	122	339	76.11	64.01	0.00
0.8	241	224	0	98	115	339	71.09	66.08	0.00
0.9	237	222	1	102	117	338	69.91	65.49	0.29
1.0	240	217	6	99	122	333	70.80	64.01	1.77

8.4 Object Recognition Testing

Histogram Intersection Testing. The Histogram Intersection Algorithm was tested against the Motherboard Component Dataset discussed previously. For this testing, the dataset was trained with sample images and then the algorithm was used to attempt to recognize the images. The size of the images varied by 10% and the time taken for the recognition was recorded. This would be used to assess how scaling of the image affects the accuracy of the algorithm. Also the luminance component was removed from the image in an attempt to remove the effect of light intensity changes on the image. The test was then redone with these changes to determine the impact of these changes on the performance of the module. The testing images were labelled before testing, and the accuracy was calculated based on how many of the predicted labels matched the pre-labels of the images. Based on the results, best average accuracy achieved for the Histogram Intersection without the luminance removal was 51% and it occurred at a scale of 0.8 as seen in Fig. 4. The accuracy of this method increased when the luminance component of the images was removed to about 74% and the recognition accuracy of each component was also increased as seen in Fig. 5. The comparative accuracy of both methods can be seen in Fig. 6.

Bag of Features Testing. The Bag of Features method was tested using the Motherboard Component Dataset discussed previously. To test this algorithm, the Bag of Features model was trained with discussed feature point detectors. First, it was trained with SIFT features, then with SURF features and last ORB features. The training was accomplished with the training component dataset discussed in the previous section. During testing, images were also scaled down by increments of 10% to assess the impact of scaling on this method of object recognition. Accuracy of each method of feature point detection was also determined. This was accomplished by manually labelling the test images and comparing these output of the Bag of Features model predictions. The SIFT performed the best at a scale of 0.2. The results obtained for the accuracy for each component can be seen in Fig. 9. At this scale, the average accuracy for all components was 95%. The SURF features, however, performed the best with this model at a scale of 0.8. At this scale, it achieved an average accuracy of 97%. The results for this is presented in Fig. 11. Finally, the orb features was able to achieve a the max accuracy of 96% at a scale of 0.2. The accuracy for each individual component can be seen in Fig. 10. A comparison of the accuracy of all the methods and over changes in scale is presented in Fig. 12. From this it can be seen that, at a 0.2 scale factor, the ORB Bag of Features achieved its peak accuracy. It can also be seen that the SURF and SIFT bag of features achieved an even higher accuracy than the ORB at certain scale factors. This was, however, a marginally better performance. A comparison of the average recognition time for each feature point technique with the Bag of Features Model is presented in Fig. 13. From this, it can be deduced that for a comparable accuracy the recognition time is shorter for the ORB bag of features method, making it the best method for this solution.

Local Binary Patterns - Support Vector Machine. The Local Binary Patterns algorithm was also tested using the Motherboard Component Dataset. The algorithm was implemented first using the training dataset discussed above, which contained images of the different motherboard components. To test the performance of this method, the radius of the Local Binary Pattern operator was varied by increments of 10 pixels. Also the image was scaled at increments of 10%. Just as before, the testing images were pre-labelled and the Support Vector Machine Training was used to label the images. The accuracy computed just as before using the number of correct labels divided by the total number of images. The LBP SVM performed achieved a peak accuracy of 78% when it had a scale of 0.4 and radius of 10. The recognition accuracy for each component at the peak accuracy is presented in Fig. 7. The average recognition time results for the support vector implementation of the LBP is shown in Fig. 8.

Overall System Testing. The overall recognition system was tested using the Motherboard Image dataset that was discussed. This testing was done to assess the accuracy of the final recognition system and also the speed of operation. Using the best preforming algorithms at their maximum performance, configurations were determined by testing and reviewing the results. During this testing, the number of correct recognition cases over the total number of images was assessed. Also the time taken to process each image on average was recorded. Lastly a confusion matrix was developed for the system so that the performance can be more deeply analyzed.

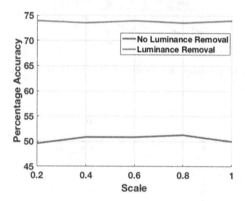

Fig. 4. Showing the recognition accuracy of both histogram intersection methods

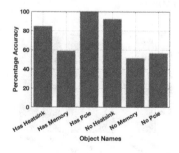

Fig. 5. Showing the recognition accuracy of the histogram intersection method for each component with luminance removal

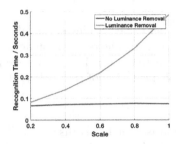

Fig. 6. Showing the comparison of average recognition time for the histogram methods

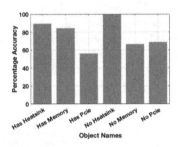

Fig. 7. Showing the recognition accuracy of the LBP at 0.4 scale and radius 10 – support vector machine.

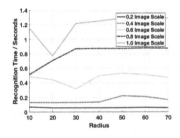

Fig. 8. Showing the average recognition time for the support vector machine implementation of local binary patterns

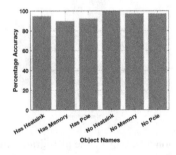

Fig. 9. Showing the recognition accuracy of the SIFT at 0.2 scale – bag of words method

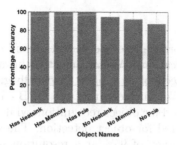

Fig. 10. Showing the recognition accuracy of the ORB at 0.2 scale – bag of words method

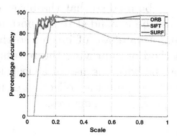

Fig. 11. Showing the recognition accuracy of the SURF at 0.8 scale – bag of words method

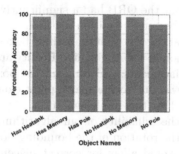

Fig. 12. Showing the average accuracy of the bag of features implementation of ORB, SIFT and SURF.

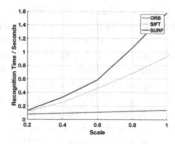

Fig. 13. Showing the average recognition time of the bag of features implementation of ORB, SIFT and SURF.

9   Conclusion

We presented a novel approach to object detection and recognition for real-time Augmented Reality applications. We implemented this algorithm in the context of an AR application for technology support to visually guide the field technicians through repair actions. We concluded that the ORB - Bag of Features method was the best suited method for object recognition, while the SIFT feature point method was the best suited for object detection. The ORB - Bag of Features method had a peak accuracy of 95% at a resolution scale of 0.2, while SIFT feature point method peaked at a resolution scale of 0.4. When compared the SIFT and SURF, Bag of Features method had a marginally better performance than the ORB method, but the ORB had a significantly lower recognition time making it the faster and better recognition method.

One significant limitation was that bounding boxes sometimes cannot be place at the desired location in the Augmented Reality application. This resulted in failed bounding box placements, which meant the boxes were sometimes not visible to the user. This was due to the sparse point cloud created by the Wikitude API, which was used for this implementation.

In order to increase the reliability of our algorithm, further improvements can be made to transfer the rotation of the bounding boxes to the Android side of the application. This would allow for correct placement of the Augmented Reality bounding boxes even under cases of extreme rotation. There is scope for exploration in the area of Augmented Reality implementations allowing for a more dense point cloud to be used so that the boxes can be more accurately drawn. The system can also be expanded to support more types of hardware systems and possibly using a database of images so that it can detect for an array of systems. One method of improving the results of the recognition and detection components may be with the use of a deep learning approach. This approach however would also require the collection of more training data, and may not scale well for unique hardware devices.

References

1. Garcia, M.L.D., Soto, D.A.P., Mihaylova, L.S.: A bag of features based approach for classification of motile sperm cells. In: 2017 IEEE International Conference on Internet of Things (iThings) and IEEE Green Computing and Communications (GreenCom) and IEEE Cyber, Physical and Social Computing (CPSCom) and IEEE Smart Data (SmartData), pp. 104–109. IEEE (2017)
2. Karami, E., Prasad, S., Shehata, M.: Image matching using SIFT, SURF, BRIEF and ORB: performance comparison for distorted images (2015)
3. Piccinini, P., Prati, A., Cucchiara, R.: Real-time object detection and localization with SIFT-based clustering. Image Vis. Comput. **30**(8), 573–587 (2012)
4. Seib, V., Kusenbach, M., Thierfelder, S., Paulus, D.: Object recognition using Hough-transform clustering of SURF features. In: Workshops on Electronical and Computer Engineering Subfields, pp. 169–176 (2012)

5. Csurka, G., Dance, C., Fan, L., Willamowski, J., Bray, C.: Visual categorization with bags of keypoints. In: Workshop on Statistical Learning in Computer Vision, ECCV, vol. 1, no. 1–22, pp. 1–2, Prague (2004)
6. O'Hara, S., Draper, B. A.: Introduction to the bag of features paradigm for image classification and retrieval. arXiv preprint arXiv:1101.3354 (2011)
7. Li, W., Chen, C., Su, H., Du, Q.: Local binary patterns and extreme learning machine for hyperspectral imagery classification. IEEE Trans. Geosci. Remote Sens. **53**(7), 3681–3693 (2015)
8. Rublee, E., Rabaud, V., Konolige, K., Bradski, G.: ORB: an efficient alternative to SIFT or SURF. In: ICCV, pp. 2564–2571 (2011)
9. Asmara, R.A., Rahutomo, F., Hasanah, Q., Rahmad, C.: Chicken meat freshness identification using the histogram color feature. In: 2017 International Conference on Sustainable Information Engineering and Technology (SIET), pp. 57–61 (2017)
10. Swain, M.J., Ballard, D.H.: Color indexing. Int. J. Comput. Vis. **7**(1), 11–32 (1991)
11. Nguyen, D.T., Zong, Z., Ogunbona, P., Li, W.: Object detection using non-redundant local binary patterns. In: 2010 IEEE International Conference on Image Processing, pp. 4609–4612 (2010)
12. Ojala, T., Pietikäinen, M., Harwood, D.: A comparative study of texture measures with classification based on featured distributions. Pattern Recogn. **29**(1), 51–59 (1996)
13. Meena, K., Suruliandi, A.: Performance evaluation of local binary patterns and it's derivatives for face recognition. In: 2011 International Conference on Emerging Trends in Electrical and Computer Technology, pp. 742–746 (2011)
14. Qin, Y., Xu, H., Chen, H.: Image feature points matching via improved ORB. In: 2014 IEEE International Conference on Progress in Informatics and Computing, pp. 204–208 (2014)
15. Lowe, D. G.: Object recognition from local scale-invariant features. In: The Proceedings of the Seventh IEEE International Conference on Computer Vision, 1999, vol. 2, pp. 1150–1157. IEEE (1999)
16. Lowe, D.G.: Distinctive image features from scale-invariant keypoints. Int. J. Comput. Vis. **60**(2), 91–110 (2004)
17. Bay, H., Tuytelaars, T., Van Gool, L.: SURF: speeded up robust features. In: Leonardis, A., Bischof, H., Pinz, A. (eds.) ECCV 2006. LNCS, vol. 3951, pp. 404–417. Springer, Heidelberg (2006). https://doi.org/10.1007/11744023_32
18. Pietikinen, M., Hadid, A., Zhao, G., Ahonen, T.: Computer Vision Using Local Binary Patterns. Computational Imaging and Vision, vol. 40, p. 222. Springer, London (2011). https://doi.org/10.1007/978-0-85729-748-8
19. Ahmad, A., Yusof, R., Mitsukura, Y.: Identifying the dominant species of tropical wood species using histogram intersection method. In: IECON 2015–41st Annual Conference of the IEEE Industrial Electronics Society, pp. 003075–003080 (2015)
20. Chernov, V., Alander, J., Bochko, V.: Integer-based accurate conversion between RGB and HSV color spaces. Comput. Electr. Eng. **46**, 328–337 (2015)
21. Chien, H.J., Chuang, C.C., Chen, C.Y., Klette, R.: When to use what feature? SIFT, SURF, ORB, or A-KAZE features for monocular visual odometry. In: 2016 International Conference on Image and Vision Computing New Zealand (IVCNZ), pp. 1–6 (2016)
22. Raguram, R., Frahm, J.-M., Pollefeys, M.: A comparative analysis of RANSAC techniques leading to adaptive real-time random sample consensus. In: Forsyth, D., Torr, P., Zisserman, A. (eds.) ECCV 2008. LNCS, vol. 5303, pp. 500–513. Springer, Heidelberg (2008). https://doi.org/10.1007/978-3-540-88688-4_37

GRASP Method for Vehicle Routing with Delivery Place Selection

Petar Afric[✉], Adrian Satja Kurdija, Lucija Šikić, Marin Silic, Goran Delac, Klemo Vladimir, and Sinisa Srbljic

Faculty of Electrical Engineering and Computing, University of Zagreb, Unska 3, Zagreb, Croatia
{petar.afric,adrian.kurdija,lucija.sikic,marin.silic, goran.delac,klemo.vladimir,sinisa.srbljic}@fer.hr

Abstract. In this paper we present a greedy randomized adaptive search procedure (GRASP) for solving a vehicle routing problem (VRP) for package delivery with delivery place selection. The problem can be solved by stepwise optimization, i.e., first selecting delivery sites and then defining routes based on that selection. Alternatively, it can be solved by jointly optimizing delivery site selection and routing. We investigate the effects of stepwise optimization in comparison to joint optimization. The evaluation results show that our proposed stepwise approach, while expectedly producing longer routes than joint approach (by 4% on average), can provide a solution 1000× faster than the previous benchmark approach. The proposed procedure is therefore well suited for the dynamic environment of package delivery which is widespread in modern cities as a consequence of e-commerce.

Keywords: Greedy randomized adaptive search procedure · Vehicle routing problem · Package delivery

1 Introduction

Humanity is increasingly using e-commerce. In modern cities, especially smart cities of the future, there is an increasing need for optimized package delivery. The motivation is both to maximize profit and to reduce our impact on the environment. In this paper we study package delivery with delivery site selection.

Schittekat et al. present an interesting problem and analysis in [1]. They tackle a problem of school bus routing (SBR) with bus stop selection. In this problem, students need to be assigned to a station from a list of potential stations and then routes need to be constructed so that all students are transported to school while covering a distance as small as possible. By jointly optimizing student station assignment and station route assignment, they produce significantly shorter routes then if they divided the process into two steps: assigning

© Springer Nature Switzerland AG 2019
D. Wang and L.-J. Zhang (Eds.): AIMS 2019, LNCS 11516, pp. 72–83, 2019.
https://doi.org/10.1007/978-3-030-23367-9_6

students to stations, and defining routes for the stations with assigned students. We noticed several things:

- This problem is equivalent to the problem of package delivery where the package can be delivered to multiple delivery sites. Since providing multiple delivery sites can produce shorter routes, such user behavior should be incentivized.
- The running time of the joint optimization approach seems quite large for the dynamic world of package delivery. We decided to investigate how time performance improves when using a stepwise approach.
- The benchmark stepwise approach presented in the above paper seems very simple, thus artificially increasing the benefit of the presented approach. We decided to investigate how a smarter stepwise approach compares to the joint approach.

The rest of the paper is organized as follows. Section 2 defines the problem in precise terms. Section 3 presents the work related to this paper. In Sect. 4, a detailed description of the proposed algorithm is given. Section 5 presents the evaluation results. Section 6 gives final comments about our work and future research possibilities.

2   Problem Definition

In this paper the problem of defining vehicle routes for delivery trucks with an addition of delivery place selection is considered. The problem can be described as follows:

- there is a single production factory,
- there are N delivery stations,
- there are M customers who will pick up their delivery at the delivery station.

Furthermore,

- each customer will visit only one delivery station, which needs to be in his or her walking range,
- each customer will pick up only one delivery package,
- all delivery trucks have the same capacity which indicates the number of packages they can carry (all packages are assumed to have the same size),
- any delivery station can be visited by only one delivery truck.

The goal is to minimize the total route length travelled by all trucks.

A mathematical description of the problem is shown in Table 1 and Eqs. 1, 2, 3, 4 and 5.

The aim is to minimize expression (1):

$$\sum_{i=1}^{N}\sum_{j=1}^{N} c_{ij} \sum_{k=1}^{T} x_{ijk} + \sum_{i=1}^{N} cp_i \sum_{k=1}^{T} xp_{ik} \tag{1}$$

Table 1. Mathematical problem description

Parameter	Description
N	Number of delivery stations
M	Number of customers
T	Number of delivery trucks
K_k	Capacity of delivery truck k specified by number of packages it can carry
c_{ij}	Cost of going from station i to station j
cp_i	Cost of going from station i to the production factory
pn_l	Number of packages picked up by customer l
s_{il}	1 if the station i is within range of customer l, otherwise 0
x_{ijk}	1 if delivery truck k travels between stations i and j, otherwise 0
xp_{ik}	1 if delivery truck k travels between stations i and the production factory, otherwise 0
y_{ik}	1 if the delivery truck k goes to station i, otherwise 0
z_{il}	1 if the customer l goes to station i, otherwise 0

While respecting the following restrictions:

$$\sum_{i=1}^{N} z_{il} s_{il} = 1 \quad \forall l \in \{1, ..., M\} \tag{2}$$

$$pn_l = 1 \quad \forall l \in \{1, ..., M\} \tag{3}$$

$$K_i = K_j \quad \forall i, j \in \{1, ..., T\} \tag{4}$$

$$\sum_{k=1}^{T} y_{ik} = 1 \quad \forall i \in \{1, ..., N\} \tag{5}$$

In this paper we present a fast greedy randomized adaptive search procedure (GRASP) heuristic algorithm for solving the described problem. The algorithm consists of two parts:

1. assigning customers to delivery stations,
2. defining routes for visiting delivery stations.

The first part is done using a greedy heuristic, while the second one is done using a specialized local search. These two steps are repeated R times and the best solution is kept.

In order to evaluate the proposed approach, we conducted extensive laboratory experiments. During the experiments we compared various approachpresented in [1]. Our results show that although a stepwise approach does, on average, produce longer routes the difference gap can be minimized from 23% to 4% while improving execution time by three orders of magnitude. In the end we give guidelines for future work on this topic.

3   Related Work

Vehicle routing is a very active field of research. An overview of research in this field is given by Vigo and Toth in [2]. A large body of work in this field is concerned with incorporating as many real world constraint as possible. This is easily seen by the amount of variation of the vehicle routing problem (VRP). There is VRP with time windows (VRPTW), inventory routing problem (IRP), production routing problem (PRP), location routing problem (LRP), inventory location routing problem (ILRP), capacitated vehicle routing problem (CVRP), split delivery routing problem (SDVRP) and many others, all of them described in [3].

However, to the best of our knowledge there does not seem to be a large body of work which studies the effect of multiple delivery site availability. Most of the work on this topic seems to be done by dealing with the school bus routing (SBR) problem since station selection is a common part of this problem. [4] describe two stepwise approaches for such problems. Location-Allocation-Routing (LAR) first selects the delivery sites and then performs routing on the selected sites. Allocation-Routing-Location (ARL) first performs routing and then performs delivery site selection.

In our paper we have decided to use the LAR strategy and implement it using a GRASP metaheuristic [5], noting that Park and Kim observed in [6] that only a few metaheuristic approaches have been tried for this problem.

4   Proposed Algorithm

As introduced before, the algorithm can be divided into two parts:

1. assigning customers to delivery stations,
2. defining routes to delivery stations.

The following sections describe each of the steps.

4.1   Assigning Customers to Delivery Stations

The main idea behind the assignment algorithm is to reduce the number of delivery stations which need to be visited while preferring delivery stations which are closer to the production factory. The algorithm (shown formally in Algorithm 1) goes as follows:

- The fitness of each station is calculated. The fitness indicates how fit a station is to be assigned to customers. It is generated in the following way:
  - For each station it is initialized to zero.
  - A constant C (controlling the relevance of the distance to the factory) is randomly generated uniformly from $[0, 10]$. For each station, the fitness is increased by C divided by the distance of the station to the production factory.

- Then, for each customer, the fitness of each reachable station is increased by a reciprocal of the number of reachable stations. In this way the fitness of stations which can be reached by a lot of customers or which are the only option for some customers are increased.
- The stations are then sorted in descending order by fitness. If the fitness difference is less then $fitness\_d\_min$, precedence is given to stations closer to the production factory. $fitness\_d\_min$ is a hyper-parameter which we usually set to 0.01.
- The stations are then iterated in the sorted order. For each station, customers which can reach it are considered.
  - If the station can be reached by a number of customers less or equal to the capacity of the truck, then all the customers are assigned to that station.
  - If more customers can reach the station, they are sorted by the number of stations they can reach in ascending order. If two customers can reach the same number of stations, precedence is given to the customer which is farther from the production factory. Customers are then assigned to the current station in the sorted order until the capacity on the truck is filled.

After all of this is done, all customers are assigned to a station. Those stations which have at least one customer assigned to them are active stations and only they are considered in the rest of the algorithm.

Algorithm 1. Assigning customers to delivery stations

$C \leftarrow getRandomValue(0, 10)$
for $station \leftarrow stations$ **do**
  $fitness[station] = C/distance[factory][station]$
end for
for $customer \leftarrow customers$ **do**
  $fconst = 1/stationsInCustomerReach[customer].Count()$
  for $station \leftarrow stationsInCustomerReach[customer]$ **do**
    $fitness[station]+ = const$
  end for
end for
$Sort(stations).Ascending().Using(fitness, distance)$
for $station \leftarrow stations$ **do**
  $customersInReach = customerInReach[station]$
  if $customersInReach <= truckCapacity$ **then**
    for $customer \leftarrow customersInReach$ **do**
      $stationFor[customer] = station$
    end for
  else
    $Sort(customersInReach).Descending()$
    $.Using(stationsInCustomerReach, distance)$
    for $i \leftarrow Range(truckCacpacity)$ **do**
      $customer = customersInReach[i]$
      $stationFor[customer] = station$
    end for
  end if
end for

4.2   Defining Routes to Delivery Stations

The goal of this step is to define truck routes for active stations which are as short as possible while respecting the truck capacity constraint. This problem can be divided into two subproblems:

- determining which stations are grouped to the same route,
- determining the best possible order of visiting the stations in the route.

The developed algorithm can be divided into three separate steps:

1. preprocessing,
2. initial solution generation,
3. solution optimization.

Preprocessing involves iterating over all stations and defining routes for stations which cannot be combined with any other station due to the capacity constraint. These stations and routes are no longer taken into consideration in further optimization.

Initial solution generation is done using a greedy heuristic which does the following:

1. it selects a station which is not yet assigned to any route and creates a route for it,
2. then it iterates over the rest of the unassigned stations and calculates which of the *satisfiable* stations is closest to the set of stations currently in the route. A station is *satisfiable* if the distance between the station and the route is smaller than between the station and the factory.
3. If the closest station is found, it is added to the current route; otherwise that is the end of the current route creation.
4. The previous steps are repeated as long as there are active unassigned stations.

The described algorithm is shown in Algorithm 2. Each of the defined routes is optimized using a greedy heuristic TSP (travelling salesman problem) solver which will be described later.

Solution optimization is done using local search. The search is defined by the following properties.

- An incomplete neighborhood consists of one element which is generated by doing one of the following:
  - switching a station from one route to another,
  - selecting two stations from different routes and swapping the stations between the two routes,
  - joining two routes into one,
  - breaking a route into two routes at a random point.

Algorithm 2. Initial solution generation

```
rout = {}
while activeStations.IsEmpty() == false do
    station = activeStations.RemoveAt(0)
    route.Add(station)
    routeExpanded = true
    while routeExpanded do
        routeExpanded = false
        closestToRoute = NULL
        for activeStation ← activeStations do
            distanceToRoute = Infinity
            for routeStation ← route do
                if distance[factory][activeStation]>distance[activeStation][routeStation] then
                    distanceToRoute =
                    Min(distanceToRoute, distance[activeStation][routeStation])
                end if
            end for
            if closestToRoute.distanceToRoute > distanceToRoute then
                closestToRoute = activeStation
                closestToRoute.distanceToRoute = distanceToRoute
            end if
        end for
        if closestToRoute! = NULL then
            rout.Add(closestToRoute)
            routeExpanded = true
        end if
    end while
    tspSolver.Optimize(rout).Using(distance)
    routes.Add(route)
    route = {}
end while
```

There is a small probability (a parameter called *repetitionChance*) that another modification occurs after each modification.

- Routes are re-optimized using a TSP solver in each iteration as soon as they are manipulated.
- The objective function is the sum of lengths of all routes.
- The stopping condition is reaching a maximum number of iterations or a maximum number of stagnant iterations. These are defined using hyperparameters *maxIterationCount* and *maxStagnationCount*.

The defined algorithm is shown in Algorithm 3.

Algorithm 3. Solution optimization

```
maxIterationCount = 1000000
maxStagnationCount = 100000
bestDistance = CalculateDistance(routes, distance)
while  +  + generationNumber  <  maxIterationCount AND stagnation  <
maxStagnationCount do
    neighbor = Manipulate(routes, distance)
    neighbourDistance = CalculateDistance(neighbor, distance)
    if neighbourDistance < bestDistance then
        routes = neighbour
        bestDistance = neighbourDistance
        stagnation = 0
    else
        stagnation + +
    end if
end while
```

The result produced by this step are the final routes. We are left to describe the TSP solver used in our problem.

A TSP solver is used to optimize the generated routes. This TSP solver uses the following greedy heuristic.

- If it is given three or less nodes, a list of the given nodes is returned as the solution.
- Otherwise, three random nodes are taken and declared the current optimal route. Then the following is iteratively done:
  - select a random node,
  - iterate over each edge of the current optimal route and calculate the distance change if that edge is removed and two new ones are added connecting the previously randomly selected node,
  - remove the edge which produced the minimal change in distance.

  This is repeated as long as there are nodes which are not in the route.
- Finally it returns the created route.

The described algorithm is shown in Algorithm 4.

Algorithm 4. TSP solver procedure

---

if $nodes.Count() \leq 3$ **then**
   $RET nodes$
end if
$route = \{nodes.RemoveAt(random),$
$nodes.RemoveAt(random), nodes.RemoveAt(random)\}$
while $nodes.IsEmpty() == false$ **do**
   $node = nodes.RemoveAt(random)$
   $bestEdgeChange = Infinity$
   $bestEdge = NULL$
   for $edge \in Edges(route)$ **do**
      $edgeChange = CalculateChange(route, edge, node)$
      if $edgeChange < bestEdgeChange$ **then**
         $bestEdge = edge$
         $bestEdgeChange = edgeChange$
      end if
   end for
   $route.Add(node).ByBreaking(bestEdge)$
end while

---

5   Results

For our experiments, we use the dataset presented in [1] and give our results relative to the results presented in that paper. The dataset contains 112 problem instances, with the number of customers ranging from 25 to 800, the number of stations ranging from 5 to 80, and the maximum allowed walking distance ranging from 5 to 40. For each value of the repetition parameter, we solve each instance 100 times and take the average solution route length and calculation time as the results for that instance.

Figure 1 shows the average solution route length increase produced by our algorithm when compared to the results of the joint presented in [1]. At a 100 repetitions our algorithm produces, on average, 4% longer routes. This is clearly superior compared to the 23% longer routes produced by the stepwise method reported in [1].

Figure 2 shows the solution route length increase in relation to the instance maximum walking distance constraing. As the maximum walking distance varies from 5 to 40, the increase in the route length for our solutions varies from -0.54% to 4.5% at 100 repetitions. Our results again outperform results in [1] which reports that, when varying the maximum walking distance from 5 to 40, the route length increases from 1.4% to 63.4%.

In addition, Figs. 3 and 4 present the relation between station/customer count and route length increase. As the amount of stations varies from 5 to 80, the increase in the route length for our solutions varies from 0% to 8.31% at 100 repetitions. As the amount of customers varies from 25 to 800, the increase in the route length for our solutions varies from 0% to 6.98% at 100 repetitions.

The time performance results depict the logarithm of time decrease in order to improve readability. Figure 5 shows the time decrease of our algorithm when compared to [1]. Our algorithm (on average) takes $e^{7.02} \approx 1100\times$ less time at 100 repetitions, which is clearly a superior result. The time decrease is due to the problem simplification which occurs as a consequence of the stepwise approach.

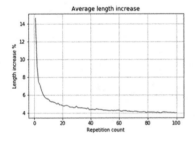 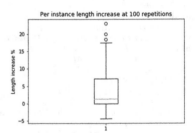

Fig. 1. Average solution route length increase

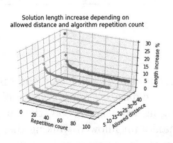 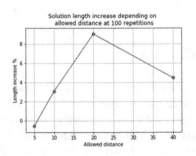

Fig. 2. Solution quality in relation to walking distance

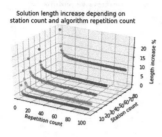
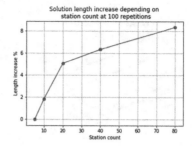

Fig. 3. Solution quality in relation to station count

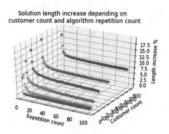
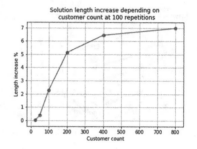

Fig. 4. Solution quality in relation to customer count

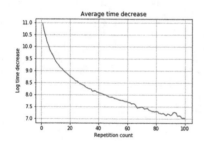
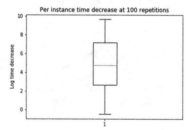

Fig. 5. Average time decrease

Figures 6, 7 and 8, show how the running time depends on the maximum walking distance, the number of stations, and the number of customers. As the maximum walking distance varies from 5 to 40, the time decrease for our algorithm varies from $e^{7.07} \approx 1171.13\times$ to $e^{6.82} \approx 913.75\times$ at 100 repetitions. As the number of stations varies from 5 to 80, the time decrease for our algorithm varies from $e^{2.01} \approx 7.47\times$ to $e^{8.53} \approx 5036\times$ at 100 repetitions. As the number of customers varies from 25 to 800, the time decrease for our algorithm varies from $e^{5.11} \approx 165\times$ to $e^{7.8} \approx 2436\times$ at 100 repetitions.

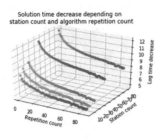 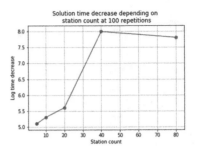

Fig. 6. Solution time decrease in relation to station count

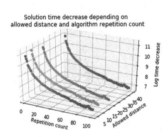 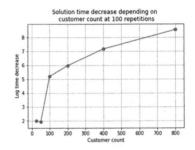

Fig. 7. Solution time decrease in relation to customer count

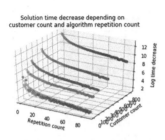 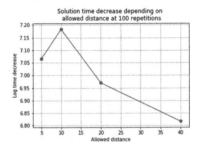

Fig. 8. Solution time decrease in relation to maximum walking distance

6   Conclusion

In this paper, a fast GRASP-based heuristic algorithm for vehicle routing with delivery place selection is presented. The evaluation results have shown that the proposed algorithm is, on average, three orders of magnitude faster than benchmark, thus showing that stepwise optimization can be much faster than joint optimization for this problem. We have also shown that using a smart stepwise approach can significantly reduce the performance gap with respect to the joint approach. Namely, with the proposed algorithm the gap has been reduced from 23% to 4%. In future work, our aim will be to increase the solution quality while maintaining or only slightly sacrificing the speed of the algorithm.

Acknowledgment. This research has been partly supported by the European Regional Development Fund under the grant KK.01.1.1.01.0009 (DATACROSS).

The authors acknowledge the support of the **Croatian Science Foundation** through the *Reliable Composite Applications Based on Web Services* **(IP-01-2018-6423)** research project.

The Titan X Pascal used for this research was donated by the NVIDIA Corporation.

References

1. Schittekat, P., Kinable, J., Sörensen, K., Sevaux, M., Spieksma, F., Springael, J.: A metaheuristic for the school bus routing problem with bus stop selection. Eur. J. Oper. Res. **229**(2), 518–528 (2013)
2. Toth, P., Vigo, D.: An overview of vehicle routing problems, pp. 1–26 (2001)
3. Archetti, C., Speranza, M.G.: A survey on matheuristics for routing problems. EURO J. Comput. Optim. **2**(4), 223–246 (2014)
4. Laporte, G., Nobert, Y., Taillefer, S.: Solving a family of multi-depot vehicle routing and location-routing problems. Transp. Sci. **22**(3), 161–172 (1988)
5. Feo, T.A., Resende, M.G.C.: Greedy randomized adaptive search procedures. J. Glob. Optim. **6**(2), 109–133 (1995). https://doi.org/10.1007/BF01096763
6. Park, J., Kim, B.I.: The school bus routing problem: a review. Eur. J. Oper. Res. **202**(2), 311–319 (2010)

Indexed Search

Erdal Kose[(✉)]

Department of Computer Sciences and Engineering,
Fairleigh Dickinson University Teaneck Campus, New Jersey, USA
ekose@fdu.edu

Abstract. The domain of Artificial Intelligence (AI) Search algorithms is a well-studied area. A variety of AI search algorithms have been developed in the past decades. Some of them are considered to be among the main AI search algorithms such as Best First Search, A*, Iterative Deepening Search, etc. The others use these main algorithms as a basis and include more heuristics to generate newer algorithms such as Iterative Deepening A* (IDA*), Branch and Bound Search, etc. the innovation of this research is a new approach to the AI search algorithms, we called it indexed search. The methods assigns integer indices to the states of the problem and instead of searching for the goal state, it searches for the index of the goal state. Once the index of a goal state found, we convert that index from decimal base to the base of the branching factor of the problem, and this new number is the solution path from goal to the start node. The new approach eliminates the Closed List which employed for most AI search algorithms to store the explored nodes. The new approach also generates a solution path faster than the respective versions of them and it also use less memory space.

Keywords: Search algorithms · A* search · Breadth First Search · Heuristic · State space

1 Introduction

Search is a problem solving mechanism in AI, and the choice of search procedure is a prescription for determining in what order the nodes in a problem are to be generated and examined. In blind search techniques, this procedure is achieved by searching for a goal without using any information. On the other hand, heuristic search techniques use partial information about the problem domain to guide the search from a start node towards a goal node. The algorithm terminates if a solution is found or no solution has been found. If the algorithm employed heuristics it is called a heuristic search. If it does not use any heuristics then it is called a blind search algorithm.

Each node in a search tree is a state of a search problem; the *state space* [12, 13] is a set of states and operators that maps states to states. Search problems can be represented with a graph $G(N, V)$, where N is a set of nodes such that $N = \{1, 2, 3, 4, \ldots n\}$, and V is a set of vertices connecting nodes such that $V = \{a_1, a_2, a_3 \ldots a_m\}$. A vertex is $a_t = (i, j) \in V$. A path P is a subset of N where each node of the path is connected, e.g. $P = \{n_1, n_2, n_3 \ldots n_n\}$ [12]. The cost of travel from vertex i to j is $c(i, j)$. The purpose of

© Springer Nature Switzerland AG 2019
D. Wang and L.-J. Zhang (Eds.): AIMS 2019, LNCS 11516, pp. 84–100, 2019.
https://doi.org/10.1007/978-3-030-23367-9_7

search algorithms is to find a desirable path that maps a start node to a goal node by applying suitable operations to each state of a search tree.

There is many search methods available in the literature, such as some newer methods by Kose 2018 [1], Sturtevant et al. 2018 [2], and Chen et at. 2017 [3]. For older search methods, see any AI textbook [12, 13]. However, For the purpose of this research, in the following sub-sections, we briefly described Breadth First Search (BFS) and A* search algorithms. After that, we will introduce a new approach to the search algorithms; we referred to it as *Indexed Search*. Finally, we will compare the implementation of fifteen puzzles with BFS and A* with the implementation of newer techniques; Indexed Breadth First Search (IBFS) and Indexed A* Search (IA*).

1.1 Breadth First Search (BFS)

The most regular form of the Breadth First Search (BFS) employs two lists for maintaining a solution called the Open and Closed List. The Open List is for storing the frontiers of a solution tree, and the Closed List is for storing the nodes, which have already been explored. There are two reasons to maintain the Closed List: first, to prevent duplication. While the search proceeds, cycles may occur. Most search algorithms employ a Closed List to prevent cycles and duplicate nodes. Secondly, the Closed List is used to build the solution paths after a goal node has been reached. As the BFS explores nodes in the order of their distance from the root, it generates nodes level by level from top to bottom until a solution has been found. As such, all the nodes at level j are expanded before the nodes at level $j + 1$ are expanded. BFS is guaranteed to find a solution if any solution is available [11]. It is also guaranteed to find the shortest path to the root. See any AI textbook for further information about BFS [4, 12, 13].

1.2 A* Search Algorithm

A* search algorithm is a well-known form of the Best First Search. The A* search minimizes the total estimated solution cost by using an evaluation function f(n).

$$f(n) = g(n) + h(n) \tag{1}$$

- g(n) is the actual cost of reaching a node n from a start node
- h(n) is the heuristic estimation for getting from the node n to the goal

A* maintains two lists, which are called the Open, and Closed List. The Open List is a priority list that contains the frontier nodes that will be expanded in the next iteration. Before a node is inserted into the Open List, its weight is evaluated by a heuristic function *f(n)* as shown in Eq. 1. The difference between the estimated value and the real value is the error rate of *h(n)*. The nodes in the Closed List are already expanded and removed from the Open List.

If the first element in the Open List is not a goal node, the algorithm generates its descendants. If an examined node is already in the Open or Closed List, the algorithm ensures to retain the one which leads to the shortest path. The A* algorithm stops searching if it meets the goal node or the Open List is empty. In the first case, the algorithm returns the solution path leading to a goal; in the second case, the algorithm returns no solution path.

If the A* algorithm employs an admissible[1] heuristic function, then the A* algorithm will generate optimal solutions [8]. A* algorithm can solve problems which have a small state space search tree but for problems which have a large search domain, the A* algorithm faces a memory problem. There are many new forms of A* and BFS search algorithms and their applications contributed by Geethu [7], Ariel et al. [5, 6], and Zhou [15]. However, for the sake of our research, we will only investigate and implement the basic form of A* search. For further information about A* search, see Kopec [8], Zhang [14], Russell [13], and Korf [9, 10].

2 Indexed Search

The contribution of this research is a new type of search method that eliminates the overhead of saving the explored nodes, and also it constructs a solution path much easier than any regular AI search algorithms. We refer it Indexed Search. In the following sections, we will develop two forms of Indexed Search; but it can be applicable to any AI search algorithm.

Most AI search algorithms maintain a list structure to save the explored nodes; this list is usually called Closed List. There are two reasons to maintain the Closed List: first, to prevent the duplications and possible cycles. Secondly, the Closed List is used to build the solution path after a goal node has been reached.

The Indexed Search algorithm eliminates Closed List and provides some methods to resolve the two main reasons to save explored nodes. Instead of using a Closed List, our new approach uses indices (see Sect. 2.2) to generate a solution path after a goal node has been reached, it also uses some heuristics to avoid duplications and cycles (see Sect. 2.3). There are two main advantages of eliminating the Closed List:

1. Save space.
2. Simplify the process of generating a solution path.

If the possible node generation operators are well defined for some problem domain, then we can build a strategy, which prevents duplication. For example, for sliding puzzle problems, such as Fifteen Puzzle, a node may be generated as a result of Left, Right, Up or Down moves. If we could track this, we can prevent possible duplications and cycles that may loop back from deeper levels back to ancestors. For example as shown in Fig. 1, if Left move creates node n and a Right move of node n will cycle back to its parent node m. This is a simple cycle that can be prevents by any regular search algorithms. However, the loops that include more than three nodes would not be avoided without searching Open List and Closed List for possible duplicate nodes as shown in Fig. 2.

---

[1] A heuristic is admissible if it finds the shortest path to a goal node if it exists.

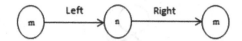

Fig. 1. Prevent looping back to parent node

Fig. 2. Loops may occurred in deeper levels.

The pure regular form of search methods, such as BFS and Depth First Search, does not track the information about how nodes are generated, and they demonstrate a lack in labelling the node generation. Indexed Search method tracks node moves by employing a parameter (see Sect. 2.1).

As we have described above, the policy of generating nodes without keeping track of how nodes are generated may create cycles. For example, if the child of a Left move is a Right move, then this will loop back to the parent as shown in Fig. 1. The search trees for the basic form of BFS and A* are undirected graphs. However, both methods eliminates cycles and duplications by searching through the Closed List for the newly generated node. If the newly generated node is in the Closed List, then the node will be discarded without adding it to the Open List. Otherwise it will be added to the Open List. Some forms of these methods check for duplicate nodes before including a node to the Open List. This mechanism adds a lot of search overhead when the search tree becomes larger. The second purpose of the Closed List is to build the solution path after a solution has been found. The algorithm does that by searching for ancestors of the examined node back from goal toward to start node. Once the start node reached, the method returns the solution path.

The Indexed Search algorithm employed two main mechanisms to prevent duplications and build a solution path. First, it tracks how a new node generated, and second it assigns an index to each new created node. These two parameters guide the search to avoid cycles and build the solution path easily. The following two subsections explore these two mechanisms.

2.1   New Node Generation

Indexed search employs a new parameter p for tracking how a node is generated from a parent node. For example, in Fig. 3, the node a is a result of a "1" move, so that for node a, the parameter p is "1". The node b is a result of a 0 move, so that p for node b is "0", etc.

The basic structure of a node N for Indexed Search is characterized by the 3-tuple {S, p, Index}, where:

- S is the state of the node.
- p is the parameter for tracking how the node generated.
- *Index* is the location of the node in the Frontier List.

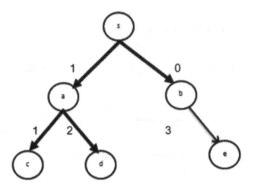

Fig. 3. Label nodes with a parameter p.

We do not keep track of the parent nodes. The parameter **p** of the nodes must be a legal move, and **p** must be an integer. For a problem **P**, if the maximum branching factor is b then p is: $0 \leq p < b$. For example, for Fifteen Puzzle, the possible moves are {0, 1, 2, 3}, we can make the following assignment for parameters of the Fifteen Puzzle; {left ==0, right ==1, down ==2, up ==3}, so that the possible p values for fifteen puzzle are $p = \{0, 1, 2, 3\}$. If the branching factor of a problem X is six, then the possible *p's* are {0, 1, 2, 3, 4, 5}, each generated state of X must be labeled with any of these values.

2.2   Creating Indices

The Frontier list is used to save the unexplored nodes. The index of a node is the location of the node in the Frontier List as illustrated in Fig. 4. For example, the first node in the list has index 0, and second node in the list has index 1 so on. We can calculate the index of a node N by the following formula.

$$i = b \times (j + 1) + p \tag{2}$$

- i is the index of N (new generated node)
- j is the index of parent of N
- p is the parameter that we will assign to N
- b is the branching factor of the problem.

0	1	2	.	.	.	156	.	.	.	.	b^{d-1}	b^d

Fig. 4. Indices of Nodes in the frontier list

For example, as shown in Fig. 3, the index of node **a** is 2, the branching factor of the problem is 4, then the index of node **c** is:

i = 4 × (2 + 1) + 1

i = 13.

We use indices to produce the solution path. Once the index of the goal node is known, the next step is to find the solution path. To generate the solution path, you must follow the following steps:

1. Convert the index of goal node to the base of maximum branching factor.
2. Switch each parameter p (described in the Sect. 2.1) to its dual move.
3. Reverse the final number to produce the solution path.

For example, for the Fifteen Puzzle, if the index of a goal node is $(98645766)_{10}$, then to generate the solution path from start node toward the goal node, we must follow the above steps:

1. Convert the index from decimal to base 4 which is the branching factor of fifteen puzzle $(98645766)_{10} \equiv 11320103130012$
2. Switch Each Parameter P to Its Dual Move: 0023102021103
3. Reverse the final number: 3011202013200

Hence, the solution path for this problem will be; *up, left, right, right, down, left, down, left, right, up, down, left, left.*

How to define the dual moves[2] depends on the implementation and on the problem domain. Parameter *p* and their dual for Fifteen Puzzle are shown in the Table 1.

Table 1. Parameter *p* and their dual for fifteen puzzle

Move	Left	Right	Down	Up
p	0	1	2	3
Dual p	1	0	3	2
Dual move in world	Right	Left	Up	Down

If the solution domain of a problem is a map from states to states, then each state in state space graph should have a coordinate or index in the map. We claim if we know the index of a goal node, then we can generate the solution path as we have described above. With Indexed Search, we have redefined the task of search algorithms; the new task is to find the index of a goal state on the map. Once we know the location of goal state in the map, then the problem solved by converting the index of goal state to the base of branching factor of the search tree. This policy will take care of building the solution path after a goal node is reached.

2.3 Prevent Duplications and Cycles

One of the purposes of retaining the parameter *p* (see Sect. 2.1) is to prevent duplications at shallow levels and the possibility of cycles that we have described above. However, it does not prevent cycles that might occur at deeper levels. In the Fifteen

---

[2] A dual move is the opposite move of a move. For Fifteen Puzzle, Right move's dual is Left move, Up move's dual is the Down move vies versa.

Puzzle example, the loops may occur at depths 1, 6, 7, 8, and so on. To prevent duplications, we employed the following steps:

1. Before adding a new generated node in to the Frontier List, we must search for its duplicated node in the Frontier List.
2. if its duplicated node is in the Frontier List then;
    a. Label the duplicated node with a new parameter
    b. discard the new generated node
3. If the duplication of the new node is not in the Frontier List, then add the new node in to the Frontier List.

This policy will prevent duplications. However, it will not prevent cycles. To avoid cycles, we employed the following strategy: If a node N is labeled with duplicated parameter (see the above steps), in the next iteration when N expanded, it will not generate its duplicated node. This heuristic prevents possible cycles For Example If a node N is already in the frontier list, and its duplication N' is generated. The N' would not be added to the frontier list because N with the same state is already in the Frontier List (see Fig. 5)

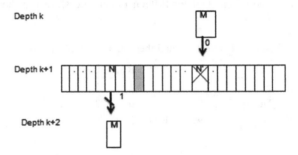

Fig. 5. Check Duplicate Nodes and Prevent Cycles. N is a new generated node, N' is N's duplication, M is child of N and parent of N'.

3   Algorithm Components

Indexed Search uses only one list to track the frontier nodes and the parameters that we have described in the above section. We called this list the Frontier List or Open list. We do not save explored nodes, any node that generated at depth 1, depth 2 ... depth *d-1* will be discarded, only nodes that are created at depth *d* will be saved for further investigation as shown in Fig. 6.

In addition to these parameters, depending on the implementation, you can add some other parameters as well. For example, for one of our implementations we kept track of the depth of nodes and for preventing cycle we kept track of another parameter (see Sects. 2.1, 2.2).

In the purpose of experiments we have developed and implemented two form of Indexed search; Indexed Breadth First Search (IBFS) and Indexed A* Search (IA*).

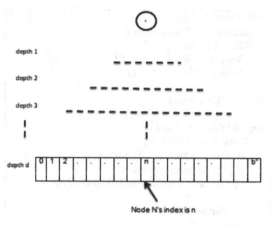

Fig. 6. Frontier List

In the following two subsections we will briefly describe the steps of IBFS and IA* algorithms.

4 Indexed Breadth First Search (IBFS)

The IBFS algorithm works as follows: First, the start node is expanded, and the parameters for each child nodes are calculated. Before new nodes are added to the frontier list, we check for any duplication. If there is no duplication and the new node's state is not a goal node, then we add the new node to the end of Frontier List. In the next iteration, the first element from Frontier List is examined. The procedure proceeds until a goal node is reached or the Frontier List is empty. The explored nodes are discarded. See Fig. 7 for IBFS algorithm's Pseudocodes.

In this section, we have shown that IBFS differs from BFS in that it uses two parameters to eliminate the Closed List employed by BFS. The IBFS algorithm does not track the Closed List as the BFS does. This policy saves memory and time. By tracking the index of frontiers, the IBFS algorithm eliminates two reasons for using the Closed List.

Now we will theoretically analyze the benefits of eliminating the Closed List.

Lemma 3.1: IBFS algorithm uses less space and time then BFS.

Proof 3.1: BFS has to save all the generated nodes; the explored nodes in Closed List and the nodes, which are generated but have not been explored in the Open List. When algorithm generates nodes at depth d, all the nodes at depth $d-1$ must be explored and saved in Closed List, so that the size of Closed List is:

$$b^0 + b^1 + b^2 \ldots b^{d-2} + b^{d-1} \tag{3}$$

```
IBFS(Node S, Node G) {
    Add S to the Frontier List L
    While L is not empty {
        Node N= First Element of L
        Expand ( Node N, List L)
    }
Return "No solution
}
Expand (Node N, List L) {
    While N has Children{
        Create the State of all children
        Calculate the parameters
        If (the new generated node is a duplicated
            node){
            discard it
        } else{
            if (N == G)
                Return solution path
            else
                add node to the end of L
        }
    }
}
```

Fig. 7. Pseudocodes for IBFS. S is the Start State and G is the Goal State. Expand Methods creates new nodes and check for solution node.

The nodes that are generated at depth d, but have not been explored yet must be stored in Open List for future investigation so that the size of Open List is b^d. Hence, the total number of nodes generated are;

$$b^0 + b^1 + b^2 \ldots b^{d-2} + b^{d-1} + b^d \qquad (4)$$

If x is $b^0 + b^1 + b^2 \ldots b^{d-2} + b^{d-1}$

Then

$b^0 + b^1 + b^2 \ldots b^{d-2} + b^{d-1} + b^d = x + b^d$ (by Eqs. 3 and 4)

Therefore, number of node stored by BFS is: $x + b^d$.

IBFS is only storing frontier nodes in to the Frontier List which is same as the Open List employed by BFS. Therefore, the memory used by IBFS is: b^d.

$$\left(b^d\right) < \left(x + b^d\right) \qquad (5)$$

Hence, BFS use more space then IBFS (by Eq. 5).

Suppose storing the explored nodes uses x amount of memory in bytes, and it takes t amount of CPU time to store each node, then BFS will take $x * t$ more time to solve a problem, because IBFS does not store the explored nodes. Therefore, IBFS uses less time to solve a problem. In addition to this fact, IBFS does not search through Closed List for duplicates; instead, it uses some heuristics to eliminate duplications and cycles. Hence, it will take less time to solve problems.

4.1 Indexed a* Search

The regular form of A* search algorithm is a kind of heuristic BFS algorithm, which employed a heuristic function to evaluate the nodes before inserting them into the Open List. The heuristic function of A* algorithm is defined in the Eq. 1. At each iteration, the node with minimum evaluation value is expanded. The nodes which are expanded and do not lead to a solution path move to a list called the Closed List, and the newly generated nodes move to a list called Open List. The purpose of the Closed List is to avoid duplicated nodes and to build the solution path after a goal node is reached. If the employed heuristic function is admissible, then the A* algorithm finds optimal path.

To build a regular form of Indexed A* search algorithm, we adopted the policy of IBFS instead of BFS. Therefore, the new form of A*algorithm is call Indexed A* search algorithm. The difference between IBFS and IA* is that, with IBFS the nodes are examined on a First In Last Out manner (FILO), but with IA* we save and expand nodes by evaluating their heuristic values, we always first examine the node which is closer to a goal node. See Fig. 8 for Pseudocodes for IA* search method.

```
IA* (Node S, Node G){
    Calculate S's Heuristic Value
    Add S to the Frontier List L
    While ( L is not empty){
        Node N= First Element of L
        Expand ( Node N, List L)
    }
}
Expand (Node N, List L ){
    While (N has Children){
        Create N's children
        If any children are duplicated
            discard
        else {
            if any N's child is a solution
                return solution path
            else
                add N' children to the list L  by their
                heuristic value h
        }
    }
}
```

Fig. 8. Pseudocodes for IBFS. S is the Start State and G is the Goal State.

5 Experimental Results and Implementations

We have implemented Fifteen Puzzle with Breadth First Search (BFS), Indexed Breadth First Search (IBFS), A*, and Indexed A* (IA*) Search Algorithms and compared the results. The following sub-sections demonstrate the results and implementation details.

6 Comparing IBFS with BFS

When we implement Fifteen Puzzles with IBFS we represent a node with 5-tuples (see Fig. 9).The node for IBFS includes the node depth, its state, parameter p, Duplication Parameter (dupFlag), and node Index as shown in Fig. 9. The parameter p is used for preventing first level duplication and creating child node index, the "DumFlag" variable is used for preventing deeper duplication and also used for pruning paths that are already generated. Index is used for creating solution path from goal node to start node.

```
class Node {
    int[] board;
    int p;
    long index;
    int DupFlag;
    int depth;
}
```

Fig. 9. IBFS Node Representation of Fifteen Puzzles

```
Public class Node {
    int[] board;
    Node parent;
    int depth;   }
```

Fig. 10. BFS Node Representation of Fifteen Puzzle

BFS Implementation: The node structure for BFS includes node depth, its parent node, and the state of the node as shown Fig. 10. For both implementations, the employed lists structures were linked lists. For BFS we have employed two linked lists called Closed List and Open List, the Closed List is used for keeping explored nodes and Open List is used for nodes that have been created but not explored yet. For IBFS we have employed one linked list called Frontier List, which is similar to Open List that we have used for BFS, it used for keeping nodes that created but have not explored yet.

For the first implementation of BFS, we checked for duplicates by comparing the new created node with the nodes in the Closed List, if there is a duplication, we discard the new created node; otherwise, we add the new node to the Open list. With the second implementation of BFS, each new node was compared to both lists (Open and Closed) to check duplications. If an identical state was found, the less efficient path to this state was deleted and the most efficient path was kept in the appropriated list.

IBFS Implementation: when we implement IBFS algorithm, we employed two policies to prevent duplication nodes of IBFS shown below: First, by using the move way parameter *p,* we prevented a node to generate its parent. For example if a Right move generates a Left move, this will loop back to the Right movie's parent node. Whenever a repeated state has been found, we save the node which is closer to the goal. Secondly, we used "DupFlag" parameter to prevent loops (see Sect. 2.2). The "Index" variable is used to generate the solution path. The aim of IBFS algorithm is to find the index of a goal node into the frontier list. Once the index of goal node is found, we can generate a solution path by converting the index from decimal numbers to the base of the branching factor of the problem.

Table 2. IBFS's performance and the size of frontier list by the solution depth. This version of IBFS employs a mechanism to check duplicate nodes.

Depth	Size of frontier list (checks for duplicate nodes)	Time
11	3941	<1 s
12	7820	<1 s
13	15593	1 s
14	30948	28 s
15	61173	2 m and 10 s
16	119768	9 m

Table 2 shows the results of IBFS implementation with the feature of checking duplicate nodes. If a duplicate node is found, the best node is added to the Frontier List and the "DupFlag" variable is set for pruning the path to the duplicate node.

Experimental results show that searching for duplicate nodes makes the BFS and IBFS slower than their respective versions, which do not check for repeating nodes. The size of the frontier list depends to the depth of the goal node. The time need to generate the solution is directly correlated to the time to search for duplicated nodes, and the time to create and save nodes.

Table 3. IBFS's performance and the size of frontier list by the solution depth. This version of IBFS does not employ any policy to check duplicate nodes.

Depth	Size of frontier list (without checking duplicate nodes)	Time
11	4667	<1 s
12	9888	<1 s
13	21047	<1
14	44973	1 s
15	95930	1 s
16	204217	2 s
17	434697	3 s
18	925983	4 s
19	1973339	10 s

Table 3 shows the results of IBFS by implementing the Fifteen Puzzle. With this implementation we excluded the duplication check policy. As you can see from Table 3 generating nodes becomes faster and the size of frontier list increases dramatically, but the problem is that there are a lot of duplicates.

Tables 4 and 5 show the results of BFS by implementing the Fifteen Puzzle. The two main differences between our IBFS and regular BFS are that: the node representation of BFS is different from our IBFS, and secondly, BFS employs a Closed List to maintain the nodes already explored and do not lead to a goal node, IBFS employed only one list for frontier nodes and discards the explored nodes.

Table 4. BFS's performance and the size of open and closed lists by the solution depth. This version of BFS employs a mechanism to check duplicate nodes in open and closed list.

Depth	Size of open list	Size of closed	Nodes generated	Time
11	3755	3976	7730	1 s
12	7808	7693	15501	10 s
13	15545	15501	31046	>1 m
14	30822	31045	61867	>8 m
15	60842	61866	92911	>25 m

Table 5. BFS's performance and the size of Open and Closed Lists by the solution depth. This version of BFS employs a mechanism to check duplicate nodes only in the Closed List.

Depth	Size of Open List	Size of Closed	# Nodes generated	Time
11	4269	3976	8245	1 s
12	8704	8244	16948	4 s
13	17663	16948	34611	30 s
14	36177	34610	70786	>3 m
15	73006	70786	143792	>13 m

The results from Tables 2, 3, 4, 5, and 6 show that the IBFS is faster for solving same puzzle states, and it uses less memory by omitting the Closed List. BFS algorithms cannot explore deeper into the search tree. However, IBFS can search to deeper levels as well. If you omit the duplication node checking policy then IBFS can generate frontiers up to depth 21.

Table 6 and Chart 1 shows that BFS used more memory than IBFS to keep track of the nodes. If the goal node is in deeper layers then BFS is unable to find a solution path, it ran out of memory.

When we apply IBFS and BFS to the same instance of Fifteen Puzzles, for some puzzles, which have a goal state in shallow levels, both algorithms find a solution very quickly. However, for puzzles, which have a goal state in deeper levels, IBFS finds a solution faster than BFS, and for some instances BFS was unable to find a solution at all, see Chart 2.

Table 6. Compare the space used for BFS and IBFS.

Depth	Total number of nodes stored by IBFS	Total number of nodes stored by BFS
11	3941	8245
12	7820	16948
13	15593	34611
14	30948	70786
15	61173	153792
16	119768	No solution

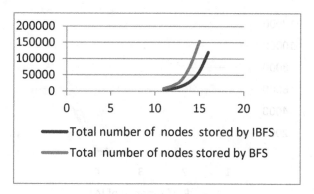

Chart 1. Compare total number of nodes stored by IBFS and BFS. The horizontal coordinate shows the depth of the goal node and the vertical coordinate shows the number of nodes generated.

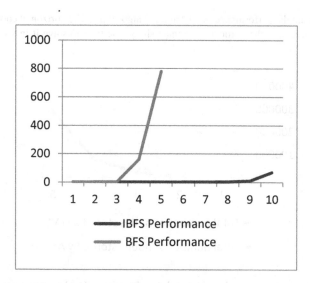

Chart 2. Performance of IBFS and BFS by applying to same instance of Fifteen Puzzles. The horizontal coordinate shows the puzzle instances, and the vertical coordinate shows the time to solve it in second.

6.1   Comparing IA* with A*

Implementation of IA* is similar to the IBFS. The only difference is that IA* tracks heuristic evaluation of a node and the frontier list is ordered by the heuristic evaluation values. The best node is added to the front of the list.

We only present experimental results for IA* and A* algorithms which allow duplications. If we add a duplication check mechanism when we try to solve some examples of the Fifteen Puzzle, the algorithms become extremely slow which is normal due to the fact that the A* algorithm usually is not employed to solve Fifteen Puzzles.

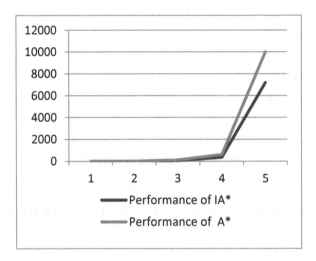

Chart 3. Compare the performance of IA* and A* algorithms. The horizontal coordinate shows the puzzle instances, and the vertical coordinate shows the time to solve it in second.

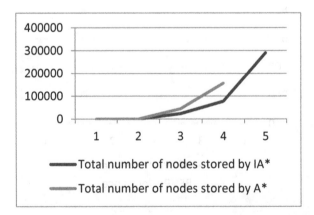

Chart 4. Compares storage used by IA* and A* algorithms. The horizontal coordinate shows the puzzle instances, and the vertical coordinate shows the number of nodes generated.

Results from Chart 3 show that; IA* and A* solve the puzzles that have a goal state at shallow levels approximately at the same amount of time, but if the goal state is on deeper levels, A* becomes extremely slow or cannot reach to goal state at all. However, IA* is able to solve some instance of this puzzles.

Results from Chart 4 shows IA* uses less memory than A* by completely eliminating the Closed List. And also A* is unable to solve some instances of fifteen puzzle however IA* can solve this instances.

The A* algorithms cannot solve Fifteen Puzzle Problems which have a goal node deeper than 50 moves. However IA* is able to solve some instances that have goal state deeper than 50 moves.

7   Conclusions and Future Works

We have introduced a new type of search algorithm that assigns an index to each node in its Frontier List, and after a goal node reached the algorithm covert the goal's index from decimal to the base of branching factor of problem to find the solution path. We have defined and implemented two types of indexed search algorithms; Indexed Breadth First Search (IBFS) and Indexed A* (IA*) search methods. These newer techniques enable the elimination of the Closed List employed by the standard BFS and A* algorithms. Our experimental results show that IBFS algorithm generates a solution faster than the standard BFS. It also needs less memory than the BFS. Additionally, the IA* algorithm generates a solution slightly faster than the A* algorithm and it needs less space than the A*.

The main approach of traditional AI search methods to solve a problem is to build a search space by creating new nodes, and storing these nodes in data structures for further investigation. The search proceeds according to heuristic function and the steps of the algorithm. The search terminate once the goal node reached or assigned time expired to find a solution. The Indexed Search redefined the task of search algorithms; the new task is to find the index of a goal state. Each state in the state space assigned an index, the search terminates once the index of the goal node is found. The Indexed search also does not keep track of explored nodes.

In the future, we are planning to develop more versions of Indexed search algorithm such as Indexed Iterative deepening search and to compare the results with respective other type of algorithms. We also plan to apply Indexed Search to some other industrial problems.

References

1. Kose, E.: Sub Goal Oriented A* Search. In: Aiello, M., Yang, Y., Zou, Y., Zhang, L.-J. (eds.) AIMS 2018. LNCS, vol. 10970, pp. 95–105. Springer, Cham (2018). https://doi.org/10.1007/978-3-319-94361-9_8
2. Sturtevant, N.R., Felner, A.: A brief history and recent achievements in bidirectional search. In: The Thirty-Second AAAI Conference on Artificial Intelligence AAAI (2018)

3. Chen, J., Holte, R.C., Zilles, S., Sturtevant, N.R.: Front-to-end bidirectional heuristic search with near-optimal node expansions. In: IJCAI (2017)
4. Bolac, L., Cytowski, J.: Search Methods for Artificial Intelligence. Academic Press, Cambridge (1992)
5. Felner, A., Moldenhauer, C., Sturtevat, N., Schaeffer, J.: Single-Frontier Bidirectional Search. AAAI, Atlanta (2010)
6. Felner, A., Ben-Yair, A., Kraus, S., Netanyahu, N.: Finding the shortest path with A* in an unknown physical environment. J. Artif. Intell. Res. **21**, 631–670 (2004)
7. Geethu, E.M.: Direction based heuristic for pathfinding in video games. Procedia Comput. Sci. **47**, 262–271 (2015)
8. Kopec, D., Marsland, T.A., Cox, J.: The Computer Science and Engineering Handbook, 2nd edn. In: Tucker, A. (ed.), pp. 1–26. CRC Press, Boca Raton (2004). Chapter 26
9. Korf, R.E.: Linear-space best first search. Artif. Intell. **62**(2), 41–78 (1993)
10. Korf, R.E.: Depth-first iterative deepening: an optimal admissible tree search. Artif. Intell. **27**(1), 97–109 (1985)
11. Luger, G.F., Stubblefield, W.A.: AI Algorithms, Data Structures, and Idioms in Prolog, List, and Java. Pearson Education, Inc., Boston (2009)
12. Luger, G.F.: Artificial Intelligence Structures and Strategies for Complex Problem Solving, 6th edn. Addison Wesley, Boston (2008)
13. Russell, S.J. Norvig, P.: Artificial Intelligence: A Modern Approach, 2nd edn. Prentice Hall, Upper Saddle River
14. Zhang, W.: State Space Search-Algorithms Complexity Extensions and Applications. Springer, Heidelberg (1999). https://doi.org/10.1007/978-1-4612-1538-7. (2003)
15. Zhou, R., Hansen, E.A.: Breadth-First Heuristic Search. AAAI, San Jose (2004)

Cognitively-Inspired Agent-Based Service Composition for Mobile and Pervasive Computing

Oscar J. Romero[✉][iD]

Carnegie Mellon University, Pittsburgh, OA 15213, USA
oscarr@andrew.cmu.edu
http://www.cs.cmu.edu/~oscarr/

Abstract. Automatic service composition in mobile and pervasive computing faces many challenges due to the complex and highly dynamic nature of the environment. Common approaches consider service composition as a decision problem whose solution is usually addressed from optimization perspectives which are not feasible in practice due to the intractability of the problem, limited computational resources of smart devices, service host's mobility, and time constraints to tailor composition plans. Thus, our main contribution is the development of a cognitively-inspired agent-based service composition model focused on bounded rationality rather than optimality, which allows the system to compensate for limited resources by selectively filtering out continuous streams of data. Our approach exhibits features such as distributedness, modularity, emergent global functionality, and robustness, which endow it with capabilities to perform decentralized service composition by orchestrating manifold service providers and conflicting goals from multiple users. The evaluation of our approach shows promising results when compared against state-of-the-art service composition models.

Keywords: Service composition · Pervasive middleware · Cognition

1 Introduction and Motivation

In Mobile and Pervasive Computing (MPC), a *Service* can be defined as any hardware or software functionality (resources, data or computation) of a smart device that can be requested by other devices for usage [18]. *Service composition* refers to the technique of creating composite services by the aggregation of atomic, simpler and easily executable services. Despite the existence of MPC middleware for automatic service composition [9,10,18,24], there are still some challenges that need to be tackled, as we illustrate in the next example:

Alice and Bob are planning to have a theme party at their home next weekend (high-level goal), so they need to coordinate some tasks among them. To achieve this goal, they interact with a user application (e.g., a personal assistant [25], a chatbot [28], etc.) connected to a MPC middleware installed on their mobile

© Springer Nature Switzerland AG 2019
D. Wang and L.-J. Zhang (Eds.): AIMS 2019, LNCS 11516, pp. 101–117, 2019.
https://doi.org/10.1007/978-3-030-23367-9_8

and wearable devices (e.g., smartphones, smartwatches, tablets, etc.), which act as Service Providers. The high-level goal, which will lead to the creation of a composite service, may be decomposed into 3 sub-goals: buy-food, buy-beer, and buy-home-decoration. There is also a set of atomic services that are hosted by service providers: get-location, find-place, calculate-distance, who-is-nearer, share-shopping-list, go-to-place. Now, each sub-goal is accomplished by the composition of a sequence of services, e.g.: buy-food = {get-location(user) → find-place(supermarket) → calculate-distance(user, supermarket) → who-is-nearer(market, users) → share-shopping-list(users) → go-to-place(user, market)}.

Given the previous example we focus on five challenges, so service composition should: (1) consider preferences from multiple users; (2) coordinate the interaction between services hosted by different service providers; (3) consider resource scarcity in smart devices [21]; (4) perform dynamic adaptation to unpredictable changes occurring in the environment; (5) deal with both short-term and long-term user's goals. Performing service composition while taking into account a myriad of variable factors as described above (e.g., users, services, service providers, QoS values, context, etc.), makes the problem become intractable even for approaches that use dynamic composition. The main issue with these approaches is that they propose solutions focused on optimality (e.g, graph-, rule-, and workflow-based solutions), which do no consider limitations imposed by the decision-making process (specially on smart devices), revealing their inability to process and compute the expected utility of every alternative action when variable factors grow in size (combinatorial explosion). Therefore, we propose a cognitively-inspired approach based on bounded rationality, which centers on the fact that perfectly rational decisions are often not feasible in practice because of the intractability of the problem, the limited computational resources, and time constraints; instead, our approach seeks satisfactory solutions rather than optimal ones. Thus, our main contributions are twofold: (1) We propose *COPERNIC*, a cognitively-inspired agent-based service composition middleware, as a first approach to addressing the five challenges described above (i.e., multiple users, decentralized coordination, and inexpensive, dynamic, and long-short term composition) using a bounded rationality approach; and (2) We develop a prototype of *COPERNIC* and evaluate its performance against to state-of-the-art service composition models. This paper is organized as follows: Sect. 2 outlines the system architecture. Section 3 details our approach, and Sect. 4 reports the experimental results. Sections 5 and 6 presents the related work and the conclusions, respectively.

2 Overview

2.1 Preliminaries

As considered in the literature [3], we distinguish two types of services: *abstract* and *concrete* services. Formally, a concrete service cs_i is a tuple $\langle cs_i^{in}, cs_i^{out}, cs_i^{prec}, cs_i^{postc}, cs_i^{QoS}, cs_i^{ctx} \rangle$ that performs a functionality by acting on input data (cs_i^{in}) to produce output data (cs_i^{out}), with pre-conditions (cs_i^{prec}), post-conditions (cs_i^{postc}), Quality of Service requirements (cs_i^{QoS}), and contextual information. An abstract service as_i is a tuple $\langle as_i^{pre}, as_i^{post}, as_i^{cs} \rangle$ realized by several concrete services that offer the same functionality $(as_i^{cs} \in \{cs_{(i,1)}, cs_{(i,2)}, ...,$ $cs_{(i,n)}\})$ with preconditions (as_i^{pre}) and postconditions (as_i^{post}) such that $\forall cs_{(i,j)}$, $cs_{(i,k)} \in as_i^{cs}/(as_i^{pre} = cs_{(i,j)}^{pre} \cap cs_{(i,k)}^{pre}) \wedge (as_i^{post} = cs_{(i,j)}^{post} \cap cs_{(i,k)}^{post}).$

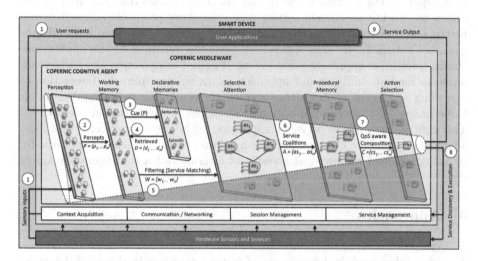

Fig. 1. *COPERNIC*'s overall architecture (single device). The white cone illustrates how a continuous stream of data is filtered out so only the most relevant elements are retained for the composition while the others are either discarded or put on hold until they receive more activation to become participants.

2.2 System Architecture

Figure 1 depicts the overall architecture of *COPERNIC*, though it is worth noting that it does not reflect yet the distributed nature of our model. The *COPERNIC* Agent is a cognitive module inspired by architectural principles defined by the Common Model of Cognition (CMC) [13,20], a computational model that captures a consensus about the structures and processes that are similar to those found in human cognition. Next, we briefly describe *COPERNIC*'s pipeline (Fig. 1) and its realization on the CMC model. In *Step 1*, the *Perception* module makes sense of the agent's current state by processing both external (e.g., user requests) and internal (i.e., signals from other modules) sensory inputs, categorizing that information, and recognizing situations where a set of abstract services may be triggered. In *Step 2*, the *Perception* module outputs a set of symbolic structures (percepts) that are stored in a Working Memory (WM) for further processing as abstract service inputs. In *Step 3*, the WM cues the declarative memories (i.e., *Episodic Memory* that retrieves information about historic performance of services, context, etc., and *Semantic Memory* that retrieves service definitions, user preferences, etc.) and stores local associations in *Step 4*. In *Step 5*, the content of the WM is filtered out by the attention mechanism so the agent only focuses on the most relevant information needed for matching abstract services. In *Step 6*, goals are decomposed and abstract services compete and cooperate (creating coalitions) among them in order to get the focus of attention. In *Step 7*, the *Procedural Memory* executes a set of heuristics to dynamically bind abstract services to concrete services by validating the QoS requirements. In *Step 8*, the *Action Selection* chooses the most appropriate action to execute a concrete service using discovery protocols adapted to the heterogeneous nature of the environment (the process is repeated until all subgoals are satisfied). In *Step 9*, service's output is returned to the application. Unlike traditional approaches that create uPFRont composition plans which are prone to inadaptability, in our approach, plans emerge from the interaction of cascading sequences of **cognitive cycles** corresponding to perception-action loops (steps 1–8) where compositional conditions are validated in every cycle. This contribution allows service composition to be more reactive, robust, and adaptive to dynamic changes while composition plans are generated on-the-fly by using minimal resources as a result of filtering out a continuous stream of data.

3   Approach

A. Perception
The perception module defines a set of feature detectors in charge of detecting and classifying the sensory inputs, i.e., there are different feature detectors to identify external stimuli (i.e., user requests) and internal stimuli (i.e., user's context, physical context – sensor readings, and service QoS). Feature detectors create *percepts*, units of perceived information with a symbolic representation (key-value pairs, e.g., <location, home>) and an activation level. Percepts activation rapidly decay over time (when not re-stimulated) according to the following inverse sigmoid function: $p_{act_i} = \frac{sal_i}{\log_2 cc_i}$, where p_{act_i} is the activation for percept i, sal_i is the salience of the stimulus (the quality by which a percept stands out from its neighbors), and cc_i the number of cognitive cycles since the last time the percept received activation. Salience is a numeric value between 1–10 (being 10 the most salient stimulus) and serves for designers to add some relevance to perceived information, e.g, a "user request" percept may have a higher salience (so it should last longer) whereas "Temporary WiFi disconnection" may have a lower salience. This module outputs a set of percepts $P = \{p_1...p_n\} \mid \forall p_i \in PR$, where PR is a set of premises such that $as^{pre} \cup cs^{pre} \subseteq PR$.

B. Short-term Working Memory (WM)
WM holds previous percepts not yet decayed away, and local associations from declarative memories that are combined with the percepts to understand the current state of the composition. Information written in the WM may reappear in different cognitive cycles until it fades away. To that purpose, WM defines a limited storage capacity (default: 7 units [16]) and a recency-based decay function that keeps active a limited number of units, expressed as a base-level activation

function [2]: $B_i^w = iB_i^w + \sum_{l=1}^{n} t_l^{-d}$, where i is a WM unit (w_i), l is the lth setting of w_i, t_l is the time since lth unit was presented, iB_i^w is the initial value of activation, and d is a decay parameter that reflects differences in WM units volatility, e.g., dynamic changes on *user context* happen more often than changes on *user preferences*, so the former should have a higher decay value, whereas the latter should have a lower one, which makes user context obsolete quicker than user preferences. If B_i^w is above a threshold ($B_i^w > t_w$) then w_i will be used as an input for service matching, i.e., $w_i \subseteq (as^{pre} \cup cs^{pre}) \subseteq PR$.

C. Long-term Episodic Memory (EM)

EM is a content-address-able associative memory that records temporal sequences of user and system events. *COPERNIC* defines 3 types of EM: (1) *User EM* that stores user past actions (e.g., Bob searched for nearby beer shops after doing the shopping); (2) *Service Provide EM* that stores historic data of service and service provider performance (efficiency, reliability, QoS, reputation, failures, etc.); and (3) *Network EM* that stores neighboring updates, network hops, etc. Any unit written to the WM cues a retrieval from EM, returning prior activity associated with the current entry. We used a Sparse Distributed Memory (SDM) [11], a high-dimensional space that mimics a human neural network. SDM is lightweight, random (it retrieves service associations in equal time from any location), content-addressable (it finds complete contents using content portions), and associative (it finds contents similar to a cue).

D. Long-term Semantic Memory (SM)

SM is intended to capture the meaning of concepts and facts about: (1) service descriptions; (2) the world (e.g., <Home><is-a><place>); and (3) the user (e.g., preferences, goals, etc.). SM is implemented using a Slipnet, an activation passing semantic network, where each concept is represented by a node, and each conceptual relationship by a link having a numerical length, representing the "conceptual distance" between the two nodes involved, which is adjusted dynamically. The shorter the distance between two concepts is, the more easily pressures can induce a slippage (connection) between them. Nodes acquire varying levels of activation (i.e., measure of relevance to the current situation in the WM) and spread varying amounts of activation to neighbors. Let $B_i^s = B_{i-1}^s + \sum_{j=0}^{n}(k - L_{i,j})$ such that B_i^s and B_{i-1}^s are the current and previous activations of node i, respectively; k is a constant for regulation of spreading activation; and $L_{i,j}$ is the conceptual length between nodes i and j. Traditional semantic-driven approaches for service composition use ontology-based description languages, however, these static representations do not account for the dynamicity of the environment, require the use of semantic reasoners and ontologies, and lack a mechanism to represent conceptual distance. The declarative module outputs a set of premises $D = \{d_1...d_n\} \mid \forall d_i \in PR$.

E. Selective Attention (SA)

Based on Posner's theory of attention [15], our SA filters out a continuous stream of content from WM while carrying out three attentional functions: (1) maintaining an alert state (e.g., SA gives priority to salient information like context and

QoS); (2) focusing agent's senses on the required information (e.g., to discover *get-location* service and bring it into composition, SA needs to focus on changes on GPS readings); and (3) the ability to manage attention towards goals and planning (e.g., SA focuses on the high-level goal "plan a party at home" and its corresponding sub-goals). SA uses a Behavior Network (BN) [14] , a hybrid system that integrates both a connectionist computational model and a symbolic, structured representation. BN defines a collection of behaviors (nodes) that compete and cooperate among them (through spreading activation dynamics) in order to get the focus of attention. In *COPERNIC*, each behavior maps to a single abstract service as, and *"service discovering/matching"* is modeled as an emergent property of activation/inhibition dynamics among all abstract services. Revisiting the formal definition of an abstract service as_i, we have the tuple: $\langle as_i^{pre}, as_i^{add}, as_i^{del}, as_i^{\alpha} \rangle$, where as_i^{pre} is a list of preconditions that have to be true before the service becomes active, as_i^{add} and as_i^{del} represent the expected (positive and negative) postconditions of the service in terms of an "add" and a "delete" lists, and as_i^{α} is the level of activation. If a WM unit w_i is in as_i^{pre} then there is an active link from w_i to as_i. If the goal g (i.e., a user request or any sub-goal stored in WM) is in as_i^{add} then there is an active link from g to as_i. There is a successor link from service as_i to service as_j for every WM unit such that $w_i \in as_i^{add} \cap as_i^{pre}$. A predecessor link from as_j to as_i exists for every successor link from as_i to as_j. There is a conflicter link from as_i to as_j for every WM unit such that $w_i \in as_j^{del} \cap as_i^{pre}$. Additionally, the model defines five global parameters that can be used to tune the global behavior of the network: π is the mean level of activation, θ is the threshold for becoming active, ϕ is the amount of activation energy a WM unit injects into the network, γ is the amount of energy a goal injects into the network, and δ is the amount of activation energy a protected goal takes away from the network. These global parameters make it possible to mediate smoothly between service selection criteria, such as trading off goal-orientedness for situation-orientedness, adaptivity for inertia, and deliberation for reactivity (see Listing 1.1).

```
input: a set of WM units W, a set of goals G, cognitive cycle t
output: selected abstract service AS
A := set of registered abstract services //A = {as_1...as_n}
M_j := nil //∀as ∈ A, j ∈ W | M_j = ∑_{i=1}^n #(as_i^pre ∩ j)
X_j := nil //∀as ∈ A, j ∈ W | X_j = ∑_{i=1}^n #(as_i^add ∩ j)
U_j := nill //∀as ∈ A, j ∈ W | U_j = ∑_{i=1}^n #(as_i^del ∩ j)
for each abstract service as_i in A do:
   AW_(i,t) := ∑_j φ · (1/M_j) · (1/#(as_i^pre)) //compute activation from current WM state (AW)
   AG_(i,t) := ∑_j γ · (1/X_j) · (1/#(as_i^add)) //compute activation from goals (AG).
   TG_(i,t) := ∑_j δ · (1/U_j) · (1/#(as_i^del)) //take activation away from achieved goals (TG)
   BW_(i,t) := ∑_j as_i^{α(t-1)} · (1/X_j) · (1/#(as_i^add)) //spread activation energy backward (BW)
   FW_(i,t) := ∑_j as_i^{α(t-1)} · (φ/γ) · (1/X_j) · (1/#(as_i^add))) //spread activation energy forward
   as_(i,t).act := EW_(i,t) + EG_(i,t) - TG_(i,t) + BW_(i,t) + FW_(i,t) //total activation for as_i
end for
return AS := max_act(A)
```

Listing 1.1. Pseudocode for the Spreading Activation Dynamics of *COPERNIC*'s Attentional Mechanism (see Section F.)

F. Procedural Memory (PM)

PM defines a set of heuristics (in the form of productions) to: (1) discover and match concrete services based on contextual information and QoS attributes; and (2) adjust the BN parameters in order to make the global behavior be more adaptive (i.e., deliberative vs. reactive, goal-oriented vs. situation-oriented, etc.) depending on the task requirements. Suppose there are two concrete services associated to "get-location" abstract service (e.g., Bob's phone hosts cs_p and Bob's smartwatch hosts cs_w), and each concrete service has 2 QoS features: accuracy and latency. The accuracy of cs_p is better since it uses fused location algorithms and its GPS sensor provides more precise readings, but its latency is higher than cs_w, so at a given moment, a heuristic production might prefer to match cs_w, even if this is not as accurate as cs_p, just because it can deliver a faster response during time-sensitive compositions. Regarding tuning BN parameters, PM applies the following heuristics [19] to keep the balance between: (1) goal-orientedness vs. situation-orientedness, $\gamma > \phi$; (2) deliberation vs. reactivity, $\phi > \gamma \wedge \phi > \theta$; (3) bias towards ongoing plan vs. adaptivity, $\phi > \pi > \gamma$; and (4) to preserve sensitivity to goal conflict, $\delta > \gamma$. The corresponding values are dynamically adapted over time and using a *reinforcement learning mechanism* based on the heuristic utility. Utility learning for a heuristic i after its nth usage is: $U_i(n) = U_i(n-1) + \alpha[R_i(n) - U_i(n-1)] + \epsilon$, where α is the learning rate (default [2]: 0.2), $R_i(n)$ is the effective reward value given to heuristic i for its nth usage, ϵ is a temperature (level of randomness) that is decreased over time, i.e., $\epsilon = 1/e^{(n/k)}, k = 0.35$ (determined empirically [2]).

G. Action Selection (AS)

AS processes different kind of actions: (1) internal actions such as goal setting (it adds new goals to both the WM and SA modules); and (2) external actions such as triggering a device's effector/actuator, and invoking the discovery mechanism to look up a concrete service and then execute it. AS uses a scheduler mechanism to sort (by priority) and execute actions in the future.

H. Cognitive Cycle

In mapping to human behavior [13], *COPERNIC*'s cognitive cycles operate at roughly 50 ms, although the actions that they trigger can take significantly longer to execute. A cognitive cycle starts with sensing and usually ends with selection of an internal or external action. The cognitive cycle is conceived as an active process that allows interactions between the different components of the architecture. Deliberation, reasoning, and generation of plans in *COPERNIC* take place over multiple cascading cognitive cycles in the current situation (i.e., multiple overlapping cycles iterating at an asynchronous rate, see Listing 1.2).

```
input: set of sensory inputs SI, set of user goals G
output: selected concrete service CS
P := nil //set of salient percepts (P = {p_1..p_n})
W := nil //set of active units in the WM (W = {w_1..w_n})
D := nil //set of retrieved declarative units (D = {d_1..d_n})
A := set of registered abstract services (A = {as_1..as_n})
C := set of registered concrete services (C = {cs_1..cs_n})
R := nil //set of resulting actions
```

```
while remaining goals G > 0 do: //cognitive cycle i
  P_i := detect, classify and temporarily store SI and G
  W_i := add salient percepts to WM (W_i = W_(i-1) ∪ P_i)
  D_i := cue and retrieve declarative memories using the content of WM
  W_i := add declarative units to WM (W_i = W_i ∪ D_i)
  W_i := decay and filter WM units (W_i = W_d, where W_d ⊆ W_i)
  A_i := focus attention and do service matching (A_i = W_i ∩ A^pre)
  C_i := apply heuristics (PM) and select concrete service candidates (Ci = A_i ∩ QoS)
  CS := select a concrete service
  R_i := wrap CS execution as an action and add it to the set of actions
  a := prioritize actions R_i and pick the most relevant
  if a is of type ''service-execution'' then execute concrete service's action a.CS
  else execute internal action
end while
```

Listing 1.2. Pseudocode for COPERNIC's Cognitive Cycle (see Fig. 1)

I. Session Management

This module manages shared sessions across multiple user's *Devices* (service providers). A running instance of *COPERNIC* is hosted by each device. Using proximity discovery protocols, devices are grouped by physical nearness into *Groups*. For instance, on Fig. 2, Group *"bob-with-me"* represents the devices that Bob carries with him whereas *"bob-home"* represents a Group of devices at Bob's home. Groups belonging to the same user are logically grouped into *Sessions*, where each Session guarantees that multiple ubiquitous devices can share information and collaborate in a distributed, inexpensive and robust fashion.

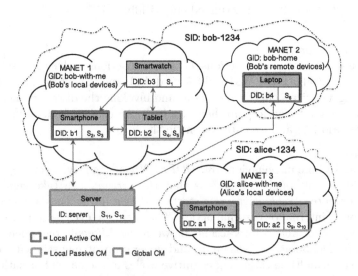

Fig. 2. Infrastructure-less MPC environment. *COPERNIC* agents are distributed across different local networks (MANET) and collaborate during composition. DID: Device ID, GID: Group ID, SID: Session ID, $S_1..S_n$: Services.

J. Service Management

Service management (i.e., service discovery, service coordination, and management of the information flow between service components) is performed by a *Composition Manager* (CM). Service management tasks are distributed on an as-needed basis among multiple *Composition Managers* (CMs) in both infrastructure-based and infrastructure-less networks. Unlike traditional approaches, where transferring the control from one CM to another does not consider fatal failures that prevent such transference, our approach is based on a Binary Star pattern that serves for primary-backup node failover. That is, *COPERNIC* chooses two CMs per Group, one works in active mode while the other one in passive mode. Both active and passive CMs monitor each other and if the active CM disappears from the network, then the passive one will take over as active CM and send a request for another device to join as a passive CM. Using a ranking function based on four levels of device capabilities, as show in Table 1, *COPERNIC* is able to determine which devices will be the active and passive CMs, that is: $R_{cm} = Pri_{cm} \times Per_{cm}$, where R is the ranking of CM cm, Pri is a level-based priority function (i.e., Level-0 = 0... Level-3 = 3), and Per is a CM performance function based on composition completeness, composition time, etc.

Table 1. Composition manager levels

Feature	Level-0	Level-1	Level-2	Level-3
COPERNIC version	Minimal	Lightweight	Full	Full
Resources (CPU, memory)	Scarse	Limited	Rich	Rich
Can act as CM?	NO	YES	YES	YES
Cross-session composition?	NO	NO	NO	YES
Example devices	Sensors	Wearables	Smartphone, Laptop	PC, server

It is worth noting that only Level-3 can perform *global cross-session compositions* (i.e., involving multiple users and sessions), though Level-2 and Level-1 can still perform *local compositions* (i.e., within a group) so the whole composition task is distributed among multiple CMs, as shown in Fig. 2. Each Local CM tailors a partial composition plan that satisfies the needs of its user by using local resources and services; then a Global CM, which can see the whole picture, receives as inputs partial plans from Local CMs and makes "good enough" decisions using the available information. By good enough we mean that, rather than trying to look for an optimized solution, CMs exploit opportunities that contribute to the ongoing goal/plan while adapting to unpredictable changing situations. Figure 3 illustrates how CMs make good enough decisions as a result of the spreading activation dynamics coordinated by *COPERNIC* cognitive agents.

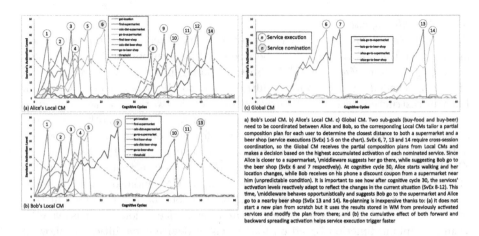

a) Bob's Local CM. b) Alice's Local CM. c) Global CM. Two sub-goals (buy-food and buy-beer) need to be coordinated between Alice and Bob, so the corresponding Local CMs tailor a partial composition plan for each user to determine the closest distance to both a supermarket and a beer shop (service executions (SvEx) 1-5 on the chart). SvEx 6, 7, 13 and 14 require cross-session coordination, so the Global CM receives the partial composition plans from Local CMs and makes a decision based on the highest accumulated activation of each nominated service. Since Alice is closer to a supermarket, \middleware suggests her go to there, while suggesting Bob go to the beer shop (SvEx 6 and 7 respectively). At cognitive cycle 30, Alice starts walking and her location changes, while Bob receives on his phone a discount coupon from a supermarket near him (unpredictable condition). It is important to see how after cognitive cycle 30, the services' activation levels reactively adapt to reflect the changes in the current situation (SvEx 8-12). This time, \middleware behaves opportunistically and suggests Bob go to the supermarket and Alice go to a nearby beer shop (SvEx 13 and 14). Re-planning is inexpensive thanks to: (a) it does not start a new plan from scratch but it uses the results stored in WM from previously activated services and modify the plan from there; and (b) the cumulative effect of both forward and backward spreading activation helps service execution trigger faster

Fig. 3. Spreading activation dynamics for the example described in Sect. 1

4   Evaluation

A. Experimental Setup

We implemented the dynamic composition overlay on the NS-3 simulator using the experimental settings on Table 2. We compared *COPERNIC* against two state-of-the-art decentralized service composition models: GoCoMo, a goal-driven service model based on a decentralized heuristic backward-chaining planning algorithm [5]; and CoopC, a decentralized cooperative discovery model that employs a backward goal-driven service query and forward service construction mechanism but does not support runtime composite service adaptation [8].

Table 2. Experimental settings

Setting	Value
Number users (1 goal/user)	1, 2
Service density (# providers)	sparse (**SD-S**): 20, medium (**SD-M**): 40, dense (**SD-D**): 60
Composition length	5 services (**CL-5**), 10 services (**CL-10**)
Node mobility	slow (**M-S**): 0–2 m/s, medium (**M-M**): 2–8 m/s, fast (**M-F**): 8–13 m/s
Number of services	Abstract: 10, Concrete: 40 (4 per abstract service)
Communication range	250 m
Sem. matchmaking delay	0.2 (s) [5]
Sample per experiment	100 runs
Node movement	Random walking Monte Carlo model
Pre/post-cond per service	Random (1-4)

We run 2 different experiments and measured the composition efficiency using 4 different metrics: composition time (**CT** in seconds), average memory usage of all service providers involved in the composition (**MU** in Kb), a planning failure rate (**PFR**) calculated as the ratio of the number of failed planning processes to the number of all the issued requests during the simulation cycles, and the execution failure rate (**EFR**) computed as the ratio of the number of failed executions to the number of all the successful plans.

B. Flexibility of Service Composition

This scenario evaluates the flexibility of *COPERNIC*, GoCoMo, and CoopC during the generation of service composites while varying node mobility, service density, and service complexity (composition length). This scenario uses the configuration presented in Table 2 and only one user. The experimental results are shown in Table 3 (blue and red cells are the best and worst measurements for each category, respectively). Overall, GoCoMo got the lowest failure rates (PFR), followed by *COPERNIC* and then by CoopC, though *COPERNIC*'s composition time (CT) and memory usage (MU) were the lowest in comparison to the other two approaches. In particular, GoCoMo got a lower failure rate (12–38%) than *COPERNIC* when the mobility was slow. This difference dropped to 7–13% in fast-mobility high-density scenarios thanks to *COPERNIC* is less sensitive to mobility changes because the information about participant services is stored in the WM and gradually fades away, so when, for instance, a service provider disappears and reappears later in time, the probability that this service provider is still in the WM is high (due to its activation may have not decayed entirely), so it will be able to promptly participate again in the composition without producing significant planning failures. In comparison with CoopC, *COPERNIC* got 12–25% less failures due to CoopC's does not support runtime adaptation and poorly handles mobility and density changes. Regarding composition time, *COPERNIC* tailored composite services up to 42% faster than GoCoMo and up to 71% faster than CoopC; and it used up to 72% less memory than GoCoMo and up to 84% less memory than CoopC. The reason for this significant reduction in composition time and resource consumption is that *COPERNIC* is continuously filtering out the stream of incoming information (sensory stimuli), which keeps it into reasonable margins of resources usage, despite of the dynamism of the environment. It is worth noting that *COPERNIC* did not show a significant difference in memory usage when using a composition length of either 5 or 10 services (-4%–11%) in comparison with GoCoMo (60%–190%) and CoopC (157%–201%), which suggests that our approach could be smoothly scaled up.

C. Adaptability of Service Composition

In this scenario we simulated 2 users with one goal each. Then, in the middle of the composition users switched their goals (switch point). We measured the ability (in terms of planning and executing failure rates) of both *COPERNIC* and GoCoMo to adapt to the new situation and replan a different composite service for both users while using different settings for mobility, density, and composition length. In this experiment we did not consider CoopC due to it

Table 3. Flexibility of service composition

			M-S			M-M			M-F		
			SD-S	SD-M	SD-D	SD-S	SD-M	SD-D	SD-S	SD-M	SD-D
COPERNIC	CL-5	PFR (%)	18.2	3.7	1.1	17.5	1.4	1.4	21.1	3.3	1.1
		CT (sec)	0.9	0.5	0.8	1.1	1.2	1.2	1.1	1.4	1.4
		MU (Kb)	63	81	93	67	86	93	73	88	98
	CL-10	PFR (%)	17.8	3.7	1.1	17.7	1.5	0.5	19.7	3.8	1.4
		CT (sec)	1.2	0.6	0.8	1.2	1.2	1.1	1.2	1.3	1.9
		MU (Kb)	70	86	92	70	73	85	78	89	94
GoCoMo	CL-5	PFR (%)	13.1	3.3	0.6	16.1	1.2	0.3	18.0	3.1	0.9
		CT (sec)	1.3	0.7	0.9	1.3	1.4	1.4	1.3	1.3	1.4
		MU (Kb)	79	93	112	78	93	110	80	94	114
	CL-10	PFR (%)	16.2	2.3	0.8	24.7	1.1	0.4	22.1	3.5	1.3
		CT (sec)	2.1	2.2	2.2	2.2	2.3	2.3	2.3	2.4	2.4
		MU (Kb)	213	273	314	201	287	308	221	286	345
CoopC	CL-5	PFR (%)	16.2	2.4	0.8	21.9	1.3	2.3	24.5	3.7	1.2
		CT (sec)	1.8	1.9	1.9	1.9	1.8	2.1	1.9	2.1	2.2
		MU (Kb)	114	245	367	121	239	353	117	275	359
	CL-10	PFR (%)	24.0	2.3	1.3	25.2	2.4	1.2	31.8	4.2	1.6
		CT (sec)	4.1	4.2	4.2	4.5	4.7	4.9	5.0	5.1	5.5
		MU (Kb)	325	476	593	332	488	605	345	497	657

cannot perform runtime service composition adaptation. Also, for the sake of simplicity, we only used a composition length of 5 services. Since GoCoMo lacks both multi-goal and multi-user composition processing, we had to run simultaneously 2 instances of GoCoMo with one goal each, and then switched the goals at the specific switch point. The individual measurements of both instances were added up, this makes GoCoMo more comparable against *COPERNIC*. In order to demonstrate the adaptability of *COPERNIC*, we used two different configurations for its attentional mechanism. A configuration is defined as a tuple of values corresponding to the Behavior Network's parameters described in Sect. 4.E, such that $C_i = \langle \theta_i, \pi_i, \phi_i, \gamma_i, \delta_i \rangle$. Configuration C_1 uses the default values for the attentional mechanism: $C_1 = \langle 30, 20, 20, 20, 20 \rangle$, while configuration C_2 uses values discovered by the utility learning mechanism (described in Sect. 4.F) after 100 test runs: $C_2 = \langle 22, 27, 42, 23, 18 \rangle$. Results are presented in Table 4.

Table 4. Adaptability of service composition

		M-S			M-M			M-F		
		SD-S	SD-M	SD-D	SD-S	SD-M	SD-D	SD-S	SD-M	SD-D
COPERNIC - C1	PFR (%)	23.1	5.2	2.1	21.1	4.3	1.9	21.9	4.8	2.0
	EFR (%)	45.2	22.6	15.9	69.4	31.2	21.4	78.5	43.9	37.0
	CT (sec)	5.8	4.2	3.1	6.1	4.4	3.7	6.4	4.5	3.9
	MU (Kb)	85	93	110	90	102	117	95	111	123
COPERNIC - C2	PFR (%)	20.7	4.7	1.6	18.5	3.6	1.4	19.8	4.2	1.7
	EFR (%)	38.5	17.3	11.3	58.2	19.3	14.9	63.8	29.8	26.6
	CT (sec)	4.2	3.1	2.3	5.5	3.9	2.9	5.6	4.0	3.1
	MU (Kb)	84	93	109	91	103	115	96	112	120
GoCoMo	PFR (%)	20.3	4.2	1.4	18.1	3.5	1.1	19.1	3.9	1.6
	EFR (%)	43.5	18.2	13.2	67.4	24.2	16.8	76.3	35.7	32.4
	CT (sec)	5.4	3.9	3.2	5.9	4.3	3.5	6.6	4.6	3.9
	MU (Kb)	428	536	678	544	623	701	598	703	812

Despite the fact that GoCoMo had lower planning failure rates than *COPER-NIC* (12%–42% and 2%–11% in comparison with C_1 and C_2 respectively), the memory required by it to complete the compositions was considerable higher (up to 5.7 times higher) than both configurations of *COPERNIC*. One of the main reasons for this significant divergence in memory usage is that GoCoMo's service discovery mechanism uses a cache to store the progress of resolving split-join controls for parallel service flows, which results in resource-intensive processes creating multiple potential execution branches. On the contrary, *COPER-NIC* does not keep a record of multiple execution branches and does not store in memory different workflows for each fork of the plan; it keeps in memory only one single plan that is created on-the-fly, that is, when goals or sensory stimuli (internal signals and user requests) change then it adapts to the new situation by spreading more activation to those nodes (e.g., perception, WM, and attentional nodes) that should participate in the new plan, which becomes more attractive than the current plan. Additionally, *COPERNIC* does not replan at every time step. The "history" of the spreading activation also plays a role in the service selection since the activation levels are not reinitialized at every time step (instead, they are accumulated over time, so when changing the focus to another goal, services that may participate in the new goal reuse their current activation and continue accumulating activation on top of it). Furthermore, it is important to highlight that the cost of recomposing is significantly reduced by *COPERNIC* thanks to its distributed nature where multiple agents decompose the whole problem into smaller planning objectives. Similar to the previous experiment, one of the drawbacks of our approach is that its failure rate was higher than GoCoMo's one due to the attention mechanism could dismiss some crucial information pieces at any point affecting the final decision. Now, comparing the results of both configurations of *COPERNIC*, we can observe that in general C_2 outperforms C_1. We can infer that if γ (the amount of energy a goal injects into the attentional mechanism) $> \phi$ (the amount of energy that the WM units inject into the attentional mechanism) then *COPERNIC* will be more goal-oriented and less sensitive to changes in the current state (e.g., changes in mobility). On the contrary, if $\phi > \gamma$ then the system will be more sensitive to changes in the current state rather than changes in the goals. Also, if δ (the amount of activation energy a protected goal takes away from the system) is significantly greater than γ then the system will keep a stubborn position, that is, it will try to always stick with the original plan (protected goal) and will be reluctant to refocus its attention to the new goal. On the contrary, if γ is considerable greater than δ then the system will be continuously switching from one goal to another and never will conclude any plan. Finally, reducing the activation threshold θ may help the system make faster decisions (reactive behavior), useful during time-sensitive composition; by contrast, increasing θ will slow down the reasoning process (deliberative behavior), useful for long-term composition planning. Therefore, the utility learning mechanism has to find a proper ratio between these parameters so the performance of the system is improved. The learning mechanism found a tradeoff between the parameter and discovered that, in order to make the system sensitive to both current-state changes (e.g., mobility, perceived stimuli, etc.) and goal changes, without switching indefinitely between goals, and with the ability to undone previously reached (protected) goals in order to refocus on new goals (replanning), then γ should be slightly greater than δ at a ratio of $\approx$ 4:3; ϕ should be greater than γ at a ratio of $\approx$ 2:1; and $\phi > \pi > \gamma$ where ϕ is greater than π at a ratio of 14:9. When using values beyond those ratios (as C_1 does), *COPERNIC*'s planning and execution failure rates increased considerably in comparison with GoCoMo.

As a side note, the way CoopC (and other baseline service composition models) addresses faults in composition is for the system to restart the whole process if any service has failed during the execution, of course, this solution is unable to utilize the partial results. Unlike CoopC, *COPERNIC* neither creates a long-term plan upfront, nor constructs a search tree. Instead, plans are tailored on-the-fly through activation accumulation, so that it does not have to start from scratch when one path does not produce a solution, but smoothly moves from one composition plan to another. As a result, the computation of the composition plan is much less expensive. Creating a long-term plan in advance would require too much time (especially for a cognitive agent operating in a rapidly changing MPC environment), instead, plans are emergently created by *COPERNIC* as a result of multiple cascading cognitive cycles. The main differences between our approach and both GoCoMo and CoopC are that our approach can mediate smoothly between deliberation and reactivity by determining (through learning) a tradeoff between $\phi, \gamma, \delta, \pi$ and θ; and that it can perform deliberative composition by accessing long-term intentions stored in the episodic memory. It is worth noting that there is a multiple correlation between resource consumption, execution failure rate, and planning failure rate, so the more *COPERNIC* filters out the information required for the composition the lesser resources are required during composition, the faster the composite service will be generated and, therefore, the lower the execution failure rate will be. That is, if a composite service can be planned and replanned quickly and without requiring too many resources (as *COPERNIC* does), then the discrepancies between planning and execution will be minimized and, as a consequence, the execution failure rate will be minimized as well. However, the more the information is filtered out the higher the planning failure rate will be due to the cognitive agent may dismiss critical information pieces during planning.

5   Related Work

In the existing literature, there are mainly two different techniques of drafting a composition plan [18]. The first one utilizes the classical planning techniques used in AI (e.g., HTN, petri-nets, state charts, rule-based, multi-agent systems, π-calculus, etc.). Under this approach [7,23], the composition of atomic services into a composite service is viewed as a planning and optimization problem. The second technique uses workflows, in which a composite service is broken down into a sequence of interactions between atomic services [4]. The third technique uses direct mappings between user requests and service descriptions without needing intermmediate representations such as ontologies [22]. In general, first and second approaches either rely on conditional plans and can therefore handle only a limited range of non-deterministic action outcomes, or have the queries about unknown information explicitly included in the predefined service composition procedure. These plans use to be computationally expensive, have to deal with composition length and strive to optimize the resources involved. Our service composition model is not as expensive as traditional approaches because plans are constructed emergently on-the-fly as the result of both the spreading activation dynamics defined at multiple overlays of the system, and the cognitive mechanism for filtering out and focusing on the most relevant information. To reduce composition and execution failures while dealing with complex user requirements, existing service composition techniques investigate flexible composition planning mechanisms, and service execution policies such as: open service discovery approaches and dynamic service planning approaches. A graph-based service aggregation method [1, 26] models services and their I/O parameters in an aggregation graph based on the parameter dependence of the services. It dynamically composes services to support a task in a workflow when a direct match between the task and a single service does not exist. Such a workflow may need to be generated offline by a domain expert or a composition planning engine, which is inconvenient when a change is required at runtime. Dynamic service planning approaches such as [12,17] use classic AI-planning algorithms, such as forward-chaining and backward-chaining for dynamic composition planning, and usually employ a bi-direction planning algorithm to find a path with the smallest cost from the dependency graph. However, these approaches require central service repositories to maintain service overlays, and have no support for dynamic composition replanning for composition failures. AI-planning algorithms like Haley [27], and a fuzzy TOPSIS method [6] have been investigated for dynamic composition planning and have features for automatic re-planning to handle failures. However AI-planning algorithms rely on central composition engines that have not yet been applied on mobile devices. In addition, they need to re-generate a new plan for failure recovery, which is time-consuming and not suitable for dynamic environments.

6   Conclusions and Future Work

We described *COPERNIC*, an agent-based model for service composition in MPC environments. Our main contribution is the implementation of a cognitive model that efficiently and dynamically orchestrates distributed services under highly changing conditions. Our approach focuses on bounded rationality rather than optimality, allowing the system to compensate for limited resources by filtering out a continuous stream of incoming information. We tested our model against state-of-the-art service composition models while modifying mobility, service density and composition complexity features, and the promising results demonstrated that a cognitively-inspired approach may be suitable for pervasive environments where resources are scarce and the smart devices have computational and hardware constraints. Our future work will mainly focus on tightly integrating a context-awareness feature into our model so cognitive agents can make more accurate decisions during service selection.

References

1. Al-Oqily, I., Karmouch, A.: A decentralized self-organizing service composition for autonomic entities. ACM Trans. Auton. Adapt. Syst. **6**(1), 7:1–7:18 (2011)
2. Anderson, J.R., Bothell, D., Byrne, M.D., Douglass, S., Lebiere, C., Qin, Y.: An integrated theory of the mind. Psychol. Rev. **111**(4), 1036 (2004)
3. Balzer, S., Liebig, T.: Bridging the gap between abstract and concrete services a semantic approach for grounding owl-s. In: Semantic Web Services (2004)
4. Ben Mokhtar, S.: Semantic Middleware for Service-Oriented Pervasive Computing. Ph.D. thesis, Université Pierre et Marie Curie - Paris VI Dec 2007
5. Chen, N., Clarke, S.: Goal-driven service composition in mobile and pervasivecomputing. Serv. Comput. **11**(1), 49–62 (2018)
6. Cheng, D.Y., Chao, K.M., Lo, C.C., Tsai, C.F.: A user centric service-oriented modeling approach. World Wide Web **14**(4), 431–459 (2011)
7. Davidyuk, O., Georgantas, N., Issarny, V., Riekki, J.J.R.: MEDUSA: middleware for end-user composition of ubiquitous applications. In: Ambient Intelligence
8. Furno, A.: Efficient cooperative discovery of service compositions in unstructured p2p networks. In: Parallel Processing (2013)
9. Ibrahim, N., Mouël, F.L.: A survey on service composition middleware in pervasive environments. CoRR abs/0909.2183 (2009)
10. Immonen, A., Pakkala, D.: A survey of methods and approaches for reliable dynamic service compositions. SOCA **8**(2), 129–158 (2014)
11. Kanerva, P.: Sparse Distributed Memory. MIT Press, Cambridge (1988)
12. Khakhkhar, S., Kumar, V., Chaudhary, S.: Dynamic service composition. CS and AI **2**(3), 32–42 (2012)
13. Laird, J.E., Lebiere, C., Rosenbloom, P.S.: A standard model of the mind: toward a common computational framework across artificial intelligence, cognitive science, neuroscience, and robotics. AI Mag. **38**(4), 13 (2017)
14. Maes, P.: How to do the right thing. Connection Sci. **1**(3), 291–323 (1989)
15. Michael, P.: Cognitive Neuroscience of Attention. Springer, New York (2011)
16. Miller, G.A.: The magical number seven, plus or minus two: Some limits on our capacity for processing information. Psychol. Rev. **63**(2), 81–97 (1956)
17. Oh, S., Lee, D., Kumara, S.R.T.: Effective web service composition in diverse and large-scale service networks. IEEE Trans. SC **1**(1), 15–32 (2008)
18. Raychoudhury, V., Cao, J., Kumar, M., Zhang, D.: Middleware for pervasive computing: a survey. Pervasive Mob. Comput. **9**(2), 177–200 (2013)
19. Romero, O.: An evolutionary behavioral model for decision making. Adapt. Behav. **19**(6), 451–475 (2011)
20. Romero, O.J.: CogArch-ADL: toward a formal description of a referencearchitecture for the common model of cognition. Procedia Comput. Sci. **145**, 788–796 (2018)
21. Romero, O.J., Akoju, S.: An efficient mobile-based middleware architecture for building robust, high-performance apps. In: ICSA. In press (2018)

22. Romero, O.J., Dangi, A., Akoju, S.: NLSC: unrestricted natural language-based service composition through sentence embeddings. In: SCC (2019)
23. Santofimia, M.J., Fahlman, S.E., del Toro, X., Moya, F., López, J.C.: A semantic model for actions and events in ambient intelligence. AI **24**(8), 1432–1445 (2011)
24. Stavropoulos, T.G., Vrakas, D., Vlahavas, I.: A survey of service composition in ambient intelligence environments. Artif. Intell. Rev. **40**(3), 247–270 (2013)
25. Tomazini, L., Romero, O.J., Hruschka, H.: An architectural approach for developing intelligent personal assistants supported by NELL. In: ENIAC (2017)
26. Wang, Z., Xu, T., Qian, Z., Lu, S.: A parameter-based scheme for service composition in pervasive computing environment. In: CISIS, pp. 543–548 (2009)
27. Zhao, H., Doshi, P.: A hierarchical framework for logical composition of web services. Serv. Oriented Comput. Appl. **3**, 285–306 (2009)
28. Zhao, R., Romero, O.J., Rudnicky, A.: SOGO: a social intelligent negotiation dialogue system. In: Intelligent Virtual Agents (IVA) (2018)

Accelerating Deep Learning Inference on Mobile Systems

Darian Frajberg[✉], Carlo Bernaschina, Christian Marone, and Piero Fraternali

Dipartimento di Elettronica, Informazione e Bioingegneria, Politecnico di Milano, Piazza Leonardo da Vinci, 32, Milan, Italy
{darian.frajberg,carlo.bernaschina,christian.marone, piero.fraternali}@polimi.it

Abstract. Artificial Intelligence on the edge is a matter of great importance towards the enhancement of smart devices that rely on operations with real-time constraints. We present PolimiDL, a framework for the acceleration of Deep Learning on mobile and embedded systems with limited resources and heterogeneous architectures. Experimental results show competitive results with respect to TensorFlow Lite for the execution of small models.

Keywords: Deep Learning · Mobile sensing · Acceleration · Mobile devices · Embedded systems · Continuous vision

1 Introduction

The recent success of Deep Learning (DL) has boosted its application to many areas, with remarkable results that are influencing people's lives [20]. Typical implementations of DL models focus on the maximization of accuracy for a given task, and architectures to achieve such an objective have become significantly deeper and more complex over time [10,25]. Powerful workstations with Graphics Processing Units (GPUs) were fundamental for the success of DL, making their computationally expensive training possible. On the other hand, even though resources of embedded systems, such as smartphones, tablets, wearable devices, drones and Field Programmable Gate Arrays (FPGAs), are rapidly improving, they are still not completely suitable for the deployment of big and complex models. Furthermore, the use of remote cloud services for the execution of models has its own drawbacks due to the use of the network, such as cost, availability, latency, and privacy issues [5]. These limitations promote the interest in compact architectures for accelerating execution, by optimizing computation, storage, memory occupation, and energy consumption. The efficient execution of DL on the edge can benefit areas such as robotics, autonomous vehicles, augmented reality, health monitoring and digital assistance, which rely on smart devices with real-time constraints.

© Springer Nature Switzerland AG 2019
D. Wang and L.-J. Zhang (Eds.): AIMS 2019, LNCS 11516, pp. 118–134, 2019.
https://doi.org/10.1007/978-3-030-23367-9_9

In this work, we present PolimiDL, a framework for accelerated DL inference on mobile and embedded systems. PolimiDL speeds-up the execution time of ready-to-use models, by applying multiple optimization methods, and increases efficiency of operations without impacting accuracy. Its implementation is very generic, with neither hardware nor platform specific components, and supports devices with very heterogeneous architectures. The development of PolimiDL was started with the goal of deploying DL models on mobile devices, when no other stable solutions were available. It is currently deployed in PeakLens[1] [6], a real world AI-enhanced augmented reality (AR) mobile app for the identification of mountain peaks, with +370k installs. Experimental results demonstrate the effectiveness of PolimiDL to accelerate inference time, achieving competitive results with respect to TensorFlow Lite on a set of DL models and across multiple mobile devices.

The contributions of the paper can be summarized as follows:

- We introduce the problem of DL acceleration for devices with limited resources and discuss the design requirements of solutions capable of supporting a wide spectrum of device architectures.
- We propose a framework (PolimiDL) for DL acceleration that improves performance on mobile devices and embedded systems without accuracy loss.
- We release a public implementation of the framework in an open repository[2].

The rest of the paper is structured as follows: in Sect. 2, we discuss the related work; in Sect. 3, we introduce the requirements; in Sect. 4, we present PolimiDL; and in Sect. 5 we describe the evaluation of the framework; finally Sect. 6 concludes and gives an outlook on the future work.

2   Related Work

Compression Techniques. Compression techniques target large scale architectures and aim at reducing the number of parameters and floating point operations (FLOPs), possibly tolerating small accuracy drops in favor of execution acceleration and optimization of computational resources, storage, memory occupation and energy consumption. Quantization [27] reduces numerical precision of CNNs to accelerate run-time performance and reduce storage and memory overhead, with minor accuracy loss. Pruning [8] removes redundant connections, thus the number of weights, and proved to efficiently compress state of art models by one order of magnitude. Alternative options include knowledge-distillation [11] to compress and transfer knowledge from complex models to simpler ones, and tensor decomposition methods [17] followed by low-rank approximation, for the reduction and compression of weights. The effectiveness of compression depends on the size and redundancy of the original model and most compression techniques are applied either after or at training-time. Post-training compression

---

[1] https://www.peaklens.com.
[2] https://github.com/darianfrajberg/polimidl.

is easy to apply, but may induce a sensible accuracy loss, especially when no fine-tuning is performed on the models afterwards. On the other hand, training-aware compression tends to achieve better results, but requires more time and it is more complex to apply.

Optimized Model Architectures. Lightweight architectures with compact layers pursue the design of an optimized network topology, yielding small, fast and accurate models, suitable for resource-constrained devices. SqueezeNet [15] is a first-generation optimized CNN architecture, with modules composed by small Convolutional kernels; it achieves the same accuracy as AlexNet [18] with 50 times less parameters and can be effectively compressed on disk. MobileNet [12] is a family of efficient models for mobile vision applications, which perform different trade-offs of accuracy, computation and number of parameters. Such models, released by Google, are based on Depthwise Separable Convolutions [4] and outperformed most of previous state-of-the-art models. MobileNet v2 [22] further improves MobileNet, by incorporating inverted residual connections. Recently, reinforcement learning has been also exploited for the discovery of efficient building blocks, to support the design phase. Tan et al. [26] proposed MnasNet, an automated neural architecture search that exploits a multi-objective reward to address both accuracy and latency measured in real-world mobile devices.

Hardware Acceleration (HA). HA is the use of dedicated hardware to complement general-purpose CPUs and perform computationally intensive work more efficiently, e.g. by favoring specific operations and data-parallel computation. Digital Signal Processors (DSPs), GPUs and, more recently, Neural Processing Units (NPUs) are examples of it. Prominent mobile system on chip (SoC) vendors have incorporated specialized hardware for accelerated AI inference, focusing on vector and matrix-based instructions. Nonetheless, such instructions and the access to them depend on the proprietary Software Development Kits (SDKs) of each vendor, which are incompatible and impair the porting of acceleration solutions. Given the need of standardization, Google has recently published the Android Neural Networks API[3] (NNAPI), which defines a layer of abstraction that provides unified access to DL run-time acceleration. Its support for current devices is still limited due to its availability from Android 8.1 and requires specialized vendor drivers, otherwise computation falls back to the CPU. Similarly, recent versions of OpenGL[4] and Vulkan[5] were introduced for GPU-based efficient computations, but their support is reduced for older devices and depend on vendors' implementation. From iOS 8, Apple devices feature the Metal API[6], designed to maximize performance and let developers access HA. Apple has the advantage of targeting a limited and relatively homogeneous set of devices, while having full control over the production, which simplifies integration and support.

---

[3] https://developer.android.com/ndk/guides/neuralnetworks.
[4] https://www.opengl.org.
[5] https://www.khronos.org/vulkan.
[6] https://developer.apple.com/metal/.

Heterogeneous Computing Scheduling. While HA relies on dedicated physical components designed to speed-up specific operations, heterogeneous computing scheduling comprises the design of strategies to efficiently coordinate and distribute the workload among processors of different types [1]. Previous research works [14,19] have proposed DL scheduling techniques for embedded systems. Results show a good level of optimization, with accuracy loss up to 5%. However, for maximum efficiency, these methods require specific drivers (e.g., to support recent versions of OpenCL) or custom implementations for different architectures with direct access to hardware primitives.

Mobile DL Frameworks. Frameworks for the execution of DL models on mobile and embedded systems pursue optimized deployment on devices with limited resources, by managing memory allocation efficiently and exploiting the available hardware resources at best. We built PolimiDL, our own optimized framework for DL acceleration on mobile devices and embedded systems, when no efficient off-the-shelf solutions were available; recently, some new tools were released, such as TensorFlow Lite[7], Caffe2[8], and Core ML[9]. Training is performed off-board, with mainstream tools such as TensorFlow, Caffe or MXNet, and the resulting models is converted into the format of the mobile framework for deployment. Open Neural Network Exchange Format[10] (ONNX) proposes the standardization of models definition, to simplify the porting of models trained with different tools. Furthermore, CoreML already exploits Metal HA on iOS devices, while NNAPI support for Android frameworks and devices is still not totally stable nor fully integrated.

Benchmarking. Performance benchmarking measures indicators to compare run-time architectures. For mobile DL, relevant metrics include accuracy, execution time, memory overhead, and energy consumption. Shi et al. [24] assessed the performance of various open-source DL frameworks, by executing different models over a set of workstations with heterogeneous CPU and GPU hardware. The work [23], defines guidelines to asses DL models on Android and iOS devices, and [9] studies the latency-throughput trade-offs with CNNs for edge Computer Vision. Finally, Ignatov et al. [16] present a publicly available Android mobile app to benchmark performance on a set of DL Computer Vision tasks. Scores are calculated by averaging performance results over all the devices and the corresponding SoCs evaluated.

3   Requirements

Before introducing the architecture and use of PolimiDL, we pinpoint the requirements for its development. When dealing with specific hardware architectures

---

[7] http://www.tensorflow.org/mobile/tflite.
[8] http://caffe2.ai/docs/mobile-integration.html.
[9] http://developer.apple.com/documentation/coreml.
[10] https://onnx.ai.

and vendors, maximum performance can be reached by developing ad-hoc optimised solutions. Nonetheless, such approach may comprise scalability and maintenance, when targeting many heterogeneous architectures and devices, as in the case of the Android market nowadays. Moreover, as highlighted in Sect. 2, current acceleration approaches still have limitations: 1. HA primitives are still not completely standardized and stable, but are tightly dependent on SoC vendors; 2. cloud-offloading can imply cost, availability, latency and privacy issues; 3. retraining or modifying the architecture of ready-to-use models can be extremely time-consuming; 4. post-training compression of already small models can detriment accuracy. Under the above mentioned drivers, the requirements at the base of PolimiDL can be summarized as follows:

1. **Focus on execution.** It should be possible to train a model using tools already known to the developer. The framework should focus just on execution concerns, without the need of re-training.
2. **Minimum dependencies.** It should be possible to execute an optimized model independently of the Operating System, hardware platform or model storage format.
3. **Easy embedding.** It should be possible to embed the framework and optimized models into existing applications easily, without the need of ad-hoc integration procedures.
4. **End-to-end optimization.** Optimization should be applied as early as possible and span the model life-cycle (generation, compilation, initialization, configuration, execution).
5. **Offline support.** Computation should occur only on-board the embedded system, without the need of a network connection for work off-loading.
6. **No accuracy loss.** The acceleration for constrained devices should not reduce accuracy w.r.t. to the execution on a high performance infrastructure.

4   The PolimiDL Framework

PolimiDL aims at speeding-up the execution time of ready-to-use models by applying multiple optimizations that increase the efficiency of operations without modifying the model's output. Its implementation is highly generic, with neither hardware nor platform specific components; this enables performance gains on heterogeneous devices and simplifies maintenance, eliminating the need of targeting different platforms by means of different tools. It is written in C++ and can be compiled for all major platforms, requiring only a very simple interface layer to interact with the platform-specific code. PolimiDL exploits multi-threaded execution, based on the STL Concurrency Extensions[11], and SIMD instructions, based on the well-known Eigen Library[12]. Figure 1 illustrates the general workflow of the proposed framework, with its main stages (in red) and data/artifacts (in green), showing the stage in which each optimization takes place. The pipeline

---

[11] https://isocpp.org/wiki/faq/cpp11-library-concurrency.
[12] https://eigen.tuxfamily.org.

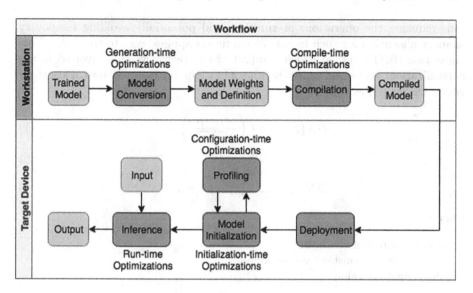

Fig. 1. PolimiDL's workflow. (Color figure online)

starts by training a model via some external DL framework, such as TensorFlow or Caffe2, on a workstation or cloud accelerated learning infrastructure, such as Google Cloud[13]. The trained model is converted into a PolimiDL compatible format, while applying generation-time optimizations. Next, the model is compiled for the target architectures and compile-time optimizations are applied, enabling SIMD instructions where supported. Once the model is deployed on the target device, an initialization stage applies initialization-time optimizations to determine the best memory layout. The first time a model is deployed, the initialization step can include the profiling of the model, which enables configuration-time optimizations to determine the best scheduling approach. Finally, the model is ready to process inputs by applying run-time optimizations, which involve dynamic workload scheduling to speed-up inference.

4.1 Generation-Time Optimizations

Layers Fusion. Consecutive in-place layers with identical filter size can be fused into one single layer, thus reducing the number of iterations over the cells of an input matrix. Such technique has been applied to fuse multiple combinations of layers, such as Batch Normalization/ReLu6 and Bias/ReLu. Potentially, Batch Normalization/ReLu6 fusion can be further extended by incorporating a Pointwise Convolution beforehand, taking into account that such combination of layers is frequently used for Depthwise Separable Convolutions.

Weights Fusion. Layers applying functions with constant terms comprising multiple weights can be pre-computed and encoded as unique constant weights,

---

[13] https://cloud.google.com/products/ai/.

thus reducing the operations at run-time and potentially avoiding temporary memory allocation for such layers. Weigh fusion applies, e.g., to the Batch Normalization (BN) layer, in which a subset of the vector weights involved in the normalization, scale and shift steps ($\gamma, \sigma^2, \epsilon$) can be factored into a constant vector weight (ω) as follows:

$$BN(x_i) = \gamma * \left(\frac{x_i - \mu}{\sqrt{\sigma^2 + \epsilon}} \right) + \beta \tag{1}$$

$$\omega = \frac{\gamma}{\sqrt{\sigma^2 + \epsilon}} \tag{2}$$

$$BN(x_i) = \omega * (x_i - \mu) + \beta \tag{3}$$

where:

- x_i is the input of the layer
- γ, μ, σ^2, β are constant vector weights
- ϵ is a constant value

Weights Rearrangement. Layers' weights, which are multidimensional matrices, are generally stored as linear arrays ordered by a default schema (e.g., output channel, row, column and input channel). PolimiDL stores the weights in different ways based on the layer type. Weights associated to predefined Convolutional layer types are stored in an order such that Eigen's GEMM matrix operations do not require any memory reshaping at run-time. These optimizations are executed automatically and transparently to the developer, who need not know their details.

4.2   Compile-Time Optimizations

Fixed Network Architecture. The architecture of a model is fixed at compile-time, which enables the compiler to perform per-layer optimizations. As an example, Convolutional layers can exploit loop-unrolling [13], because the number of channels and the kernel size are known at compile-time, potentially generating different machine code for each configuration of layer parameters. This approach can be seen as a limiting factor, because the model architecture cannot be updated at run-time or by simply changing a configuration file. However, it is important to notice that changing the model architecture is not expected to occur after the model has been deployed. Besides, in PolimiDL a model can be compiled as a set of Shared Objects (.so) files for the corresponding target architectures (armeabi-v7a, x86 and arm64-v8a for Android), enabling model updates by a simple file replacement. Given a fixed model architecture, PolimiDL supports the update of layer weights at run-time. When the run-time update of weights is not required, then the weights can be stored together with the network architecture, by embedding them in the .so files; this avoids the overhead of loading them from secondary memory, as opposed to TensorFlow Lite, where architecture and weights are stored as an external file loaded from disk.

Shared Memory Allocation & "tick-tock" Piping. Efficient memory allocation and management is critical in embedded systems, where the amount of memory is limited and access time is slower than in workstations. Exploiting spatial locality [2] to reduce cache misses can decrease inference time and energy consumption significantly. For this purpose, layers in PolimiDL do not own the memory they read inputs from, write outputs to, or use to store intermediate results: memory is injected as a dependency from the layer scheduler. Given this organization, the memory required by a model can be reduced to just 3 areas: 1. Layer Input 2. Layer Output 3. Temporary data. These areas are properly sized at run-time, to contain the largest layer in the model. A disadvantage of this approach is the need to copy the output of a layer back into the input area to feed it to the next layer. PolimiDL alleviates this inconvenience by inverting the input and output buffers of subsequent layers. With this schema, data goes back and forth between the two buffers in a "tick-tock" fashion. Tick-tock buffer swapping is skipped for "in-place" layers, i.e., layers that can use the same buffer area for both input and output: they do not trigger an input/output buffer flip. ReLu layer is a clear example, because it performs value-wide operations enabling in-place modifications. Furthermore, given the fixed model architecture, layer piping can be computed at compile-time via the template meta-programming capabilities of C++, without incurring in any run-time costs.

4.3 Initialization-Time Optimizations

Memory Pre-allocation. Pre-allocating memory buffers to contain the layers of a complete model without memory reuse may be feasible for server computation, but is certainly not the best option for embedded systems with hardware constraints. We have shown how the proposed framework reduces this memory requirements via shared buffers and the "tick-tock" piping. PolimiDL further reduces memory requirements by fusing the 3 buffers (input, output and temporary) into a single one. During initialization, each layer is queried about its memory requirements: input size, output size and temporary data, which can differ based on hardware capabilities, e.g., number of threads, or input size, in the case of Fully Convolutional Networks. A single buffer is allocated and sized to contain data of the most demanding layer. The upper and lower end of the buffer are used as input/output areas respectively, following the "tick-tock" strategy, while the area in between is used for the temporary data. This approach further reduces memory requirements as a single memory cell can store input, output or temporary data in different layers.

Small Tasks for Low Memory Consumption. While some layers require little or no temporary memory to work efficiently, others have a space-time trade-off. As an example, Convolutional layers can exploit SIMD instructions if their 3D input is unrolled into 2D matrices, where each row is the linearized input to the kernel. While unrolling the entire input and exploiting Eigen's SIMD and cache optimization capabilities may reduce the computation time significantly, it also increases the memory requirements of the layer by increasing the size of the temporary buffer. In these cases, PolimiDL does not perform a full input unroll, but divides the operation into smaller tasks, which can be executed independently. In this way, the temporary memory required by the tasks has a fixed size.

4.4   Configuration Time Optimizations

Scheduling Optimization. PolimiDL features a task scheduler, explained in detail in Sect. 4.5, which enables layers to divide the workload into tasks executed by different threads. The optimal size for a scheduled task may vary depending on the specific layer, the underlying architecture, or even on the input size for Fully Convolutional Neural Networks. Task sizes can be considered as parameters, which can be: 1. set to a default value, which may not be optimal 2. inferred by executing a profiling routine during initialization, which may increase the initialization time 3. inferred once for all on the specific device, stored and loaded at subsequent initialization steps. The profiling for each layer is performed by assessing the execution time of different task sizes. A full exploration of the task size space is not possible, given the high time and computation requirements. The sizes used during the assessment are generated by a power law heuristics. Task sizes may be bounded to a maximum value, dictated by the available temporary memory. It is important to notice that the available temporary memory may be more than the one requested at initialization time. This is because the buffer is initialized to contain the largest layer and, as a consequence, layers with smaller footprint can exploit the extra temporary memory.

4.5   Run-Time Optimizations

Dynamic Workload Scheduling. Static and even distribution of workload among available cores does not represent the most suitable solution, due to the unpredictable nature of mobile resources availability, more evident in asymmetric architectures such as ARM big.LITTLE [3]. A static scheduling strategy can under-utilize resources, wasting processing power. Conversely, dynamic multi-threaded scheduling of tasks can adapt well to different contexts and allows cores to be better exploited. Tasks are forwarded to a fixed size thread-pool (by default the number of workers is set to $max(1, \#cores - 1)$). In PolimiDL, during the development of a layer, it is possible to opt-out from dynamic scheduling or to enable it just when profiling shows a significant improvement. Dynamic scheduling should not be applied blindly, as computational intensive layers, such as Convolutions, perform better when dynamically scheduled, while others, such as ReLu, may perform worse due to memory bottlenecks. Therefore, dynamic scheduling is disallowed by default for layers that would be harmed by it.

4.6   Layers Coverage

Table 1 summarizes the layers supported by PolimiDL and their features[14].

---

[14] Given the open source release of PolimiDL, the supported layers may be subject to modifications and further extensions.

Table 1. Layers supported by PolimiDL.

Layer name	In place	Temporary memory	Schedulable
Convolution	No	Yes	Yes
Depthwise convolution	No	Yes	Yes
Pointwise convolution (out channels ≤ in channels)	Yes	Yes	Yes
Pointwise convolution (out channels > in channels)	No	No	Yes
Max pooling	No	Yes	No
Average pooling	No	Yes	Yes
Batch normalization	Yes	No	Yes
Bias	Yes	No	No
ReLu	Yes	No	No
ReLu6	Yes	No	No
Softmax	Yes	No	No

Fully Connected layers can be supported by introducing a standard Convolution in which the corresponding kernel size is equal to the expected layer input size. Given an expected input size of 1x1xN, such operation can be managed efficiently by using a 1x1xNxM Pointwise Convolution, where N represents the input channels and M the output classes.

4.7 Limits to Generalization

The applicability of PolimiDL to a specific model is subject to the support of the required layers and to the availability of a converter from the source DL framework format. PolimiDL currently supports conversion from the Tensor-Flow format. Furthermore, features such as batch inference, model quantization and the inclusion of additional layers may require adaptations of the architecture design; for example, residual skip connections would require more complex buffers piping. Shared object libraries with self-contained weights declared as variables can be used for small models, common in embedded systems; but they may suffer from compilation constraints when big models, such as VGG-16 [25], are involved. Finally, PolimiDL currently runs on CPU only and does not support GPU processing, due to the still limited and non-standard access to it, which would require multiple implementations.

5   Evaluation

5.1   Experimental Setup

The evaluation benchmarks inference execution time of DL models on heterogeneous embedded systems, comparing PolimiDL with the state-of-the-art solution for edge inference: TensorFlow Lite[15]. Measurements are collected by means of an Android benchmark application, implemented by extending TensorFlow Lite's sample application[16] to support multiple experiments. The use of multiple devices and models is critical for performance evaluation, given the non-linear correlation between hardware features and tasks characteristics [16].

The evaluation process is conducted as follows:

- Initialization and pre-processing times are not considered in the overall processing time.
- One warm up inference run is executed before the actual measurements.
- 50 consecutive inference iterations are executed and averaged to reduce variance.
- Three complete evaluation sessions with all models and devices are averaged, to further reduce variance.
- Models are run on mobile devices having above 80% of battery charge and pausing for 5 mins between executions.

Models. Evaluation exploits hardware with limited resources and models with a small-size architecture achieving a good trade-off between accuracy and latency. Three models with diverse characteristics, listed in Table 2, are evaluated.

Table 2. Models used for evaluation.

Model	Task	Mult-adds	Parameters	Input size
PeakLens original	Semantic segmentation	2G	429K	$320 \times 240 \times 3$
PeakLens optimized	Semantic segmentation	198M	21K	$320 \times 240 \times 3$
MobileNet	Object classification	569M	4.24M	$224 \times 224 \times 3$

PeakLens original [7] is a Fully Convolutional Neural Network model [21] for the extraction of mountain skylines, which exhibits a good balance between accuracy, memory consumption, and latency; it is exploited in the implementation of PeakLens, a real-world AR application for mountain peak recognition on mobile phones. The model was trained with image patches for binary classification, by adapting the LeNet architecture as shown in Table 3, and can be applied to pixel-wise classification of full images.

PeakLens optimized is a modified version of the PeakLens model replacing standard Convolutions with Depthwise Separable Convolutions, inspired by MobileNet [12]. The optimized version improves accuracy and performance and reduces the number of parameters by one order of magnitude. The architecture is shown in Table 4: each Depthwise Separable Convolution block consists of a sequence of Depthwise Convolution, Relu, Pointwise Convolution, and Relu.

---

[15] The latest stable version at the time of writing is tensorflow-lite:1.13.1.
[16] https://github.com/tensorflow/tensorflow/tree/master/tensorflow/lite/examples/android/app.

Table 3. PeakLens original model.

Layer type	Input shape	Filter shape	Stride
Conv	$29 \times 29 \times 3$	$6 \times 6 \times 3 \times 20$	1
Pool (max)	$24 \times 24 \times 20$	2×2	2
Conv	$12 \times 12 \times 20$	$5 \times 5 \times 20 \times 50$	1
Pool (max)	$8 \times 8 \times 50$	2×2	2
Conv	$4 \times 4 \times 50$	$4 \times 4 \times 50 \times 500$	1
ReLU	$1 \times 1 \times 500$	-	1
Conv	$1 \times 1 \times 500$	$1 \times 1 \times 500 \times 2$	1

Table 4. PeakLens optimized model.

Layer type	Input shape	Filter shape	Stride
Conv	$29 \times 29 \times 3$	$3 \times 3 \times 3 \times 32$	1
ReLU	$27 \times 27 \times 32$	-	1
Depthwise separable conv	$27 \times 27 \times 32$	$3 \times 3 \times 32 \times 32$	2
Depthwise separable conv	$13 \times 13 \times 32$	$3 \times 3 \times 32 \times 64$	1
Depthwise separable conv	$11 \times 11 \times 64$	$3 \times 3 \times 64 \times 64$	2
Depthwise separable conv	$5 \times 5 \times 64$	$3 \times 3 \times 64 \times 128$	1
Conv	$3 \times 3 \times 128$	$3 \times 3 \times 128 \times 2$	1

MobileNet [12] is a well-known state-of-the-art CNN architecture for efficient inference on mobile devices, developed by Google for diverse tasks, such as image classification and object detection. Multiple versions of MobileNet trained on ImageNet are publicly available[17], among which the biggest version has been chosen for evaluation (MobileNet_v1_1.0_224).

Devices. Six distinct Android devices with heterogeneous architectures are used, Table 5 lists the devices and their characteristics.

Configurations. Multiple configurations are tested to analyze the impact of the scheduler thread pool size. #*threads* is the number of usable threads, which depends on the device (see Table 5). The evaluated configurations comprise:

- **min(4,#threads):** the thread-pool has a maximum of 4 workers, which is TensorFlow Lite's default configuration.
- **max(1,#threads-1):** the thread-pool employs all available threads but one.
- **#threads:** the thread-pool comprises all threads, for maximum parallelism.

---

[17] https://github.com/tensorflow/models/blob/master/research/slim/nets/mobilenet_v1.md.

Table 5. Devices used for evaluation.

Device	Android Version	Chipset	CPU	RAM (GB)
Asus ZenFone 2 ZE500CL (Z00D)	5.0	Z2560 Intel Atom	2-cores 1.6 GHz (4 threads)	2
Google Pixel	9.0	MSM8996 Qualcomm Snapdragon 821	2-cores 2.15 Ghz Kryo + 2-cores 1.6 Ghz Kryo (4 threads)	4
LG G5 SE	7.0	MSM8976 Qualcomm Snapdragon 652	4-cores 1.8 GHz Cortex-A72 + 4-cores 1.2 GHz Cortex-A53 (8 threads)	3
LG Nexus 5X	8.1	MSM8992 Qualcomm Snapdragon 808	4-cores 1.44 GHz Cortex-A53 + 2-cores 1.82 GHz Cortex-A57 (6 threads)	2
Motorola Nexus 6	7.0	Qualcomm Snapdragon 805	4-cores 2.7 GHz Krait (4 threads)	3
One Plus 6T	9.0	SDM845 Qualcomm Snapdragon 845	4x 2.8 GHz Kryo 385 + 4x 1.8 GHz Kryo 385 (8 threads)	6

5.2   Experimental Results

We report the experimental results obtained with TensorFlow Lite and PolimiDL for each combination of model, device, and configuration.

Table 6 reports the results for *PeakLens original* model. PolimiDL outperforms TensorFlow Lite in almost all cases (highlighted in green), with reductions of up to 57.32% (Motorola Nexus 6); TensorFlow Lite performs better (highlighted in red) just in one device (LG Nexus 5X) with a single configuration. Overall, PolimiDL consistently reduces average execution time by above 30%.

Table 7 reports the results for *PeakLens optimized*. This model is smaller, yet more accurate than the original one. PolimiDL outperforms TensorFlow Lite and reduces inference time significantly. This is due to the design of memory management, which exploits well spatial locality and reduces cache misses. The performance gain is highly consistent: execution times are reduced on average of more than 62% in all the configurations. Improvement is particularly sensible for low-end devices, such as ZenFone 2, where the reduction is greater than 77%.

Finally, Table 8 reports the results for *MobileNet*. Performance of the two frameworks are quite comparable, but PolimiDL reduces overall execution time. The most significant gains are achieved on the ZenFone 2 and Nexus 6 devices. TensorFlow Lite performs slightly better (not over 5%) on certain settings involving devices with big. LITTLE architecture (LG G5 SE and LG Nexus 5X).

Table 6. Experimental results of PeakLens original model.

Device	TensorFlow Lite (ms)			PolimiDL (ms)		
	Min (4,Threads)	Max (1,Threads-1)	All Threads	Min (4,Threads)	Max (1,Threads-1)	All Threads
Asus ZenFone 2	1352.67	1672.67	1353.00	936.00 (-30.80%)	1138.00 (-31.96%)	936.67 (-30.77%)
Google Pixel	207.67	255.33	210.33	145.00 (-30.18%)	171.00 (-33.03%)	145.00 (-31.06%)
LG G5 SE	418.67	290.00	272.67	273.00 (-34.79%)	209.00 (-27.93%)	200.33 (-26.53%)
LG Nexus 5X	423.67	370.33	336.33	432.33 (+2.05%)	342.33 (-7.56%)	282.33 (-16.06%)
Motorola Nexus 6	336.67	505.33	337.67	169.00 (-49.80%)	215.67 (-57.32%)	168.33 (-50.15%)
One Plus 6T	176.00	144.33	145.33	104.00 (-40.91%)	91.00 (-36.95%)	89.00 (-38.76%)
			Average	(-30.74%)	(-32.46%)	(-32.22%)

Table 7. Experimental results of PeakLens optimized model.

Device	TensorFlow Lite (ms)			PolimiDL (ms)		
	Min (4,Threads)	Max (1,Threads-1)	All Threads	Min (4,Threads)	Max (1,Threads-1)	All Threads
Asus ZenFone 2	740.67	807.67	743.33	166.00 (-77.59%)	179.33 (-77.80%)	167.67 (-77.44%)
Google Pixel	82.00	95.00	82.67	30.00 (-63.41%)	35.33 (-62.81%)	31.00 (-62.50%)
LG G5 SE	185.67	138.33	138.00	94.33 (-49.19%)	68.00 (-50.84%)	70.67 (-48.79%)
LG Nexus 5X	204.33	193.00	181.00	84.67 (-58.56%)	80.33 (-58.38%)	77.00 (-57.46%)
Motorola Nexus 6	140.33	225.67	135.67	52.33 (-62.71%)	66.00 (-70.75%)	49.00 (-63.88%)
One Plus 6T	66.67	68.67	66.33	22.00 (-67.00%)	22.67 (-66.99%)	22.33 (-66.33%)
			Average	(-63.08%)	(-64.59%)	(-62.73%)

Despite the fact that PolimiDL features dynamic scheduling, it is the Operating System the ultimate responsible of the allocation of tasks to workers and low frequency cores seem to be prioritized for this model and devices. Nonetheless, the average execution time, when using all threads but one, is reduced by ≈16%.

The activation of NNAPI has been assessed in TensorFlow Lite for the supported devices, but results are not reported due to unstable performance. NNAPI reduces execution time on the Google Pixel, but doubles it on the LG Nexus 5X.

In conclusion, experimental results demonstrate the potential of PolimiDL by showing competitive results with respect to the well-known TensorFlow Lite

Table 8. Experimental results of MobileNet model.

Device	TensorFlow Lite (ms)			PolimiDL (ms)		
	Min (4,Threads)	Max (1,Threads-1)	All Threads	Min (4,Threads)	Max (1,Threads-1)	All Threads
Asus ZenFone 2	734.00	775.33	733.33	371.00 (-49.46%)	377.33 (-51.33%)	374.33 (-48.95%)
Google Pixel	75.67	82.33	77.00	74.00 (-2.20%)	82.67 (+0.40%)	73.67 (-4.33%)
LG G5 SE	263.67	274.67	275.67	276.67 (+4.93%)	259.00 (-5.70%)	256.33 (-7.01%)
LG Nexus 5X	217.33	225.00	223.33	222.33 (+2.30%)	234.33 (+4.15%)	226.00 (+1.19%)
Motorola Nexus 6	224.33	298.33	227.67	203.67 (-9.21%)	176.00 (-41.01%)	163.33 (-28.26%)
One Plus 6T	56.67	56.67	57.67	49.67 (-12.35%)	51.67 (-8.82%)	53.00 (-8.09%)
			Average	(-11.00%)	(-17.05%)	(-15.91%)

platform. Results are particularly improved when dealing with small models and low-power devices; this finding corroborates the potential of the proposed framework for supporting the implementation of augmented reality applications for mass market mobile phones, which is the use exemplified by PeakLens app.

6   Conclusion and Future Work

In this paper we presented PolimiDL, an open source framework for accelerating DL inference on mobile and embedded systems, which has proved competitive with respect to TensorFlow Lite on small models. Implementation is generic and aims at supporting devices with limited power and heterogeneous architectures. Future work will concentrate on adding support for more layers, quantization, and conversion from more DL frameworks. Moreover, experimentation will be extended by evaluating additional models, configurations, metrics (e.g. energy consumption and memory accesses) and devices (e.g. Raspberries and drones).

Acknowledgements. This research has been partially supported by the PENNY project of the European Commission Horizon 2020 program (grant n. 723791).

References

1. AlEbrahim, S., Ahmad, I.: Task scheduling for heterogeneous computing systems. J. Supercomput. **73**(6), 2313–2338 (2017)
2. Anderson, A., Vasudevan, A., Keane, C., Gregg, D.: Low-memory gemm-based convolution algorithms for deep neural networks. arXiv preprint arXiv:1709.03395 (2017)

3. Cho, H.D., Engineer, P.D.P., Chung, K., Kim, T.: Benefits of the big. Little Architecture. EETimes, San Francisco (2012)
4. Chollet, F.: Xception: deep learning with depthwise separable convolutions. In: Proceedings of the IEEE Conference on Computer Vision and Pattern Recognition, pp. 1251–1258 (2017)
5. Dinh, H.T., Lee, C., Niyato, D., Wang, P.: A survey of mobile cloud computing: architecture, applications, and approaches. Wirel. Commun. Mob. Comput. **13**(18), 1587–1611 (2013)
6. Fedorov, R., Frajberg, D., Fraternali, P.: A framework for outdoor mobile augmented reality and its application to mountain peak detection. In: De Paolis, L.T., Mongelli, A. (eds.) AVR 2016. LNCS, vol. 9768, pp. 281–301. Springer, Cham (2016). https://doi.org/10.1007/978-3-319-40621-3_21
7. Frajberg, D., Fraternali, P., Torres, R.N.: Convolutional neural network for pixel-wise skyline detection. In: Lintas, A., Rovetta, S., Verschure, P.F.M.J., Villa, A.E.P. (eds.) ICANN 2017. LNCS, vol. 10614, pp. 12–20. Springer, Cham (2017). https://doi.org/10.1007/978-3-319-68612-7_2
8. Han, S., Pool, J., Tran, J., Dally, W.: Learning both weights and connections for efficient neural network. In: Advances in Neural Information Processing Systems, pp. 1135–1143 (2015)
9. Hanhirova, J., Kämäräinen, T., Seppälä, S., Siekkinen, M., Hirvisalo, V., Ylä-Jääski, A.: Latency and throughput characterization of convolutional neural networks for mobile computer vision. In: Proceedings of the 9th ACM Multimedia Systems Conference, pp. 204–215. ACM (2018)
10. He, K., Zhang, X., Ren, S., Sun, J.: Deep residual learning for image recognition. In: IEEE Conference on Computer Vision and Pattern Recognition, pp. 770–778 (2016)
11. Hinton, G., Vinyals, O., Dean, J.: Distilling the knowledge in a neural network. arXiv preprint arXiv:1503.02531 (2015)
12. Howard, A.G., et al.: Mobilenets: efficient convolutional neural networks for mobile vision applications. arXiv preprint arXiv:1704.04861 (2017)
13. Huang, J.C., Leng, T.: Generalized loop-unrolling: a method for program speedup. In: Symposium on Application-Specific Systems and Software Engineering and Technology, ASSET 1999 (Cat. No. PR00122), pp. 244–248. IEEE (1999)
14. Huynh, L.N., Lee, Y., Balan, R.K.: Deepmon: mobile gpu-based deep learning framework for continuous vision applications. In: 15th Annual International Conference on Mobile Systems, Applications, and Services, pp. 82–95. ACM (2017)
15. Iandola, F.N., Han, S., Moskewicz, M.W., Ashraf, K., Dally, W.J., Keutzer, K.: Squeezenet: alexnet-level accuracy with 50x fewer parameters and< 0.5 mb model size. arXiv preprint arXiv:1602.07360 (2016)
16. Ignatov, A., et al.: Ai benchmark: running deep neural networks on android smartphones. In: European Conference on Computer Vision, pp. 288–314. Springer (2018)
17. Kim, Y.D., Park, E., Yoo, S., Choi, T., Yang, L., Shin, D.: Compression of deep convolutional neural networks for fast and low power mobile applications. arXiv preprint arXiv:1511.06530 (2015)
18. Krizhevsky, A., Sutskever, I., Hinton, G.E.: Imagenet classification with deep convolutional neural networks. In: Advances in Neural Information Processing Systems, pp. 1097–1105 (2012)
19. Lane, N.D., et al.: Deepx: a software accelerator for low-power deep learning inference on mobile devices. In: Proceedings of the 15th International Conference on Information Processing in Sensor Networks, p. 23. IEEE Press (2016)

20. Lane, N.D., Georgiev, P.: Can deep learning revolutionize mobile sensing? In: Proceedings of the 16th International Workshop on Mobile Computing Systems and Applications, pp. 117–122. ACM (2015)
21. Long, J., Shelhamer, E., Darrell, T.: Fully convolutional networks for semantic segmentation. In: Proceedings of the IEEE Conference on Computer Vision and Pattern Recognition, pp. 3431–3440 (2015)
22. Sandler, M., Howard, A., Zhu, M., Zhmoginov, A., Chen, L.C.: Mobilenetv2: inverted residuals and linear bottlenecks. In: Proceedings of the IEEE Conference on Computer Vision and Pattern Recognition, pp. 4510–4520 (2018)
23. Sehgal, A., Kehtarnavaz, N.: Guidelines and benchmarks for deployment of deep learning models on smartphones as real-time apps. arXiv preprint arXiv:1901.02144 (2019)
24. Shi, S., Wang, Q., Xu, P., Chu, X.: Benchmarking state-of-the-art deep learning software tools. In: 7th International Conference on Cloud Computing and Big Data (CCBD), pp. 99–104. IEEE (2016)
25. Simonyan, K., Zisserman, A.: Very deep convolutional networks for large-scale image recognition. arXiv preprint arXiv:1409.1556 (2014)
26. Tan, M., Chen, B., Pang, R., Vasudevan, V., Le, Q.V.: Mnasnet: platform-aware neural architecture search for mobile. arXiv preprint arXiv:1807.11626 (2018)
27. Wu, J., Leng, C., Wang, Y., Hu, Q., Cheng, J.: Quantized convolutional neural networks for mobile devices. In: Proceedings of the IEEE Conference on Computer Vision and Pattern Recognition, pp. 4820–4828 (2016)

Design of Mobile Service of Intelligent Large-Scale Cyber Argumentation for Analysis and Prediction of Collective Opinions

Najla Althuniyan[✉], Joseph W. Sirrianni, Md Mahfuzer Rahman, and Xiaoqing "Frank" Liu

University of Arkansas, Fayetteville, AR 72701, USA
{nalthuni,jwsirria,mmr014,frankliu}@uark.edu

Abstract. Issues of national and international importance attract the attention of millions of people who want to share their opinions online. These discussions among a large number of people contain rich information, from which we want to extract the crowd wisdom and collective intelligence. Most of these discussions happen in social media platforms such as Facebook and Twitter or debate-centric platforms. Social media platforms are accessible but not structured in a way to effectively facilitate these large-scale discussions, leading many discussions to be fragmented, difficult to follow, and nearly impossible to analyze collective opinions. Debate-centric platforms represent issues with binary solutions and modest analytics. In the cyber-argumentation, a sub-field of AI, argumentations platforms have been developed to facilitate online discussion effectively. These platforms provide structured argumentation frameworks, which allows for meaningful analytics models to mine the argumentation. However, few platforms have mobile service application and those that do provide only basic statistical analytics. In this paper, we present the design of a mobile application service to support intelligent cyber argumentation. This service is designed to facilitate large-scale discussion and report complex analytics on a handheld screen size. The platform has several integrated analytical models, which use AI techniques, to capture collective opinions, detect opinion polarization, and predict missing user opinions. An example of a large-scale discussion is used to demonstrate the effectiveness of bringing intelligent cyber-argumentation into the mobile space.

Keywords: Mobile app design · Mobile service · Opinion prediction · Ongoing discussion · Cyber argumentation · Collective intelligence · Opinion polarization · Fuzzy logic · Argumentation analysis

1 Introduction

People are eager to discuss local and global issues and share their opinions and views with others. Online discussion allows for massive participation from users with different personal backgrounds and perspectives. Large-scale cyber-argumentation services facilitate massive online discussion where users can post issues and viewpoints and then others respond to them. In addition, integrated AI models can analyze the

© Springer Nature Switzerland AG 2019
D. Wang and L.-J. Zhang (Eds.): AIMS 2019, LNCS 11516, pp. 135–149, 2019.
https://doi.org/10.1007/978-3-030-23367-9_10

argumentation data and capture the crowd wisdom from these discussions. These analytics help users understand extensive discussions without the need to go through the whole discussion. People mostly use social media and networking services for large-scale issue-based discussion because of its popularity and accessibility. However, social media and networking services, such as Facebook, Twitter and LinkedIn, are not explicitly designed to handle large-scale cyber-argumentation. They are not structured for substantial discussions because they are user and connection-centric, not issue-centric. Discussions on issues are fragmented, they take place in many users' local pages and/or are separated into numerous different threads, which are hard to follow and it is easy to lose track of the conversation.

Instead of using social media services for argumentation, some people use online debate services for argumentation. These debate services, such as Kialo [11], Contra [12] and Debate.com [13], are designed to handle argumentation in a user-friendly interface. However, these services have limited capabilities. Typically, they present only two-sides of the issues forcing users to either completely agree or disagree with a side. Moreover, some of these services require users to reply or comment in order to express their opinions on an issue. In certain cases, users would like to express their agreement or disagreement without the need to post a new comment or reply. For example, if a user sees that someone else has made the argument they were going to make, he/she should be able to express his/her agreement without having to make a redundant post of the same reasoning. In addition, they lack analytics to understand the discussion. While these debates services facilitate argumentation and deliberation better than social media services, they tend to lack support for mobile applications. Of the three services listed above, only Contra has a mobile application, and its mobile app presented even fewer content and analytics than its web-version. Thus, these services lack the analytical power of cyber argumentation systems and only rarely have robust mobile applications. In the aforementioned services, users cannot explicitly state the degree of agreement/disagreement on a solution for an issue or other arguments. Therefore, users feel restricted and limited in those kinds of discussions. Moreover, many of these services do not provide analytics for facilitating argumentation effectively.

There are other available services such as Quora [15] and Reddit [14] open for public questioning and discussion. Quora is a question and answering service and Reddit is a social news aggregation and discussion service. Both have downvote/upvote features for answers, but these features are intended as a judgment of quality, not a judgment of agreement or disagreement. They have a similar structure to the issue tree, but they cannot effectively facilitate many types of discussions like debates. For example, neither services have a way for users to express explicit agreement or disagreement, outside of writing it in their text. This means that the only way to tell if an idea is being supported or not is to read the text replies from every user which is very cumbersome on the reader. In addition, they provide fundamental analytics to users. They are not designed to handle online argumentation.

Researchers have developed few online debate platforms for argumentation where users can have many more choices of solutions on a single issue. These tools [1, 2, 7] can handle the argumentation better than the above-listed services, but they are not widely available and supported after their research is finished. In addition, the number of participants in these tools is small. Moreover, there are no statistics or measures regarding collective opinions about the posted issues or arguments on these platforms. Most of these platforms do not provide mobile services; and if it has, they have limited functionality.

Developing mobile services for online argumentation is a challenging task due to the limited mobile screen space and the potentially massive issue tree size. Thus, to resolve this problem, we designed a mobile service with a native application for online argumentation. This service represents the issue tree in the mobile space in a user-friendly way. The issue tree is broken down substantially-complicated question into smaller solvable ones. The root of the tree is the issue that is a question or an unsettled problem or situation under consideration to be solved. The internal nodes and leaves of the tree are suggested views or solution to the root. In this mobile application service, users can easily navigate, participate, and follow issue-based discussion and understand what is going on in discussions. It allows users to post issues, viewpoints, or arguments pertaining to different topics. Issues are user generated and can be about any topic. Under the issues, users can post different viewpoints or positions on the issue. These positions serve as solutions or stances on a given topic, depending on the nature of the issue. Unlike other argumentation services, which provided users a choice between distinct mutually exclusive positions, our service allows users to define positions that overlap or are alternatives to other positions. Everyone can react to each position or other arguments with different levels of agreement or disagreement. Moreover, users have the choice to add more arguments or counterarguments for deliberation. The resulting discussions between users highlight various aspects of the positions. The application adapted several AI models to provide meaningful statistics for users such as the collective opinions prediction and each position's polarization index. Therefore, users stay aware and well informed about the collective interactions with the system.

This paper is structured as follow: Sect. 2 is about the related work done in research for cyber argumentation. Section 3 is discussing the service components and application framework. It contains the architecture of the app and the Interface discussion. Section 4 discusses the analytics model used in this application: the collective intelligence model, the polarization index model and the collective opinions prediction model. Section 5 presents a detailed example from the data set and analyzes it. Section 6 is the conclusion and future work.

2 Related Work

There has been some academic research done on both web-based and mobile-based argumentation platforms. ArguBlogging [2] and CCSAV in [7] are examples of web-based argumentation platforms while ArgueApply [1] is an example of a mobile-based argumentation platform.

In mobile-based argumentation services, ArgueApply [1] is a mobile-based argumentation app that uses the Grappa [10] framework to evaluate different viewpoints on a specific debate. In this app, users can post statements to an ongoing discussion with five levels of agreement or disagreement. Then, the application reports all posted viewpoints and the extent to which users have accepted and rejected each viewpoint.

The result is displayed as who is right in the discussion. In debates and deliberations, rightness and wrongness are typically not evaluated based on user-feedback, but based on truth and logical reasoning. Moreover, if a user is unhappy with the results of a discussion, he could add unquestionable links that influence the outcome significantly. The discussion in cyber-argumentation systems should capture the crowd thinking and not be biased based individual tendency. This application presents modest analytics for users such as who is viewing or joining the discussion.

In web-based argumentation services, there are different design choices and presentations adapted to handle cyber argumentation. ArguBlogging [2] is designed to let users share opinions across blogs. It allows users to post arguments with two responses: agree or disagree. However, it gives users the option to provide more details (links) to support or attack the argument as evidence. It only supports two kinds of blogging sites: Tumblr and Blogger. Still, it is limited to binary sides as responses to posted arguments. No analytics or statistics are provided to the user. Another example of web-based argumentation is [7]. It uses a CCSAV, collaborative computer-supported argument visualization, platform with moderation. CCSAV platforms are a representation-centric process to consolidate the collective efforts for the creation of a shared argument map based on IBIS, Issue-Based Information System, [9] argumentation web framework. The argument map is presented to the users as a tree or network filled with arguments and counter-arguments, such as issues, claims, premises, and evidence, with different kinds of relationships, such as support, attack, warrant, etc. This kind of platforms requires skilled users because it expects users to form the argument map accurately; which for novice users can be challenging to follow [7]. It has a better visual representation for the discussion. However, it requires moderation. If a user does not map the argument accurately, the created argument gets pending until a moderator validates the issue. They estimated 1:20 as a moderator to active participants ratio [4]. In a real-time large-scale online service, it is not feasible to hire the same moderators-users ratio to process all pending posts manually.

The argumentation map in [4] had more than 200 users and more than 5000 postings (ideas, arguments and comments) in three weeks. It claimed to be large-scale deliberation. In our empirical study, there are more than 300 users and 10000 arguments in five weeks. Please refer to the Discussion section for more information on our empirical data. There is potential for it to be used by a larger user population.

According to Statista [5], there was about 13% increase in the number of mobile app downloads in 2018 than in 2017. Therefore, mobile phones are taking more focus and use from people. The mobile market growth is expecting mobile users who are using smartphones to be more than 50% of the total users by 2018. Therefore, developing a mobile-based argumentation application is a significant achievement to bring a large-scale cyber-argumentation to everyone worldwide. In this research paper, we contribute a mobile application design to support large-scale cyber-argumentation with simple design and intelligent metrics/analysis capabilities. This design allows users to view issue trees and create new issues, positions, and arguments. Moreover, it allows users to react and reply to each other based on their opinions. Finally, the application produces the collective and personal statistics and additional useful information to users as they use the system such as predicting collective opinions index and polarization index on the position level.

3 Framework

3.1 The Mobile Service Architecture

This mobile service is built on the intelligent cyber-argumentation system (ICAS) platform [3]. ICAS is a web-based argumentation platform based on informal Issue-Based Information System model [9]. The structure of the system can be viewed as multiple weighted directed trees. Each issue can be considered as a tree root. Each position addressing that issue is a child to the root, as in Fig. 1. Users can support or attack each position with an argument(s). In addition, users can support and attack each other's arguments. These arguments become children to a position or other arguments. Each argument has text and an agreement value. Each component is detailed later this section.

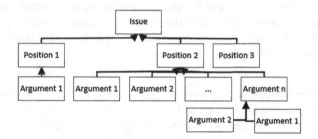

Fig. 1. Issue, positions, and arguments representation

An overview of the environment used to develop this application is given in Fig. 2. The framework of this mobile application consists of two major components, the front-end and the back-end.

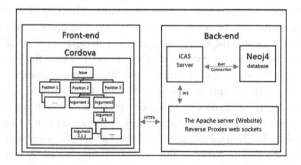

Fig. 2. App architecture and components

3.2   The Front-End

The front-end is an Android application developed by the Cordova framework and written using JQuery and HTML 5. This application requires a minimum SDK level of 28 (Android 9) as a front-end. The front-end connects to the back end using HTTPS.

3.3   User Interface

This application is taking simplicity and ease of use into consideration. The main components of the app are issues, position, arguments, reactions and analytics buttons. Below are the details of each component.

Issues

Issues are the unsolved problem or open questions for discussion. When a user is logged in to the application, the main page is loaded, as in Fig. 3(a). The main page displays a list of issues. Every user has the choice either to add a new issue or view the existing issues. A user can select any issue to view all related information. When a user selects an issue, all related positions are displayed, as in Fig. 3(b). Users can navigate to the issues list by tabbing in the home bar.

Positions

Positions are the stances or solutions for issues. Like issues, a user can select any existing position to engage to it or add a new position, as in Fig. 3(b). When a user selects a position, all related arguments are displayed. In addition, the number of replies, number of reactions and the overall agreement value of the position are shown, see Fig. 3(c). These numbers summarize the discussion size and the degree to which participants have agreed/disagreed with the position. From the position tab users can reply or react to any positions. Users can navigate or go back to the selected issue by tabbing on the issue text at the top of the screen.

Arguments and Reactions

Arguments are statements of users opinions against positions or other arguments. Arguments are made of text and agreement values. The text describes the user's argument in words and can be up to 2500 characters. The agreement value is a user-defined value that indicates the user's agreement or disagreement on the parent node. The agreement value is a real number between -1 and 1, where the sign indicates that the user is in agreement or disagreement with the parent argument and the value represents the intensity of agreement/disagreement. For example, a user may post (-0.4) as an agreement value. Since the sign is negative, it is a disagreement. The 0.4 indicates that the user is moderately disagreeing. If the agreement value is 0, it means the user is natural (indifferent) about the argument. Levels of agreements/disagreements are selected using the sliding bar as in Fig. 4. This sliding bar is divided into 11 levels, which indicate different levels of agreement. These levels are in one interval $[-1, 1]$ and are separated with 0.2 interval length. The sections are Completely Disagree (-1.0), Strongly Disagree (-0.8), Moderately Disagree (-0.6), Weakly Disagree (-0.4), Slightly Disagree (-0.2), Indifferent (0), Slightly Agree $(+0.2)$, Weakly Agree $(+0.4)$, Moderately Agree $(+0.4)$, Strongly Agree $(+0.8)$, and Completely Agree $(+1)$. This sliding bar is used to simplify the system interface to users.

Fig. 3. (a) Main page. (b) Selected issue. (c) Selected position. (d) Collective intelligence analytics. (e) Personal intelligence analytics.

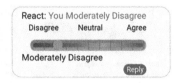

Fig. 4. The Sliding Bar

Users can add arguments by using the reply button. Arguments can be made for positions or other arguments. A position's discussion is made up of all arguments under it. Users can also interact with positions and arguments using a reaction. Reactions are statements of agreement/disagreement without any text. Reactions are used to explicitly support or attack arguments or positions using the react button as in Fig. 3(c). This helps with reducing redundant arguments in the system but still allow users to stay engaged in the discussion. To maintain the discussion's integrity, the application service does not allow standard users to delete or modify issues, positions and arguments after posting them. Instead, users can post updates to arguments and reactions they authored. An update creates a new argument with the user's modification and linked to the old argument. The old argument is still visible in the application but marked as an updated one. The application will keep both values because the old argument may have some children that are calculated in the collective intelligence index. This update's restriction is made because we do not want the author to change the issue, positions or arguments to something contradictory or unrelated to the original post. This restriction ensures transparency and encourages honesty for all users.

The Analytics Buttons
There are two analytics buttons in the application. The first button is the collective intelligence analytics button, as in Fig. 3(d). It presents meaningful numbers about the collective efforts on each position under the selected issue. It contains three collective measurements. The first one is the collective intelligence index. This index represents the overall discussion agreement for the selected position. The second index is the collective opinion index. This index reflects the users' total agreement value including the users who have not participated in a selected position, but have participated in other positions in the system. The third index is the polarization index. This index tells the user how polarized the discussion is under a selected position. More information about these indexes discussed in Sect. 4.

The second button is the personal intelligence analytics button, as in Fig. 3(e). It summaries the number of reactions and replies made by the user for each position under the selected issue. It also calculates the overall individual agreement value based on arguments and/or user reactions has made.

3.4   The Backend

The back-end consists of three major components: The Apache server, which hosts the website, the ICAS server and the Neoj4 database, as seen in Fig. 2. All analytics the applications are handled in the back end, ICAS. The Apache server connects to the ICAS server using WebSocket connection. The ICAS server connects to the Neoj4 database using the Bolt connection.

4 Collective Analytics Models

As in Table 2, the issue has four positions. Each position has more than 350 arguments. For users, to understand the discussion direction and participants attitudes, they need to read every argument in the issue tree. This is time-consuming and most likely users cannot comprehend the whole discussion. Therefore, this application design has adapted three analytics models used to make the app intelligent and informative for users. The models are the collective intelligent index, polarization index, and the prediction of collective opinions on the position level. These models use AI techniques to help users to understand the discussion event without participating. In the next subsections, there are more details about these models in the application.

4.1 Collective Intelligence Index

As stated before, users can reply and react to positions and arguments. Each reaction to a node in the application has an agreement value. This value ranges from -1 and 1. On a position level, the position or argument agreement as shown in Fig. 3(d) and (e) is calculated as:

$$Position_{overall\_agreement} = \sum_{i=1}^{N} avg(\text{argument}_i || reaction_i) \qquad (1)$$

For analytics, we need to determine the user agreement towards a position. Some users made direct reactions to positions while others made reactions to arguments. Reactions made to positions are easy to calculate their agreement value. However, for the arguments further down the tree, it is not obvious how the argument is related to the parent position. We need to derive the argument's agreement level with its parent position. For example, on position P, as shown in Fig. 5(a) is not known exactly the argument B agreement value to position P. To solve this problem, the application uses a fuzzy logic engine to reduce arguments agreement value to its parent position. In the argument reduction procedure, the fuzzy inference engine takes in two inputs and produces one output. The inputs are the agreement values of an argument to be and its parent. The output will be the new reduced agreement value for the argument to be from the fuzzy inference engine. The fuzzy inference engine uses fuzzy membership functions to quantify the linguistics agreement terms used in the application, as listed in Sect. 3. The fuzzy membership function used in the application is the piecewise linear trapezoidal function. Membership functions are defined by using four vertices of the trapezoids to define the fuzzy sets. For more explanation of the fuzzy logic engine, please refer to [3].

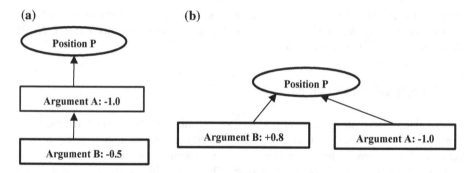

Fig. 5. (a) Position subtree before reduction. (b) Position subtree after reduction

This fuzzy logic engine uses inference rules to combine two or more inputs of the fuzzy sets. These inputs are identical to the logical operators, e.g., and, or. The inference rules are predetermined of 25 inference rules to reduce arguments agreement values. Here are two examples of the inference rules:

- If argument B supports argument A and argument A attacks position P, then argument B attacks position P (Implicit attack).
- If argument B attacks argument A and argument A attacks position P, then argument B supports position P. (Implicit support).

For more information about general argumentation heuristic rules, please refer to [3].

For example, argument A disagrees to position P with an agreement value (−1.0). Then, argument B disagrees to user A with agreement value (−0.5). From the tree visualization in Fig. 5(a), it can be inferred that argument B is supporting position P because it already disagrees with argument A. Now the application wants to determine the agreement value of argument B towards position P. The application uses a fuzzy logic engine to reduce the agreement value for nested arguments. In the application, the fuzzy logic engine reduces the agreement value of nested arguments to become direct arguments to the associated position. This engine helps in simulating all arguments into one level and connected directly to the parent position, in Fig. 5(b), more details are in [3]. This index captures the participants' thinking towards the selected position. It helps the end user to see the overall agreement value so far for the selected position from participants. This index posted to the end users as the overall agreement index. It has two attributes: a value and a color. If the index is posted with red color, it means that most of the participants are being against the selected position. If it is posted with green, it says that most of the participants are being for the selected position. The value is the overall density for this position.

4.2 Polarization Index

The polarization index, adapted from [6], measures the amount of polarization among the individual users' agreement in a given position. This index is a distribution-based index that returns a value between 0 and 1, where 0 indicates that there is no polarization and 1 indicates that there is complete polarization.

$$P_{t,norm}(\pi.y, N) = \frac{P_t(\pi,y)}{P_{max}(N)} \tag{2}$$

$$P_t(\pi,y) = \sum_{i=1}^{N} \sum_{j=1}^{N} \pi_i \pi_j I_i^\alpha \max\{|y_i - y_j| - D, 0\} \tag{3}$$

$$I_i = \log\left(\sum_{j: |y_i-y_j| \le D} \left(\pi_j * \left(1 - \frac{y_i - y_j}{D}\right)\right)\right) \tag{4}$$

The index is calculated by taking the distribution of the averaged reduced agreement value for each user as an input, represented as the pair (π, y), where y is the vector of average agreement values and π is a vector of the same length as y, where the value at π_i represents the number of users with the average agreement of y_i. To calculate the polarization index, the distribution (π, y) and the total number of users N, are given to the function $P_{t,nrom}$ in (2). The value returned by $P_{t,nrom}$ is the polarization index that is normalized by the maximum possible value for the population size N, $P_{max}(N)$.

The application has measured the polarization index for all positions; more analysis is discussed in Sect. 5. For a full reference on the polarization index, please refer to [6]. This index helps users to know if the discussion in a position is polarized or not.

4.3 Prediction of Collective Opinions

In large-scale cyber argumentation and deliberation, discussions are often incomplete. Not all users explicitly share their full positions. Therefore, it is difficult to determine the collective opinions in large-scale argumentation. If we can predict the agreement value for non-participating users, it will help us to understand the overall user attitude towards the issue or position. The application uses the cosine similarity with position correlation collaborative filtering (CSCCF) [8] model to predict the collective agreement value for all non-participating users on a particular position. To predict position p, for each user who did not participate in any discussion on this position, the application calculates their prediction value using the CSCCF model and averages all the prediction values as a collective prediction on this position.

CSCCF model integrates user agreement values on positions with their correlation values with the test position. To predict the agreement value of position t for user x, the most similar users of x are identified with respect to position t and their position t agreement values are averaged as the predicted value of position t for user x after being weighted by corresponding similarity values with the test user.

For example, assume user x has the following agreement vector $U^x = [R_1^x, R_2^x \ldots R_{t-1}^x, R_{t+1}^x \ldots \ldots R_n^x]$, where R_p^x represents the agreement value of user x at position p. The application wants to report the collective opinions predication for position t. The person-correlation coefficients between all position pairs are measured with the corresponding two tailed p values. The correlation value between position i and j is measured using Eq. (5).

$$C_{i,j} = \begin{cases} \dfrac{\sum_{k=1}^{m}(R_i^k - R_i^\wedge)*(R_j^k - R_j^\wedge)}{\sqrt{\sum_{k=1}^{m}(R_i^k - R_i^\wedge)^2}*\sqrt{\sum_{k=1}^{m}(R_j^k - R_j^\wedge)^2}} & if\ p < 0.05 \\ \\ 0 & else \end{cases} \tag{5}$$

$$\text{Similarity}\,(x,y) = \frac{\sum_{i=1,i\neq t}^{n} C_{ti}^2 R_i^x R_i^y}{\sqrt{\sum_{i=1,i\neq t}^{n} C_{ti}^2 (R_i^X)^2} + \sqrt{\sum_{i=1,i\neq t}^{n} C_{ti}^2 (R_i^y)^2}} \tag{6}$$

To measure the similarity between user x and y, at first their agreement vectors are updated with associated correlation values with test position t and then the similarity value is measured between the updated vectors (U^x, U^y). The similarity measure is the cosine similarity value between user x and y as in Eq. 6.

Users are then ranked based on their similarity values and the agreement value of position t for test user x is predicted using the top k most similar users corresponding agreement values and their similarity values with user x. More analysis is explained in Sect. 5. For more information about this model; please refer to [8]. This model predicts the collective opinion for users based on the discussion and the similarity between participants. Therefore, users can see on which direction the discussion is going.

5   Discussion and Analysis

This mobile application is capable of facilitating large-scale cyber-argumentation. Table 1 shows different nodes and content in the application. Here is a detailed example of an issue in the application.

Table 1. Data in the application

Node name	Number of records
Issues	4
Positions	16
Users	336
Arguments	10600+

5.1   Example: Issue: Guns on Campus

This issue posted with the following question: "Should students with a concealed carry permit be allowed to carry guns on campus?" and had the next four positions for users' discussion:

- Position 1: No, college campuses should not allow students to carry firearms under any circumstances.
- Position 2: No, but those who receive special permission from the university should be allowed to concealed carry.
- Position 3: Yes, but students should have to undergo additional training.

- Position 4: Yes, and there should be no additional test. A concealed carry permit is enough to carry on campus.

The discussion form the above issue is summarized in Table 2. The number of participants among all positions is about the same except for position 1. The reason for this exception could be it is more arguable than the other positions or because it was the first listed position under this issue. The same applies to the number of arguments made on each position.

Table 2. Positions statistics to the gun on campus issue

Position #	1	2	3	4
# participants	164	129	132	130
# arguments	508	386	387	355
Overall collective agreement	0.2	0.13	-0.36	0.15
Argument collective agreement	0.19	0.09	-0.34	0.14
React collective agreement	0.07	0.07	-0.12	0.06
Polarization index	0.30	0.23	0.22	0.26
Collective predication index	0.31	0.00	-0.35	0.36

The table has the overall, arguments and reactions agreement values. The reaction agreement is the collective average for users reactions towards the position without a text. The user's reaction is the user agreement degree on the posted position. The argument agreement is the collective average users reactions towards the position with a text. In this application, the user has the option to react only or to react and reply to a position or an argument. The overall collective agreement is the average users reactions to the position and all related arguments, regardless if it is with text or not. These measurements help non-participants to know about the participants' reactions to each position under the selected issue. It also informs the user about how many users have participated and arguments made so far for the selected issue. For example, position 1 seems to be more popular than position 4 because it has more number of participants and arguments than position number 4. People who like to join hot topic discussions may favor position 1 over position 4. For position 3, it seems that people are not in favor of additional training to carry a gun on campus; This position has an agreement value of -0.36.

Regarding the polarization index, the positions under the Guns on Campus issue have similar polarization values. The polarization Index for all the positions is less than or equal to 0.30. All of the positions are slightly polarized but not into a significant degree. This index helps users to have a glance about the distribution of the participant's agreement for a particular position. It leads to understanding the discussion better.

Finally, the application adapted collective opinions prediction index to predict the future of a discussion about a position. In this application, about 94 participants out of 336 have responded to all positions. Only about one-fourth of the users have participated in all discussions in the application. Incomplete discussions are the typical case for argumentation and deliberation. However, users may want to know the collective opinions prediction, which predicts what the collective user agreement would be if everyone had participated. The collective prediction index calculates the collective opinion for non-participants based on similar participants' argument, reactions to position and correlations between positions. In position 1, less than half of the users did not participate in the conversation. If they join in the future, the application would predict that they might slightly agree on the position with an agreement value 0.31.

6 Conclusion and Future Work

In this paper, we developed an innovative large-scale cyber-argumentation mobile application service. This mobile service is designed to represent the issue tree and facilitate structured discussion from multiple positions for each issue in a handheld screen size. Users can add issues, multiple positions and arguments. They can react to positions and arguments and explicitly specify degrees of their agreements/disagreements. Discussions and conversations are well organized and easy to follow and understand. In addition, this application intelligently provides analytics about the collective and personal participation based on AI analytic models such as polarization index and collective opinion prediction. These models help users stay focused and well informed about the ongoing discussions. This application is an improvement for argumentation over the existing social media and debate service.

In a real-world setting, attacks can happen in this application such as scams and trolls. However, this problem is beyond the scope of this paper and left as future research. Currently, this app is being expanded to incorporate social networking services for argumentation, automatic issues generation based on hot and daily topics. In the future, a stable version of this application is going to be published in the applications stores.

References

1. Pührer, J.: ArgueApply: a mobile app for argumentation. In: Balduccini, M., Janhunen, T. (eds.) LPNMR 2017. LNCS (LNAI), vol. 10377, pp. 250–262. Springer, Cham (2017). https://doi.org/10.1007/978-3-319-61660-5_23
2. Bex, F., Snaith, M., Lawrence, J., Reed, C.: ArguBlogging: an application for the argument web. Web Semant.: Sci. Serv. Agents World Wide Web 25, 9–15 (2014)
3. Liu, X., Raorane, S., Leu, M.C.: A web-based intelligent collaborative system for engineering design. In: Li, W.D., McMahon, C., Ong, S.K., Nee, A.Y.C. (eds.) Collaborative Product Design and Manufacturing Methodologies and Applications. SSAM, pp. 37–58. Springer, London (2007). https://doi.org/10.1007/978-1-84628-802-9_2
4. Klein, M.: Enabling large-scale deliberation using attention-mediation metrics. Comput. Support. Coop. Work (CSCW) 21(4–5), 449–473 (2012). ACM Woodstock Conference
5. Statista. www.statista.com
6. Sirrianni, J., Liu, X., Adams, D.: Quantitative modeling of polarization in online intelligent argumentation and deliberation for capturing collective intelligence. In: 2018 IEEE International Conference on Cognitive Computing (ICCC), San Francisco, pp. 57–64 (2018)

7. Iandoli, L., Quinto, I., Spada, P., Klein, M., Calabretta, R.: Supporting argumentation in online political debate: evidence from an experiment of collective deliberation. New Media Soc. **20**(4), 1320–1341 (2018). https://doi.org/10.1177/1461444817691509
8. Rahman, M.M., Sirrianni, JW., Liu, XF., Adams, D.: Predicting opinions across multiple issues in large scale cyber argumentation using collaborative filtering and viewpoint correlation. Manuscript submitted for publication (2019)
9. Kunz, W., Rittel, H.W.: Issues as Elements of Information Systems, vol. 131. Institute of Urban and Regional Development, University of California, Berkeley (1970)
10. Brewka, G., Woltran, S.: GRAPPA: a semantical framework for graph-based argument processing. In: ECAI, pp. 153–158, August 2014
11. Kialo. www.kialo.com
12. Contra app. https://contra-app.com/
13. Debate.org. www.debate.org
14. Reddit. www.riddet.com
15. Quora. www.quora.com

ResumeVis: Interactive Correlation Explorer of Resumes

Xiaohui Wang[1,2] and Jingyan Qin[1,2(✉)]

[1] School of Mechanical Engineering, University of Science and Technology Beijing,
Beijing 100083, China
qinjingyanking@foxmail.com
[2] Institute of Artificial Intelligence, University of Science and Technology Beijing,
Beijing 100083, China

Abstract. Resumes are critical for individuals to find jobs and for HR to select staffs. Almost all key events about career and demographic information are recorded on the resumes, which are commercial secrets. Too many valuable patterns can be explored from resumes. In this paper, we collect 372,829 Chinese resumes with complete attributes, such as income and Chinese ID number. Then a system called ResumeVis is developed to explore the correlations among the attributes. In the visualization system, we propose a new correlation representation – parallel coordinates with multi-valued attributes to adapt to the characteristics of resumes. Besides, user-friendly interactions, such as filter elements, reorder attributes, brushing and linking, are integrated to provide an easy-use interface. Lots of patterns and inspiring results can be found by using the system. Three case studies are illustrated as examples to validate the system usability. The system can be used as a recommendation system for job seekers and HRs.

1 Introduction

Resumes play an important role in human career. Resumes are used for employees to find jobs and for HR to select staffs. Almost all key events about career and demographic information are recorded on the resumes. Too many valuable patterns can be explored from resumes. Since resumes are commercial secrets, it is difficult to obtain the complete resumes.

Visualization techniques have already been used to assist the analysis of humanities [1], which are good at storytelling. Different aspects of humanities visualization are presented in the previous work, such as visualizing traffic data [2], table tennis data [3], E-commerce data [4]. But as far as I know, there is almost no visualizing work dedicated to resumes.

In order to obtain resumes with complete attributes, we collect resumes through the offline cooperations with as many companies as possible. For five years, 372,829 Chinese resumes are collected with complete attributes, such as income and Chinese ID number. The data distribution analysis verifies the diversity and validity of the data set. Then an interactive visualization system called

© Springer Nature Switzerland AG 2019
D. Wang and L.-J. Zhang (Eds.): AIMS 2019, LNCS 11516, pp. 150–165, 2019.
https://doi.org/10.1007/978-3-030-23367-9_11

ResumeVis is developed to explore the correlations among the attributes. There may be multiple values in one attribute of resumes, such as education experiences and work experiences. Taking the characteristics of resumes into account, we propose a new correlation representation – parallel coordinates with multi-valued attributes. Besides, user-friendly interactions, such as filter elements, reorder attributes, brushing and linking, are integrated to provide an easy-use interface. Personal perspective and correlation perspective are provided in the system. Finally, three case studies from different aspects are illustrated as examples to validate the system usability.

The main contributions include:

- A large resume data set with complete attributes is constructed, which contains 372,829 Chinese resumes and valuable attributes, such as income and Chinese ID number.
- A complete interactive visualization system is developed to explore the correlations of resumes.
- We propose a new correlation representation – parallel coordinates with multi-valued attributes, which supports multiple values in one attribute in an item.

2   Related Work

2.1   The Visualization of Humanities

The visualization techniques is good at storytelling and increasingly used to visualize humanities data [5], called digital humanities [6]. Compared with the scientific data, the humanities data is multi-dimensional and the attributes of humanities data are more complicated and diverse [7]. Different aspects of humanities visualization are presented in the previous work. For example, Xiaoying et al. visualized traffic data to find flow patterns [2]. Yingcai et al. presented a system called iTTVis to visualize table tennis data [3]. Wang developed a GIS software called "MeteoInfo" for meteorological data visualization [8]. But as far as I know, there is almost no visualizing work dedicated to resumes.

In order to mine the information hidden behind the data, interactions play an important role in information visualization [9]. There are different kinds of interactions, such as brushing [10], filtering [11], focusing and linking [12,13]. In this paper, the flexible and rich interactions are integrated in the proposed system.

2.2   The Visualization of Correlations

There are many techniques to visualize correlations, such as scatterplot matrix [14], graphs [15], maps [16] and parallel coordinates [17]. Among these visualization methods, the parallel coordinates are a common way of visualizing high-dimensional data and analyzing multivariate data [18]. It consists of n parallel lines, typically vertical and equally spaced. A data item in the data set is represented as a polyline with vertices on the parallel axes.

Some modified parallel coordinates are proposed for different visualization applications. For example, Xiaoying et.al presented the parallel coordinates with line and set, depicting attributes by lines and rectangular bars [2]. Kosara et al. proposed "parallel sets" for interactive exploring the categorical data [19]. Alexander et al. proposed "VisBricks" for multiform visualization of large, inhomogeneous data by extending the idea of "parallel sets" [20]. Graham et al. used curves to enhance parallel coordinate visualisations [21]. However, none of the above methods are suitable for resume data, in which one attribute in an item has multiple values. So in this paper, we propose an improved parallel coordinates with multi-valued attributes to adapt to the characteristics of resumes.

3   The Resume Data Set

3.1   Data Collection

There are three crucial aspects of the resumes, including the demographics, the education experiences and the work experiences. Due to the privacy and commercial secrets of resumes, there are very limited information in the online resumes. We cannot collect resumes through web crawlers, since the important information is hidden from the public. It is easy to obtain bias in the pattern mining by using the incomplete resume information. To get as much information as possible, we collect resumes through the offline cooperations with as many companies as possible to get the complete information.

Through 5 years of collection, there are 372,829 Chinese resumes in total. We organize the various sources into the unified Json format. In the Json file, each item is a resume, with dimensions in four aspects. Dimensions of the resumes are shown in Table 1, including the demographics, the education experiences, the work experiences and the training experiences.

We use the dummy coding to identify the attribute values as numbers. An employee may have multiple education experiences. So in the category of education, there are multiple education items. Each item contains the school name, the major name, the start time, the end time, and the academic qualification obtained at this school. Similarly, an employee may have multiple work experiences. Each work item contains the company name, the department name, the job name, the start time and the end time. Besides, the training experiences are taken into account, which have a direct relationship with the work experiences.

3.2   Data Distribution

Before exploring the correlations of resumes, we do the statistical analysis of data set to verify the diversity of data distribution and the validity of the data set. Since the resumes are from different sources, our collection algorithms do a lot of data integration and classification. The details will be described in the following.

Table 1. Dimensions of the resumes

Category	Dimension	Value	Description
Demographics	Gender	{1, 2}	1 = male, 2 = female
	Year of birth	number	The date of birth, obtained from the field in the resume or extracted from the ID number
	Province of birth	number	The province of birth, obtained from the ID number. The dummy coding of provinces follows the rules of ID number.
	Marital status	{1, 2, 3, 4}	1= single, 2 = married, 3 = divorced, 4 = confidential
	Email	string	The email of the contact information
	Highest education	{1, 2, 3, 4, 5, 6, 7, 8, 9}	1 = Secondary school, 2 = High school, 3 = College, 4 = Undergraduate, 5 = Master, 6 = MBA, 7 = EMBA, 8 = Ph.D, 9 = Other
	Language	{1, 2, 3, 4, 5, 6, 7, 8, 9, 10, 11}	1 = English, 2 = Japanese, 3 = French, 4 = German, 5 = Russian, 6 = Spanish, 7 = Italian, 8 = Arabic, 9 = Korean, 10 = Portuguese, 11 = Other
	Skill	string	The skills such as the softwares
	Monthly income	{1, 2, 3, 4, 5, 6, 7, 8, 9}	1 = below 1000 yuan, 2 = 1000 − 1999 yuan, 3 = 2000 − 3999 yuan, 4 = 4000 − 5999 yuan, 5 = 6000 − 7999 yuan, 6 = 8000 − 9999 yuan, 7 = 10000 − 14999 yuan, 8 = 15000 − 24999 yuan, 9 = over 25000 yuan
Education	School	string	The name of the school
	Major	string	The major when studying at this school
	Start year	number	The start year of studying at this school
	End year	number	The end year of studying at this school
	Degree	{1, 2, 3, 4, 5, 6, 7, 8, 9}	The academic qualification obtained at this school. The dummy coding of "Degree" is the same as "Highest education".
Work	Company	string	The company name
	Department	string	The department name in this company
	Job	string	The job name in this company
	Start year	number	The start year of working in this company
	End year	number	The end year of working in this company
Training	Organization	string	The name of the training institution
	Course	string	The course learned in this institution

Gender. There are 206,904 resumes with the "gender" dimension, including 104,316 females and 102,588 males. It can be seen that the proportions of men and women in the data set are balanced.

Date of Birth. Some resumes clearly show the date of birth, while some resumes record the Chinese ID number. In the Chinese ID number, the 7th number to the 14th number are the date of birth. If the explicit record of birth and the birth extracted in the Chinese ID number conflict, the date of birth is obtained from the Chinese ID number in our data collection algorithm, because the error probability of manually entering the birth is higher.

We focus on the resumes with the date of birth between 1950 to 1999, and in total 208,831 resumes meet this condition. There are 1,155 persons born in 50s (0.55% in the population), 17,595 persons born in 60s (8.43%), 110,849 persons born in 70s (53.08%), 76,663 persons born in 80s (36.71%), and 2,569 persons born in 90s (1.23%). From the distribution, we can see that 70s and 80s are the main force of the social workforce, making up nearly 90% of the total. This distribution is consistent with the distribution of the social workforce.

Marital Status. There are 187,224 resumes with the "marital status" dimension. There are 44,824 singles, which are 23.94% of the population. There are 65,148 (34.8%) married, 516 (0.27%) divorced, and 76,736 (40.99%) confidential.

Email. There are 196,609 resumes with the "email" dimension. And 5,981 different emails appear in these resumes. Most of these emails only have one resume registered. The top 9 emails with most users are 163.com (33,596), hotmail.com (30,003), sina.com (18,941), 126.com (17,988), yahoo.com.cn (14,579), qq.com (14,317), gmail.com (10,643), 263.net (9,367), sohu.com (9,136), which are in total 80.65% of the population.

Highest Education. There are 203,026 resumes with the "highest education" dimension. The distribution is shown in Fig. 1. 61.5% of the population is undergraduates and 17.78% of the population is masters. To some extent, this distribution reflects the education composition of the population.

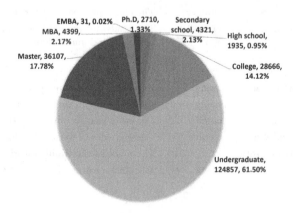

Fig. 1. The distribution of the highest education.

Language. There are 127,435 resumes with the "language" dimension. Some employees master two or more foreign languages. So there are 165,727 language items. 74.47% of the population can speak English, 13.11% of the population can speak Japanese, followed by French (4.34%), German (3.15%), Korean (1.76%), Russian (0.86%), Spanish (0.54%) and Italian (0.11%). Few people can speak other languages.

Skill. There are 59,968 resumes with the "skill" dimension, and 25,840 different skill items appear in these resumes. Some employees master two or more skills. Most of these skills are related with the computers. The top ten skills with most resumes are Visual Basic (7,694), Access (4,621), TCP/IP (4,357), FoxPro (4,328), Visual C++ (4,235), Management Information System (3,800), Java (3,479), MS-SqlServer (3,425), HTML (3,210) and Oracle (3,136).

Monthly income. The current salary is a very precious information, which is an important quantitative indicator of an employee's ability. There are 149,601 resumes with salary related information. Our data collection algorithm divided the monthly income into 9 categories, and classified each resume based on its salary related information. The distribution of the monthly incomes is shown in Fig. 2. This distribution is basically consistent with the officially released statistics of Beijing residents' income.

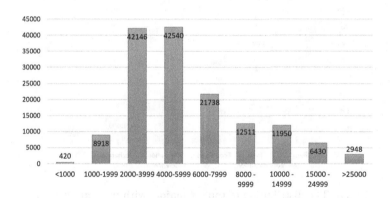

Fig. 2. The distribution of the monthly incomes.

University. The education experiences have a direct impact on the work experiences. There are 259,969 resumes with the "education" dimension. Some employees use the Chinese University names, while some employees use the English names. So the data collection algorithm combines the Chinese University names and the corresponding English names. After the data integration, there are 79,433 different universities in these resumes. The distribution of ten universities with most graduates are University of International Business and Economics (6175 graduates), Renmin University of China (5481 graduates), Beijing International Studies University (5393 graduates), Beijing University of Technology (5217 graduates), Beijing Foreign Studies University (4710 graduates), Capital University of Economics and Business (4661 graduates), Peking University

(4408 graduates), Beijing Institute of Technology (3654 graduates), Tsinghua University (3317 graduates), University of Science and Technology Beijing (3116 graduates).

All these ten universities are in Beijing, since the resumes in our data set are collected from the companies in Beijing and most people choose to work in the city where they study. There are so many different types of universities and companies in Beijing, so there is no bias to collect resumes from companies in Beijing. Besides, the number of resumes in the data set is large, which are with high qualities.

Major. There are 71 different majors in the 259,969 resumes with the "education" dimension. There are six majors with more than ten thousand graduates, which is shown in Fig. 3. The six majors are foreign languages, business administration (eg, marketing/international trade/tourism/logistics), economics (eg, financial/accounting), information science (eg, electrical/ computer/software/network/communications), mechanical (eg, automation/ industrial design) and law.

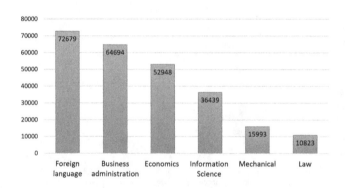

Fig. 3. The distribution of top six majors with most graduates.

Work Experiences. The work experiences are the crucial factors in the resumes. There are 174,833 resumes with the "work" dimension, which provides rich resources for further correlation exploring. Many employees have worked in more than one company. So there are 341,720 different companies in total. The top 10 companies with most employees are Lenovo (574), IBM (501), Huawei (348), Hewlett Packard (HP) China (346), Siemens China (288), CCTV (275), Bank of China (269), Beijing Organising Committee for Olympic (246) and Industrial and Commercial Bank of China (233). The statistics shows that the employee proportions in these companies are very low, for example, the proportion of IBM is 0.3%, which verifies the diversity of the work experiences in our data set and is very helpful for the correlation exploring.

There are 111,419 different types of departments in the 174,833 resumes. The top 10 departments with most employees are sales (25,418), marketing (19,368), finance (17,477), Administration (11,765), Human resource (8,699), Technical department (5,411), business (3,163), Office (2,820), engineering department (2,610) and manager office (2,130). The employees in the top four departments are more than ten thousand. Pattern mining based on one department is valuable, not to mention the entire data set.

We define some different levels of jobs and categories in each level based on the human resource expertise. For example, the levels contain sales, marketing, IT, research, finances, etc, and in the level of sales, the categories include sales manager, sales assistant, sales representative, etc. There are 1,385 different combinations in the 174,833 resumes with work experiences. The top jobs with most employees are administration - administrative assistant (20,138), other - other (18,464) administration - manager assistant/secretary/clerk (16,514), translation - English translator (10,536), sales - sales representative (10,276), sales - sales manager (10,041), finances - accountant (9,707), human resources - HR specialist/assistant (7,750), marketing - specialist/assistant (7,572) and sales - sales assistant (7,270). The abundant job categories and so many resumes with job information provide solid data support for the proposed system.

Training Experiences. There are 70,859 resumes with the "training" dimension, and 83,706 different training organizations appear in these resumes. Some employees participate in two or more training courses. Most of them are language training. The most popular training institution is New Oriental School. 3,802 employees attended the courses in New Oriental School, accounting for 5% of the population. The other two of the three most popular training institutions are Sunlands (1,447) and Beijing Foreign Studies University (1,047).

4   System Design

The screenshot of ResumeVis is illustrated in Fig. 4. There are six parts: title bar, improved parallel coordinates, introduction and controls, attribute filter, group selection and displayed attribute selection.

Title Bar. The title bar clearly shows the system name "ResumeVis: interactive correlation explorer of resumes".

A button named "keep" is used to filter and keep the items based on the attribute values. If you want to focus on some values in an attribute, you select these values by dragging vertically along the attribute axis first. Then after pressing the keep button, the items which do not meet the condition will be removed. More importantly, multiple attributes can be filtered collaboratively to support various analytical tasks. After filtering by one attribute, you can repeat the same operation to filter items by another attribute. In this way, the items are filtered by two attributes at the same time.

At the right of the title bar, there are two numbers separated by a slash. The right one is the total number of the items, while the left one is the number of the items which have been visualized in the parallel coordinates. Due to the large amount of data, the system uses the left number as a loading progress bar.

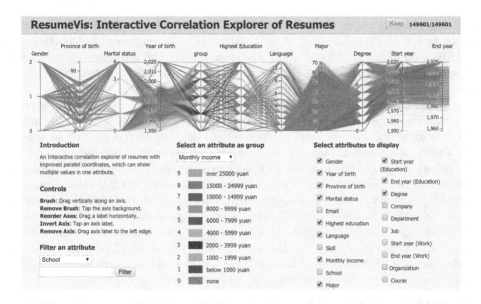

Fig. 4. The screenshot of ResumeVis.

Figure 4 shows the results by removing the items with group value "0". So there are 149,601 items in total after filtering.

Improved Parallel Coordinates. This part is the core of the system. We improve the traditional parallel coordinates to adapt to resume data. Convenient interactions are integrated in the improved parallel coordinates for flexibility, which will be explained in detail in the "interaction" subsection.

Introduction and Controls. This part shows a brief introduction of the system and the interactions for the improved parallel coordinates.

Group Selection. In the system, we can set an attribute as the group and assign different colors for all the possible values of the attribute, which helps users distinguish between different values. Only one attribute can be selected as the group at a time by selecting in the dropdown box. However, too many colors are easy to confuse. So the attributes with too many values are not allowed to be set as the group, such as the attributes "school", "company" and "job". In this system, the maximum number of possible values in the group is 71, which is the number of different majors. And the 71 different majors are encoding from 1 to 71 based on the number of employees in each major.

The color encodings for all the possible values in the group attribute and the meanings of these values are shown under the dropdown box. For example, in Fig. 4, we set the attribute "monthly income" as the group, and the color encodings and meanings of ten possible values are shown, in which "0" indicates that there is no income information.

Attribute Filter. This part is used to filter attributes, especially those with too many values. First, select an attribute in the dropdown box, then input a value and press the filter button. For example, select the attribute "school", then input the value "Tsinghua University". After pressing the filter button, the parallel coordinates will only display the items whose value of school is Tsinghua University. This part makes up the limitation of group selection.

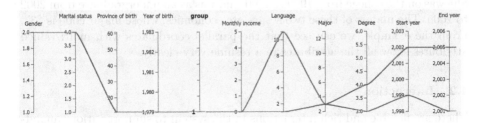

Fig. 5. An example of parallel coordinates with multi-valued attributes.

Displayed Attribute Selection. There are 21 attributes in our data set. Displaying all attributes in the parallel coordinates is too crowded. So the attribute selection part at the bottom right of the interface allows users to choose which attributes to display in the parallel coordinates by checking the corresponding check boxes. The parallel coordinates will be changed dynamically based on the user selection.

The system uses the improved parallel coordinates to depict resumes from the following two perspectives.

Personal Perspective: Sometimes we focus on one employee's resume, such as a successful person. Personal perspective is designed for this function. "Parallel coordinates with multi-valued attributes" is contributed to represent resumes, which has multiple values in one attribute. In order to protect personal privacy, the identification information such as names, Chinese ID number and emails is not visible to users.

Correlation Perspective: The parallel coordinates have an innate nature for correlation exploring. Furthermore, combined with flexible and diverse interactions, such as brush, changing axis, reordering axis, group setting, etc, the system provides rich methods of correlation exploring and helps users to obtain a more comprehensive understanding of resumes.

4.1 Parallel Coordinates with Multi-valued Attributes

In a resume, some attributes have multiple values. For example, the education experiences of an employee may include three periods, undergraduate, graduate and PhD, and the work experiences may contain multiple companies and jobs. In the standard parallel coordinates, an item is a polyline, and one attribute has only one value. So the standard parallel coordinates are not suitable for resume data. In this paper, we propose the parallel coordinates with multi-valued attributes, which can show multiple values in one attribute to meet the characteristics of resumes.

An example of parallel coordinates with multi-valued attributes is shown in Fig. 5. The employee is female and born in 1979, whose demographic information is unique. She masters two foreign languages, English and one minority language. She was on the college from 1999 to 2001 and was as an undergraduate from 2002 to 2005. The majors of these two stages are economics, whose major code is "3". From the example, we can see that the parallel coordinates with multi-valued attributes show all the attributes in a resume very clearly.

4.2   Interaction

There are flexible and rich interactions in the system to support various analytical tasks.

Brush. The brush interaction is to filter items based on attribute values by dragging vertically along the attribute axis. The brush interaction can be used with the keep button. The differences between brush and keep button are: (1) Only one attribute can be filtered at a time by using the brush interaction. If brushing the second attribute, the first brush is invalid. While using the keep button, multiple attributes can be filtered simultaneously. (2) By using the brush, the shapes and axes of the parallel coordinates stay the same, except that the items which do not meet the condition are removed. However, after pressing the keep button, the axes are adapted to the selected values and the parallel coordinates will be changed. If you want to remove brush, just tap the axis background.

Change Axis. Any combinations of all the 21 attributes in the resumes can be allowed by checking the check boxes at the bottom right of the interface. Besides, users can drag axis label to the left edge to remove one attribute.

Reorder Axis. All the axes in the parallel coordinates can be reordered in any order by dragging an attribute label horizontally at one time. If you want to see the direct correlations between two attributes, drag the attribute label horizontally to let them be next to each other.

Invert Axis. The values in each axis can be inverted upside down by tapping the axis label.

Group Settings. Each attribute with small amount of possible values can be set as the group. The group can be seen as the focus of current data analysis.

Attribute Filter. The items can be filtered by each value in any attribute.

5   Experiments

The parallel coordinates with multi-valued attributes in the system are implemented by D3.js [22] and based on the open source code [23]. The following case studies are illustrated as examples to validate the system usability.

5.1   Case Study 1: Which Attributes Related to Income?

Job seekers are most concerned about income. So we use all the items in the data set to look for the attributes related to the income. In our common sense, the higher your education, the higher your income. Another common sense is that with age, income is increasing. Is that right? In this case study, we explore the correlation among income, year of birth and highest education.

First, the attribute "monthly income" is set as the group, all the 372,829 items are displayed in different colors. The color encodings and meanings for all the monthly income types are shown at the bottom of the group selection part. Second, let the attributes "year of birth" and "highest education" be next to the attribute "monthly income" by using the axis reordering interaction. Finally, use the brush and keep button alternately to filter items by focusing on one value at a time. The specific operation is to select one value of "monthly income" by brush, then to press the keep button to only maintain the items with the specific value, finally to select all the values of "year of birth", which the filtered items fall into. The results are shown in Fig. 6.

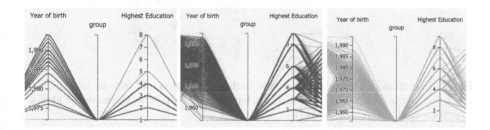

Fig. 6. Correlations among income, highest education and year of birth with monthly income as the group. The income in the left one is below 1000 yuan; the income in the middle one is between 6000 to 7999 yuan; the income in the right one is over 25000 yuan.

Figure 6 shows the correlations among income, highest education and year of birth with three values of monthly income. The left one is the result when the monthly income is below 1000 yuan. The highest education distribution mainly focuses on the secondary school, high school, college and undergraduate. There are very few highly educated. There is no item whose year of birth is below 1970. That's why we use the brush and keep button to filter items based on two attributes. We hope to expand the items along the axis as far as possible to display more clearly. The middle is the result when the monthly income is between 6000 to 7999 yuan. The distribution of highest education is relatively uniform. There are few items with EMBA as highest education, because there are few resumes that meets this condition, as shown in Fig. 1. The range of year of birth is from 1950 to 2000. The right is the result when the monthly income is over 25000 yuan. The highest education focuses on the high degrees and there are few resumes with values "secondary school" and "high school". Besides, there are many items with EMBA as highest education and more elders.

For further cross validation of correlations between monthly income and highest education, we set the attribute "highest education" as the group from another point of view. The results are shown in Fig. 7. The left one is the result when the highest education is "high school". The distribution of monthly income mainly focuses on the low incomes. There are few items with more than 1000 yuan. The right one is the result when the highest education is "Ph.D". There are more items with high income and few items with low income. So the case study validates the common sense that the higher your education, the higher your income and a certain correlation with ages.

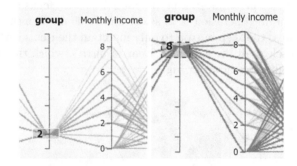

Fig. 7. Examples of correlations between highest education and income with highest education as the group. The highest education in the left one is high school; the highest education in the right one is Ph.D.

5.2   Case Study 2: Are There Differences Between Different Majors?

First, the attribute "major" is set as group. To see the correlations between each attribute and the attribute "major", drag each attribute label horizontally to let it be next to major. And press the keep button to keep items with a specific major value.

Correlations among major, language and monthly income are shown in Fig. 8(a). The distribution of language in the left image (foreign language major) is more evenly than the distributions in the other two images (information science and art). The result is in line with our understanding. Besides, there is no significant differences in the distribution of monthly income. Correlations between major and highest education are shown in Fig. 8(b). Three majors are selected,

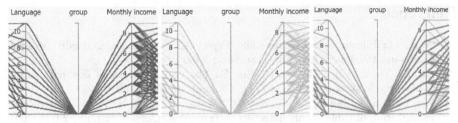

(a) Correlations among major, language and monthly income

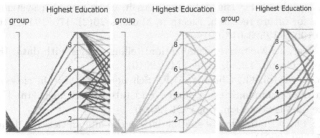

(b) Correlations between major and highest education

Fig. 8. Correlations among some attributes with major as the group. The major in the left one is foreign language; the major in the middle one is information science; the major in the right one is art.

foreign language, information science and art. We can see that the number of art doctors is obviously less than that of the other two majors. In fact, compared to other majors, there are less amount of doctoral awarding departments of art in Chinese colleges and universities.

6   Conclusion

In this paper, we propose an interactive visualization system, called ResumeVis, to explore the correlations of resumes. First, we construct a large resume data set with complete attributes, which contains 372,829 Chinese resumes and valuable attributes. The data distribution analysis verifies the diversity and validity of the data set. Then, the improved parallel coordinates with multi-valued attributes are proposed to adapt to the characteristics of resume data. Combine with the flexible and rich interactions, the system supports various analytical tasks. Finally, the case studies validate the system usability.

Acknowledgment. This work was supported by the National Natural and Science Foundation of China (61602033), the Fundamental Research Funds for the Central Universities (FRF-TP-18-007A3), USTB - NTUT Joint Research Program (TW2018004) and the grant of China Scholarship Council.

References

1. Ware, C.: Information Visualization: Perception for Design, 2nd edn. Morgan Kaufmann Publishers Inc., San Francisco (2004)
2. Shi, X., Yu, Z., Chen, J., Xu, H., Lin, F.: The visual analysis of flow pattern for public bicycle system. J. Visual Lang. Comput. **45**, 51–60 (2018)
3. Wu, Y., Lan, J., Shu, X., Ji, C., Zhao, K., Wang, J., Zhang, H.: iTTVis: interactive visualization of table tennis data. IEEE Trans. Vis. Comput. Graph. **24**(1), 709–718 (2018)
4. Akter, S., Wamba, S.F.: Big data analytics in e-commerce: a systematic review and agenda for future research. Electron. Markets **26**(2), 173–194 (2016). https://doi.org/10.1007/s12525-016-0219-0
5. Segel, E., Heer, J.: Narrative visualization: telling stories with data. IEEE Trans. Vis. Comput. Graph. **16**(6), 1139–1148 (2010)
6. Janicke, S., Franzini, G., Cheema, M.F., Scheuermann, G.: On close and distant reading in digital humanities: a survey and future challenges. In: Eurographics Conference on Visualization, pp. 1–21 (2015)
7. Jessop, M.: The visualization of spatial data in the humanities. Lit. Ling. Comput. **19**(3), 335–350 (2004)
8. Wang, Y.Q.: MeteoInfo: GIS software for meteorological data visualization and analysis. Meteorol. Appl. **21**(2), 360–368 (2014)
9. Yi, J.S., Kang, Y.A., Stasko, J.: Toward a deeper understanding of the role of interaction in information visualization. IEEE Trans. Vis. Comput. Graph. **13**(6), 1224–1231 (2007)
10. Becker, R.A., Cleveland, W.S.: Brushing scatterplots. Technometrics **29**(2), 127–142 (1987)
11. Heer, J., Card, S.K., Landay, J.A.: Prefuse: a toolkit for interactive information visualization. In: Proceedings of the SIGCHI Conference on Human Factors in Computing Systems, pp. 421–430 (2005)
12. Buja, A., McDonald, J., Michalak, J., Stuetzle, W.: Interactive data visualization using focusing and linking. In: IEEE Conference on Visualization, pp. 156–163 (1991)
13. Keim, D.: Information visualization and visual data mining. IEEE Trans. Vis. Comput. Graph. **8**(1), 1–8 (2002)
14. Elmqvist, N., Dragicevic, P., Fekete, J.D.: Rolling the dice: multidimensional visual exploration using scatterplot matrix navigation. IEEE Trans. Vis. Comput. Graph. **14**(6), 1141–1148 (2008)
15. Sauber, N., Theisel, H., Seidel, H.P.: Multifield-graphs: an approach to visualizing correlations in multifield scalar data. IEEE Trans. Vis. Comput. Graph. **12**(5), 917–924 (2006)
16. Blanco, I.D., Vega, A.A.C., Gonzlez, A.B.D.: Correlation visualization of high dimensional data using topographic maps. In: International Conference on Artificial Neural Networks (2002)
17. Wegman, E.J.: Hyperdimensional data analysis using parallel coordinates. J. Am. Stat. Assoc. **85**(1), 664–675 (1990)
18. Inselberg, A.: The plane with parallel coordinates. Visual Computer **1**(4), 69–91 (1985). https://doi.org/10.1007/BF01898350
19. Kosara, R., Bendix, F., Hauser, H.: Parallel sets: interactive exploration and visual analysis of categorical data. IEEE Trans. Vis. Comput. Graph. **12**(4), 558–568 (2006)

20. Lex, A., Schulz, H.J., Streit, M., Partl, C., Schmalstieg, D.: Visbricks: multiform visualization of large, inhomogeneous data. IEEE Trans. Vis. Comput. Graph. **17**(12), 2291–2300 (2011)
21. Graham, M., Kennedy, J.: Using curves to enhance parallel coordinate visualisations. In: Seventh International Conference on Information Visualization (2003)
22. Teller, S.: Data Visualization with d3.js. Packt Publishing (2013)
23. Kai: Nutrient Parallel Coordinates. http://bl.ocks.org/syntagmatic/3150059/ (2018) [Online]

Named Entity Recognition in Clinical Text Based on Capsule-LSTM for Privacy Protection

Changjian Liu, Jiaming Li, Yuhan Liu, Jiachen Du, Buzhou Tang, and Ruifeng Xu[✉]

Harbin Institute of Technology (Shenzhen), Shenzhen 518055, China
cjliux@163.com, lijm_hitsz@163.com, liuyuhan_hitsz@163.com,
dujiachen@stmail.hitsz.edu.cn, tangbuzhou@gmail.com, xuruifeng@hit.edu.cn

Abstract. Clinical Named Entity Recognition for identifying sensitive information in clinical text, also known as Clinical De-identification, has long been critical task in medical intelligence. It aims at identifying various types of protected health information (PHI) from clinical text and then replace them with special tokens. Along with the development of deep learning technology, lots of neural-network-based methods have been proposed to deal with Named Entity Recognition. As one of the state-of-the-art methods to address this problem, Bi-LSTM-CRF has become the mainstream due to its simplicity and efficiency. In order to better represent the entity-related information expressed in the context of clinical text, we design a novel Capsule-LSTM network that is able to combine the great expressivity of capsule network with the sequential modeling capability of LSTM network. Experiments on 2014 i2b2 dataset show that the proposed method outperforms the baseline and thus reveal the effectiveness of the newly proposed Capsule-LSTM network.

1 Introduction

In clinical text, there are protected health information (PHI) such as name, phone numbers, occupation and location, etc. To protect these privacy information from disclosure, the Health Insurance Portability and Accountability Act (HIPAA)[1] promulgated in 1996 in the United States clearly stipulates that all medical text data in scientific research and business must be de-privacy processed first. To serve this purpose, the task of Clinical Named Entity Recognition (NER) is used to identify sensitive information, both the boundaries and semantic classes of target entities, and is known as Clinical De-identification.

In the early stage, NER systems for clinical purpose, such as MedLEE [1], SymText [2], MPlus [3], KnowledgeMap [4], HiTEX [5], cTAKES [6], and MetaMap [7], are rule-based. Later, machine learning based method become popular [8–10]. Among them Conditional Random Field (CRF) [11] finally takes

---

[1] https://en.wikipedia.org/wiki/Health_Insurance_Portability_and_Accountability_Act.

© Springer Nature Switzerland AG 2019
D. Wang and L.-J. Zhang (Eds.): AIMS 2019, LNCS 11516, pp. 166–178, 2019.
https://doi.org/10.1007/978-3-030-23367-9_12

the lead [12]. Up till now, CRF has been widely adopted as the final decoding layer for NER models, regardless of the underlying structure.

Frustratingly, Machine learning based method rely heavily on labour entensive feature engineering. However, along with the surge of deep learning technology, neural network approaches open a new way to the solution of NER and bring about lots of new state-of-the-arts [13–16].

Although great progress has been made in classical NER task, the application of NER system to the clinical problem have not been fully investigated, especially that of deep learning methods. As we go deeper into the problem, we find that many state-of-the-art methods appearing in traditional NER have not been fully investigated for clinical NER, especially Clinical De-identification. Actually, different from datasets in traditional NER task, clinical texts are highly formatted and entities appearing in different part of a clinical text can have different types even if they have the same surface form.

Finally, the main contribution of our study can be sumarized as follows:

- Different from previous works that model texts in sentence-level, we move the first steps towards modeling texts in document-level in Clinical De-identification.
- We designed a noval Capsule-LSTM network, which can combine the great expressivity of capsule network and the sequential modeling capability of LSTM network.
- Experiments show that Capsule-LSTMs can outperform the original LSTMs in Clinical De-identification.

2 Related Work

2.1 Named Entity Recognition

Named Entity Recognition (NER) is an important task and has been extensively studied in the literature of Natural Language Processing, which aims at identifying named entities like person, location, organization, time, clinical procedure, biological protein, etc [17].

During the early stage, most of the approaches to NER have been characterized by the use of traditional statistical machine learning methods like Decision Tree [8], Maximum Entropy Model [18], Hidden Markov Model (HMM) [19], Conditional Random Field (CRF) [9], Supporting Vector Machine (SVM) [10] and Boosting Algorithm [20], etc. Approaches that fall into this category often require labour entensive feature engineering while also severely suffer from the data sparsity problem.

With the rapid development of deep learning technology, lots of neural-network-based methods have been proposed to address the task of Named Entity Recognition to reduce the feature engineering labour. Collobert et al. [21] proposed an effective neural language model for extracting text feature, which also tested on NER task by using a CNN-CRF architecture. Huang et al. [22] proposed a Bi-LSTM-CRF model that works well on NER task. Ma and Hovy et al. [23]

and Santos et al. [24] successfully applied CNN over characters of words to incorporate character-level feature, whose outputs were then concatenated with the word-level embeddings. Chiu and Nichols et al. [13] presented a hybrid model of bi-directional LSTMs and CNNs that learns both character- and word-level features. Lample et al. [25] discarded word-level encoding and model sequence completely over character-level feature instead.

Later, Peters et al. [26], Rei et al. [27], Reimers and Gurevych et al. [28] and Yang et al. [29] either utilized external resources or applied multi-task learning paradigm. Yang et al. [14] systematically investigated the effect of combining discrete feature and continuous feature for a range of fundamental NLP tasks including NER. Cetoli et al. [30] incorporated prior knowledge of dependency relation between words and measure the impact of using dependency trees for entity classification. The benchmark of NER has been pushed to a new state-of-the-art.

More recently, Seyler et al. [31] performed a comprehensive study about the effect of the importance of external knowledge. Zhang et al. [15] introduced lattice LSTM to NER task and to alleviate the segmentation error in Chinese. Zukov Gregoric et al. [16] distributed the computation of a LSTM cell across multiple smaller LSTM cells to reduce the total number of parameters.

2.2   Clinical De-Identification for Privacy Protection

Clinical De-identification is very much like traditional NER and has been a hot topic in clinical natural language processing for a long time. The task of Clinical De-identification was first presented by Uzuner et al. [32], and require NER system to identify and anonymize protected health information that appears in clinical notes. The dataset they used was released as part of 2006 i2b2 event.

The history of Clinical De-identification is very similar with that of Name Entity Recognition, where there is also a shifting process from rule-based system to machine learning, and then to deep learning. In the earlier stage, almost all system for Clinical De-identification were based on machine learning [33]. Stubbs et al. [34] made a full reviews over automatic de-identification systems that appeared in 2014 i2b2 de-identification track, among which all systems are based on machine learning methods and many have used Conditional Random Field for inference.

Later, researchers are resorting to deep learning approaches such that large amount of human labour can be avoided. Wu et al. [35] developed a deep neural network to recognize clinical entities in Chinese clinical documents using the minimal feature engineering approach and outperform the previous state-of-the-art. Liu et al. [36] investigated the performance of Bi-LSTM-CRF with character-level encoding over clinical entity recognition and protected health information recognition.

However, different from traditional NER task, clinical texts are highly formatted and entities appearing in different part of a clinical text can have different types even if they have the same surface form. Up till now, the problem of Clinical De-identification is still far from being solved.

In our study, we try to tackle the problem in document-level, treating each document as an single instance. Then, we introduce a novel Capsule-LSTM network that combine both the expressivity of Capsule Network and the sequential modeling capability of LSTM network. And finally, to justify our methods, we have chosen the latest 2014 i2b2 dataset, which was distributed as part of the i2b2 2014 Cardiac Risk and Protected Health Information (PHI) tasks.

3 Proposed Approach

3.1 Overall Architecture

The basic model architecture follows the general structure of Bi-LSTM-CRF, which encodes sentences using conventional bi-directional long-short term memory (Bi-LSTM) network and model target label using conditional random field (CRF).

Practically, named entities are usually comprised of out-of-vocabulary words, which can greatly damage the performance of a NER system. Therefore, in addition to word embedding, we also incorporated a character-level Bi-LSTM for better representing out-of-vocabulary words, just as many previous works have done. (See Fig. 1)

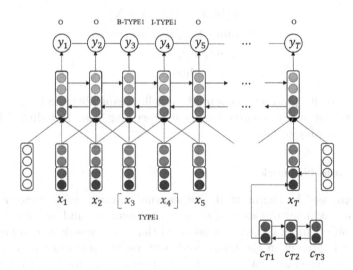

Fig. 1. The Architecture of our Bi-LSTM-CRF with character-level Bi-LSTM encoding. In the figure, we demonstrated how an input document $\langle x_1, x_2, x_3, x_4, \ldots, x_T \rangle$ was encoded, and how named entity $\langle x_3, x_4 \rangle$ of type TYPE1 can be identified via BIO tagging scheme, where x_3 was labeled B-TYPE1 while x_4 was labeled I-TYPE1.

Usually, there are two available tagging schemes, 'BIOES' or 'BIO', from which we prefer 'BIO' for its simplicity as it will incur less parameters to learn. Under the 'BIO' tagging scheme, an identified entity is defined as a sequence of words with the first word labeled with 'B' and any other trailing word labeled with 'I'. As is shown in Fig. 1, The input document $X = \langle x_1, x_2, x_3, x_4, \ldots, x_T \rangle$ with annotated entity $\langle x_3, x_4 \rangle$ of type TYPE1 (TYPE1 is an entity type, such as NAME, PHONE, etc). Then the target label sequence is $X = \langle y_1, y_2, y_3, y_4, \ldots, y_T \rangle$, where the target labels for the entity $\langle x_3, x_4 \rangle$ is $\langle y_3, y_4 \rangle$ with $y_3 = $ B-TYPE1, which means x_3 is the start of an entity of type TYPE1, and $y_4 = $ I-TYPE1, which means x_4 is an internal word of an entity of type TYPE1.

3.2 Long-short Term Memory

Long-short term memory (LSTM) was originally proposed by Hochreiter et al. [37] to deal with the gradient explosion and gradient vanishing problem of vanilla recurrent neural network, which consists of input gate i_t, forget gate f_t, output gate f_t and cell state c_t. The computation of LSTM goes like Eq. 1.

$$
\begin{aligned}
i_t &= \sigma(W_i x_t + U_i h_{t-1} + b_i) \\
f_t &= \sigma(W_f x_t + U_f h_{t-1} + b_f) \\
o_t &= \sigma(W_o x_t + U_o h_{t-1} + b_o) \\
\tilde{c}_t &= \tanh(W_c x_t + U_c h_{t-1} + b_c) \\
c_t &= i_t \odot \tilde{c}_t + f_t \odot c_{t-1} \\
h_t &= o_t \odot \tanh(c_t)
\end{aligned}
\tag{1}
$$

Because of its powerful sequential modeling capability, LSTMs have been widely used for many natural language processing task including NER and achieved promising results.

3.3 Capsule Network

Initially proposed by Hinton et al. [38], capsule network divide vector representation into a number of capsules, or groups of neurons, and are able to better represent object in an image. It is assumed that each capsule may represent an entity that is present in the input, and neurons in the capsule may represent properties of this entity. Sabour et al. [39] apply capsule network to the task of MNIST digit classification and proposed the CapsNet that outperform previous state-of-the-art convolutional network by a large margin with the same number of parameters.

Typically, We use $\boldsymbol{u}_i$ to denote the i-th input capsule, $\boldsymbol{v}_j$ to denote the j output capsule, and W_{ij} as a bridging weight parameter between $\boldsymbol{u}_i$ and $\boldsymbol{v}_j$. The computation of CapsNet are mainly about routing, as is detailed in Algorithm 1, whose input $\hat{\boldsymbol{u}}_{j|i}$ can be obtained by $\hat{\boldsymbol{u}}_{j|i} = W_{ij}\boldsymbol{u}_i$.

Algorithm 1. Routing Algorithm of CapsNet

Input: $\hat{u}_{j|i}$, r, l
Output: v_j
for all capsule i in layer l and capsule j in layer $(l+1)$: $b_{ij} \leftarrow 0$.
for r *iterations* **do**

　|　for all capsule i in layer l: $c_i \leftarrow softmax(b_i)$
　|　for all capsule j in layer $(l+1)$: $s_j \leftarrow \sum_i c_{ij}\hat{u}_{j|i}$
　|　for all capsule j in layer $(l+1)$: $v_j \leftarrow squash(s_j)$
　|　for all capsule i in layer l and capsule j in layer $(l+1)$: $b_{ij} \leftarrow b_{ij} + \hat{u}_{j|i} \cdot v_j$

end

Following the intuition of CapsNet, we apply capsule network to NER, with the expectation that capsules inside are able to capture the information of named entities in clinical texts. More specifically, we use capsule network style computation inside LSTM, and propose a novel Capsule-LSTM.

3.4   Capsule-LSTM

The basic idea of Capsule-LSTM is to combine the great expressivity of capsule network and the sequential modeling capability of long-short term memory network.

To design such a structure, we begin by representing the cell state and the hidden state of LSTM as a groups of capsules. That is, $h_t, c_t \in \mathbb{R}^{d_h}$ becomes $H_t, C_t \in \mathbb{R}^{n_c \times d_c}$, where n_c is the number of capsules and d_c is the dimension of each capsule.

$$F_t^{j|i} = \sigma(W_F^{j|i}x_t + U_F^{j|i}H_{t-1}^i + b_F^{j|i})$$
$$I_t^j = \sigma(W_I^j x_t + \sum_i U_I^{j|i}H_{t-1}^i)$$
$$O_t^j = \sigma(W_O^j x_t + \sum_i U_O^{j|i}H_{t-1}^i)$$
$$\tilde{C}_t^j = \tanh(W_C^j x_t + \sum_i U_C^{j|i}H_{t-1}^i) \tag{2}$$
$$C_t^{j|i} = I_t^j \odot \tilde{C}_t^j + F_t^{j|i} \odot C_{t-1}^i$$
$$C_t^j = Routing(\{C_t^{j|i}\}_i)$$
$$H_t^j = O_t^j \odot C_t^j$$

3.5 Training and Inference

To train our model, we follow Collobert et al. [21] to use sentence-level log-likelihood as objective function, shown in Eq. 3.

$$Sent\text{-}NLL(\Theta) = - \sum_{i=1}^{|D_{train}|} \log p(Y_i|X_i, \Theta). \tag{3}$$

Under the convention of CRF, the label sequence probability can be rewritten as:

$$p(Y_i|X_i) = \frac{1}{Z(X_i)} \exp \left(\sum_{t=1}^{T+1} \Psi(Y_i^{t-1}, Y_i^t) + \sum_{t=1}^{T} \Phi(X_i^t, Y_i^t) \right). \tag{4}$$

Here, $D_{train} = (X_i, Y_i)_{i=1}^{|D|}$ is our training set, Θ is our set of model parameters, Ψ is the transition score between successive labels (documents are prepended with a $\langle start \rangle$ label and appended with a $\langle end \rangle$ label.), Φ is the emission score from word to label, and finally $Z(X_i)$ is the normalization term associated with input X_i. Just like the training of traditional CRF, we further add L1 and L2 regularization term to avoid overfitting. Therefore, the final loss function turns out to be:

$$L(\Theta) = Sent\text{-}NLL(\Theta) + \lambda R(\Theta), \tag{5}$$

where $R(\Theta)$ is the sum of L1 and L2 regularization term. During the training phase, we optimize our model against $L(\Theta)$ using Adam [40] algorithm with $lr = 0.005$, $\beta_1 = 0.9$ and $\beta_2 = 0.999$. And then in testing phase, we apply Viterbi algorithm to find out the label sequences with maximal probability for input documents.

4   Experimental Details

4.1 Dataset

Description. The dataset we used in our study is a corpus of longitudinal medical records, distributed as part of the i2b2 2014 Cardiac Risk and Protected Health Information (PHI) tasks, or 2014 i2b2 dataset for brevity. This dataset consists of 1304 medical records from 296 diabetic patients, and is officially splitted into training and testing set, where training set contains 790 documents while the testing set contains 514 documents.[2] Each document is a well-formatted medical record and named entities inside documents are annotated as text spans with corresponding entity types, where 22 entity types in total are concerned.

---

[2] Here, we use the word document and the phrase medical records interleaved without distinction.

Data Preprocessing. To avoid the nuance of handling raw data, we resort to the publicly available i2b2tools[3] that is developed based on the official evalution scripts of 2014 i2b2 challenge to load data. In this way, we convert raw data into conll format while keeping some formatting information such as end-of-line and indentation by introducing special tokens like $\langle eol \rangle$ and $\langle tab \rangle$. All number appearing in the data are replaced by the special token $\langle num \rangle$. The Table 1 and Fig. 2 shows some basic statistics of this dataset after data preprocessing.

Table 1. Basic statistics of 2014 i2b2 dataset.

Statistics	Train	Test
Number of Documents	790	514
Average Document Length	938.2	927.8
Total Entity Count	17405	11462
Average Entity Count	22.0	22.4

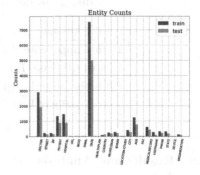

Fig. 2. Entity counts of 2014 i2b2 dataset.

4.2 Model Comparison

Evaluation Metrics. The evaluation metrics used in our study is F1 score in SemEval'13 standard, which introduced four different ways (Strict/Exact/Partial/Type) to measure precision/recall/f1 results based on the metrics defined by MUC [41]. Following previous works, we evaluate models by measuring in Strict way, which counts entity matching on exact boundary match over the surface string, regardless of the type. In our experiments, we do not implement evaluating metrics by ourselves, but use the publicly available evaluation toolkit NER-Evaluation[4].

Model Settings. In our study, the following models were compared:

- **CRF.** Traditional Conditional Random Field implemented by CRFsuite [12]. Feature template for this model is shown in Table 2.
- **Bi-LSTM-CRF.** Use conventional Bi-LSTM network for both word- and character-level encoding, and CRF for target modeling.
- **Bi-Capsule-LSTM-CRF.** Use Capsule-LSTM for word-level modeling, conventional Bi-LSTM for character-level modeling, and CRF for target modeling.

---

[3] https://github.com/danlamanna/i2b2tools.
[4] https://github.com/davidsbatista/NER-Evaluation.

To make fair comparison, we use similar hyper-parameter settings across all of the above models, where character embedding dimension is 20, character-level LSTM size is 10, word embedding dimension is 50, word-level LSTM size is 100 and word context window size is 5. As for the newly proposed Capsule-LSTM, we set the number of capsules to be 25 and the dimension of each capsule to be 4. For all models, we pretrained word embeddings using Word2Vec[5].

Table 2. Feature template for CRF baseline.

1	word unigram: w_{i+j}, $-2 \leq j \leq 2$
2	word upper case: $IsUpper(w_{i+j})$, $-2 \leq j \leq 2$
3	word title case: $IsTitle(w_{i+j})$, $-2 \leq j \leq 2$
4	whether word is digit: $IsDigit(w_i)$
5	word suffix of k characters: $Suffix(w_i, k)$, $k = 2, 3$

4.3 Results and Analysis

Overall Results. Table 3 shows the results on 2014 i2b2 dataset, whose F1 are reported (± 0.5) based on multiple runs. From this table, we can see that our newly proposed Bi-Capsule-LSTM-CRF outperform the Bi-LSTM-CRF baseline.

Table 3. Model performance over 2014 i2b2 testing set.

	Document-level			Sentence-level		
	P	R	F1	P	R	F1
CRF	92.48	81.26	86.51	90.77	76.92	83.27
Bi-LSTM-CRF	92.02	83.03	87.29	90.35	80.22	84.99
Bi-Capsule-LSTM-CRF	91.62	84.04	87.67	-	-	-

Document-level vs. Sentence-level. We compared the performance of all models in both document- and sentence-level. It is shown in Table 3 that models performs better under the document-level setting, when compared to that under the sentence-level setting, justifying our assumption that document-level context information makes a difference in recognizing entities in clinical text.

Ablation Study. For further insight into the effects of each module involved in Bi-Capsule-LSTM-CRF, we perform ablation analysis over our model under the document-level setting (Table 4).

---

[5] https://github.com/svn2github/word2vec.

Table 4. Ablation study over Bi-Capsule-LSTM-CRF.

	P	R	F1
Bi-Capsule-LSTM-CRF	91.62	84.04	87.67
w\o Capsule-LSTM	92.02	83.03	87.29
w\o character-level encoding	90.14	80.31	84.94
w\o pretrained word embedding	92.83	78.06	84.80

5 Conclusion

In our study, we design a novel neural network structure called Capsule-LSTM, which combine the great expressivity of capsule network and the sequential modeling capability of long-short term memory network. Experiments over 2014 i2b2 dataset demonstrated the effectiveness of our model.

Acknowledgments. This work was partly supported by National Key Research and Development Program of China (2017YFB0802204), National Natural Science Foundation of China under U1636103, Grant 61632011, and 61876053, Key Technologies Research and Development Program of Shenzhen JSGG20170817140856618, Shenzhen Foundational Research Funding JCYJ20170307150024907.

References

1. Friedman, C., Alderson, P.O., Austin, J.H., Cimino, J.J., Johnson, S.B.: A general natural-language text processor for clinical radiology. J. Am. Med. Inform. Assoc. **1**(2), 161–174 (1994)
2. Koehler, S.B.: Symtext: A Natural Language Understanding System for Encoding Free Text Medical Data. Ph.D. thesis (1998). AAI9829757
3. Christensen, L.M., Haug, P.J., Fiszman, M.: Mplus: a probabilistic medical language understanding system. In: Proceedings of the ACL-02 Workshop on Natural Language Processing in the Biomedical Domain. BioMed 2002, Stroudsburg, PA, USA, 2002, vol. 3, pp. 29–36. Association for Computational Linguistics (2002)
4. Denny, J.C., Irani, P.R., Wehbe, F.H., Smithers, J.D., Spickard, A. Rd.: The KnowledgeMap project: development of a concept-based medical school curriculum database. In: AMIA Annual Symposium Proceedings/AMIA Symposium. AMIA Symposium, vol. 2003, p. 195 (2003)
5. Zeng, Q.T., Goryachev, S., Weiss, S., Sordo, M., Murphy, S.N., Lazarus, R.: Extracting principal diagnosis, co-morbidity and smoking status for asthma research: evaluation of a natural language processing system. BMC Med. Inform. Decis. Mak. **6**(1), 1–9 (2006)
6. Savova, G.K., et al.: Mayo clinical text analysis and knowledge extraction system (cTAKES): architecture, component evaluation and applications. J. Am. Med. Inform. Assoc. Jamia **17**(5), 507 (2010)
7. Aronson, A.R., Lang, F.: An overview of MetaMap: historical perspective and recent advances. J. Am. Med. Inform. Assoc. **17**(3), 229–236 (2015)

8. Sekine, S., Grishman, R., Shinnou, H.: A decision tree method for finding and classifying names in Japanese texts. In: Proceeding Workshop on Very Large Corpra (1998)

9. Ratinov, L., Roth, D.: Design challenges and misconceptions in named entity recognition. In: CoNll 2009: Thirteenth Conference on Computational Natural Language Learning (2009)

10. Li, Y., Bontcheva, K., Cunningham, H.: SVM based learning system for information extraction. In: Winkler, J., Niranjan, M., Lawrence, N. (eds.) DSMML 2004. LNCS (LNAI), vol. 3635, pp. 319–339. Springer, Heidelberg (2005). https://doi.org/10.1007/11559887_19

11. Lafferty, J.D., McCallum, A., Pereira, F.C.N.: Conditional random fields: probabilistic models for segmenting and labeling sequence data. In: Proceedings of the Eighteenth International Conference on Machine Learning. ICML 2001, San Francisco, CA, USA, pp. 282–289. Morgan Kaufmann Publishers Inc. (2001)

12. http://www.chokkan.org/software/crfsuite/

13. Chiu, J.P.C., Nichols, E.: Named entity recognition with bidirectional LSTM-CNNs. Comput. Sci. **4**, 357–370 (2016)

14. Yang, J., Teng, Z., Zhang, M., Zhang, Y.: Combining discrete and neural features for sequence labeling. In: Gelbukh, A. (ed.) CICLing 2016. LNCS, vol. 9623, pp. 140–154. Springer, Cham (2018). https://doi.org/10.1007/978-3-319-75477-2_9

15. Zhang Y., Yang, J.: Chinese NER using lattice LSTM. In: Proceedings of the 56th Annual Meeting of the Association for Computational Linguistics (Volume 1: Long Papers), Melbourne, Australia, July 2018, pp. 1554–1564. Association for Computational Linguistics (2018)

16. Gregoric, A.Z., Bachrach, Y., Coope S.: Named entity recognition with parallel recurrent neural networks. In: Proceedings of the 56th Annual Meeting of the Association for Computational Linguistics (Volume 2: Short Papers), Melbourne, Australia, pp. 69–74. Association for Computational Linguistics, July 2018

17. Yadav, V., Bethard, S.: A survey on recent advances in named entity recognition from deep learning models. In: Proceedings of the 27th International Conference on Computational Linguistics, Santa Fe, New Mexico, USA, pp. 2145–2158. Association for Computational Linguistics, August 2018

18. Chieu, H.L., Ng, H.T.: Named entity recognition: a maximum entropy approach using global information. In: COLING 2002: The 19th International Conference on Computational Linguistics (2002)

19. Zhou, G., Su, J.: Named entity recognition using an HMM-based chunk tagger. In: Proceedings of 40th Annual Meeting of the Association for Computational Linguistics, Philadelphia, Pennsylvania, USA, pp. 473–480. Association for Computational Linguistics, July 2002

20. Freund, Y., Schapire, R.E.: Experiments with a new boosting algorithm. In: International Conference on Machine Learning, pp. 148–156 (1996)

21. Collobert, R., Weston, J., Bottou, L., Karlen, M., Kavukcuoglu, K., Kuksa, P.P.: Natural language processing (almost) from scratch. CoRR, abs/1103.0398 (2011)

22. Huang, Z., Xu, W., Yu, K.: Bidirectional LSTM-CRF models for sequence tagging. CoRR, abs/1508.01991 (2015)

23. Ma, X., Hovy, E.: End-to-end sequence labeling via bi-directional LSTM-CNNs-CRF. In: Proceedings of the 54th Annual Meeting of the Association for Computational Linguistics (Volume 1: Long Papers), Berlin, Germany, pp. 1064–1074. Association for Computational Linguistics, August 2016

24. Santos, C.N., Guimarães, V.: Boosting named entity recognition with neural character embeddings. CoRR, abs/1505.05008 (2015)

25. Lample, G., Ballesteros, M., Subramanian, S., Kawakami, K., Dyer, C.: Neural architectures for named entity recognition. In: Proceedings of the 2016 Conference of the North American Chapter of the Association for Computational Linguistics: Human Language Technologies, San Diego, California, pp. 260–270. Association for Computational Linguistics, June 2016
26. Peters, M., Ammar, W., Bhagavatula, C., Power, R.: Semi-supervised sequence tagging with bidirectional language models. In: Proceedings of the 55th Annual Meeting of the Association for Computational Linguistics (Volume 1: Long Papers), Vancouver, Canada, pp. 1756–1765. Association for Computational Linguistics, July 2017
27. Rei, M.: Semi-supervised multitask learning for sequence labeling. In: Proceedings of the 55th Annual Meeting of the Association for Computational Linguistics (Volume 1: Long Papers), Vancouver, Canada, pp. 2121–2130. Association for Computational Linguistics, July 2017
28. Reimers, N., Gurevych, I.: Reporting score distributions makes a difference: performance study of LSTM-networks for sequence tagging. In: Proceedings of the 2017 Conference on Empirical Methods in Natural Language Processing, Copenhagen, Denmark, pp. 338–348. Association for Computational Linguistics, September 2017
29. Yang, J., Zhang, Y., Dong, F.: Neural word segmentation with rich pretraining. In: Proceedings of the 55th Annual Meeting of the Association for Computational Linguistics (Volume 1: Long Papers), Vancouver, Canada, pp. 839–849. Association for Computational Linguistics, July 2017
30. Cetoli, A., Bragaglia, S., O'Harney, A., Sloan, M.: Graph convolutional networks for named entity recognition. In: Proceedings of the 16th International Workshop on Treebanks and Linguistic Theories, Prague, Czech Republic, pp. 37–45 (2017)
31. Seyler, D., Dembelova, T., Del Corro, L., Hoffart, J., Weikum, G.: A study of the importance of external knowledge in the named entity recognition task. In: Proceedings of the 56th Annual Meeting of the Association for Computational Linguistics (Volume 2: Short Papers), Melbourne, Australia, pp. 241–246. Association for Computational Linguistics, July 2018
32. Uzuner, Ö., Luo, Y., Szolovits, P.: Evaluating the state-of-the-art in automatic de-identification. J. Am. Med. Inform. Assoc. **14**(5), 550–563 (2007)
33. Meystre, S.M., Friedlin, F.J., South, B.R., Shen, S., Samore, M.H.: Automatic de-identification of textual documents in the electronic health record: a review of recent research. BMC Med. Res. Methodol. **10**(1), 70 (2010)
34. Stubbs, A., Kotfila, C., Uzuner, Ö.: Automated systems for the de-identification of longitudinal clinical narratives. J. Biomed. Inform. **58(S)**, S11–S19 (2015)
35. Wu, Y., Jiang, M., Lei, J., Xu, H.: Named entity recognition in Chinese clinical text using deep neural network. Stud. Health Technol. Inform. **216**, 624–628 (2015)
36. Liu, Z., et al.: Entity recognition from clinical texts via recurrent neural network. BMC Med. Inform. Decis. Mak. **17**(2), 67 (2017)
37. Hochreiter, S., Schmidhuber, J.: Long short-term memory. Neural Comput. **9**(8), 1735–1780 (1997)
38. Hinton, G.E., Krizhevsky, A., Wang, S.D.: Transforming auto-encoders. In: Honkela, T., Duch, W., Girolami, M., Kaski, S. (eds.) ICANN 2011. LNCS, vol. 6791, pp. 44–51. Springer, Heidelberg (2011). https://doi.org/10.1007/978-3-642-21735-7_6
39. Sabour, S., Frosst, N., Hinton, G.E.: Dynamic routing between capsules. In: Guyon, I., et al. (eds.) Advances in Neural Information Processing Systems 30, pp. 3856–3866. Curran Associates Inc., New York (2017)

40. Kingma, D.P., Ba, J.: Adam: a method for stochastic optimization. In: 3rd International Conference on Learning Representations. ICLR 2015, San Diego, CA, USA, May 7–9, 2015, Conference Track Proceedings (2015)
41. Chinchor, N., Sundheim, B.: MUC-5 evaluation metrics. In: Fifth Message Understanding Conference (MUC-5): Proceedings of a Conference Held in Baltimore, Maryland, 25–27 August 1993

Domain Knowledge Enhanced Error Correction Service for Intelligent Speech Interaction

Yishuang Ning[1,2,3,4]([✉]), Chunxiao Xing[1,2], and Liang-Jie Zhang[3,4]

[1] Research Institute of Information Technology, Beijing National Research Center for Information Science and Technology, Tsinghua University, Beijing 100084, China
ningyishuang@126.com

[2] Department of Computer Science and Technology Institute of Internet Industry, Tsinghua University, Beijing 100084, China

[3] National Engineering Research Center for Supporting Software of Enterprise Internet Services, Shenzhen, China

[4] Kingdee Research, Kingdee International Software Group Company Limited, Shenzhen, China

Abstract. Intelligent speech interaction systems have gained great popularity in recent years. For these systems, the accuracy of automatic speech recognition (ASR) has become a key factor of determining user experience. Due to the influence of environmental noise and the diversity and complexity of natural language, the performance of ASR still cannot meet the requirements of real-world application scenarios. To improve the accuracy of ASR, in this paper, we propose a domain knowledge enhanced error correction method which first the improved phonetic editing distance to select the candidates which have the same or similar phonetics with the error segment, and then adopts language model the find the most appropriate one from the domain knowledge set as the final result. We also encapsulate the method as a service with the Flask + Gunicorn + Nginx framework to improve the high concurrency performance. Experimental results demonstrate that our proposed method outperforms the comparison methods over 48.4% in terms of accuracy and almost 20–40 times concurrency performance.

Keywords: Error correction · Domain knowledge · Speech interaction

1 Introduction

In recent years, intelligent speech interaction systems (such as Apple Siri, Microsoft Cortana, Google Now, Amazon Alexa, and Samsung or Sougou Voice Assistant, etc.) have gained popularity in all segments of people's life and work [1]. In 2018, according to Forrest Research, 25% businesses have used the conversational user interface in which speech is the most direct and important way for communication to assist the mouse-click analytic tools. Currently, these

© Springer Nature Switzerland AG 2019
D. Wang and L.-J. Zhang (Eds.): AIMS 2019, LNCS 11516, pp. 179–187, 2019.
https://doi.org/10.1007/978-3-030-23367-9_13

systems normally transcribe speeches into their corresponding texts with automatic speech recognition (ASR) techniques at first, and then use natural language processing (NLP) techniques to extract the semantic information of utterances. However, the existing ASR techniques only model from the aspects of pronunciation and grammar, ignoring the guidance of relevant domain knowledge. Besides, due to the diversity and complexity of natural language, and the differences between human dialects and habits, the accuracy of ASR is still not high enough to meet the requirements of specific application scenarios.

To address these problems, many error correction approaches have been proposed in these years. For example, Zhou et al. [2] proposed a speech recognition error detection and correction algorithm which generates 20 candidates for each individual word, and then uses a linear scoring system to score each sentence and selects the sentence with the highest score as the final result. Mangu et al. [3] proposed a transformation-based learning algorithm which uses confusion network model to detect and correct the errors. Che et al. [4] proposed a post-editing Chinese text correction and intention recognition method for the Chinese speech interaction context. However, these methods still cannot obtain good results in specific areas.

In this paper, we propose a domain knowledge enhanced error correction approach which uses words with the same or similar pronunciations from different domains as the candidates for each individual word. We then use the combination method of Chinese phonetic editing distance and language model to select the word with the highest score as the final result. Besides, to improve the concurrency performance of multiple requests, we use the Flask + Gunicorn + Nginx [5] framework to encapsulate the algorithm as an application programming interface (API), making it take full advantage of the capability of multiple cores of the CPU. Experimental results demonstrate the effectiveness and efficiency of our proposed method.

The rest of the paper is structured as follows. Section 2 makes a brief overview of the error correction methods and points our their disadvantages. Section 3 presents the proposed framework for error correction as a service in our work. Section 4 carries out an extensive of experiments to evaluate the performance of the proposed method. Section 5 summarizes the paper and gives a brief introduction to our future work.

2   Related Work

Error correction of speech recognition has become a hot topic in NLP field. Recently, researchers from both academia and industry have proposed a variety of error correction methods for speech interaction scenarios. For example, Wang et al. [6] proposed a method which combines statistics and rules to realize the translation from Chinese phonetics to actual texts. Zhou et al. [2] proposed an error detection and correction algorithm that first generates 20 candidates for each word, and then uses a linear scoring system to evaluate each sentence and select the sentence with the highest score as the actual content. However, since

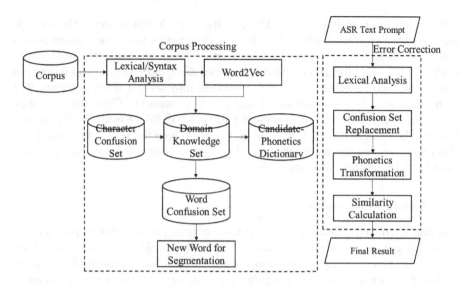

Fig. 1. Overall architecture of our proposed method.

this method only aims at specific areas, the words that can be retrieved are very limited. To solve this problem, Mangu et al. [3] proposed a transformation-based learning algorithm. In this method, a confusion network model [7] was used to detect and correct the potential errors.

Another kind of error correction algorithm is based on post-processing method [8,9]. This method adds an additional layer behind the speech recognition system to post-process the results of speech recognition. For instance, Ringger et al. [10] used a noise channel to detect and correct speech recognition results. In 2012, Bassil et al. [11] proposed a post-processing speech recognition text error correction algorithm based on Bing's online spelling recommendation. A large number of experiments in different languages verified the effectiveness of this method and improved the accuracy of text error correction. In 2016, Fujiwara et al. [12] designed a self-defined speech alphabet method to improve the speech recognition algorithm and the accuracy of word input in noisy environment. In 2018, Che et al. [4] proposed an improved phonetic editing distance [13] method to correct possible errors for the Chinese speech interaction context. However, when two candidates have the same editing distance, it will be difficult to find a suitable one.

3 Methodology

3.1 Overall Architecture

As can be seen from Fig. 1, the overall architecture of our proposed method can be divided into corpus processing phase and error correction phase. In the corpus processing phase, the utterances are first tokenized by word segmentation

[14] module. For each word, on the one hand, each character of the word is replaced by a character which has the same phonetics from the character-level confusion set to form a new word. On the other hand, the phonetics of the word is also generated to form a candidate-phonetics dictionary. In the error correction phase, the recognized text is firstly separated into several word segments. For each segment, the corresponding phonetics is generated. Then the similarity scores are calculated with the segment and each candidate from the dictionary. Finally, the candidate which has the best score is selected as the final result. In this paper, we use the weighted score of phonetic editing distance and language model [15,16] as the similarity score.

3.2   Corpus Processing

Corpus Construction. In the NLP field, corpus plays a very important role for training a model or constructing a candidate set. Although there is a huge number of universal corpora, the scales of the corpora for specific application scenarios are still very limited. To improve the accuracy of error correction, a set of text prompts that can be used in enterprise scenarios are carefully designed. This corpus contains 700 correct utterances and 196 error utterances. For the correct utterances, we further divide this corpus into four micro-scenarios, including travel application, operational data query, reimbursement and enterprise news broadcasting.

Domain Knowledge Construction. Each industry or enterprise scenario has its own unique domain knowledge [17]. This domain knowledge plays an important role in decoding the conceptual representation of user utterance for speech interaction scenarios. For each micro-scenario, to construct the relations between text prompts and core semantics, we use the dependency syntax analysis [18] to extract the core components of the utterance. We then extend the corpus with Word2Vec [4] to generate synonym words which have the same or similar semantics as the core components. Finally, the combination of the core components and their synonym words is integrated into the domain knowledge to form a specific candidate set for error correction. To improve the performance of error correction, we obtain the Chinese phonetics of each word in the domain knowledge set to form a candidate-phonetics pair dictionary at first.

Word-Level Confusion Set Generation. Since the error correction method proposed in this paper is based on word-level, the effectiveness of word segmentation will affect the accuracy of error correction. Besides, the scale of word set (called user dictionary) also plays a significant role for the main stream word segmentation algorithms such as Jieba [19] or HanLP [20] used in industrial fields. To generate a massive number of word set, we first conduct word segmentation for each utterance. Then for each segment, we replace each character with the characters which have the same or similar phonetics in the character-level confusion set, respectively. Therefore, all combinations of characters which have the same or similar phonetics with the segment will form a new word that will be put into the word-level confusion set.

Language Model Generation. When there are multiple candidates in the domain knowledge set, it will be difficult to find a suitable one. To address this problem, statistic models such as n-gram language models are usually used to evaluate the fluency of the sentence if the word is used in this case. In this paper, we use all the correct utterances to train a trigram language model with the KenLM toolkit [21].

3.3 Error Correction

For the text information output by the ASR system, we first conduct word segmentation with the same algorithm as in Sect. 3.2. To ensure the performance of word segmentation, the word-level confusion set is loaded into the word segmentation model in advance. Then we convert the text into Chinese phonetics. To prevent the impact of environmental noise and dialects, the fuzzy words are also unified. For each segment, we calculate the phonetic editing distance between the segment and each word in the domain knowledge set successively. For traditional editing distance, if the length of the two phonetics differs greatly, the distance between them cannot well represented. To solve this problem, we use the improved editing distance.

Suppose t_0 and t_i are the text segment that needs to be corrected and a word from the domain knowledge set, the distance function between t_0 and t_i can be seen in the following:

$$distance(t_0, t_i) = |len(t_0) - len(t_i)| * \left(\sum_{w \, in \, t_0} len_p(w) + \sum_{w \, in \, t_i} len_p(w) \right) / (len(t_0) + len(t_i))$$

$$(1)$$

where $len(x)$ is the number of words in x and $len_p(x)$ refers to the number of characters in phonetics of x.

Although using phonetic editing distance can usually obtain good results, when there are multiple candidates that are within the distance requirement, it will be difficult to find a suitable one. To solve this problem, we use the language model to evaluate the fluency of the sentences for each candidate further more. The word which maximize the score of the sentence will be selected as the final result.

3.4 Error Correction as a Service

To improve the concurrency of the error correction task, we use the Flask + Gunicorn + Nginx framework which has been used widely and can provide high performance in these years. As can be seen in Fig. 2, the error correction service which has used this framework is divided into 3 layers: reverse proxy layer, WSGI

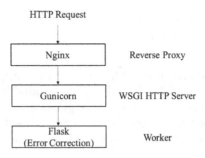

HTTP Request

| Nginx | Reverse Proxy |

| Gunicorn | WSGI HTTP Server |

| Flask (Error Correction) | Worker |

Fig. 2. The Flask + Gunicorn + Nginx error correction service framework.

HTTP server layer and worker layer. When a new HTTP request comes from the clients, it first accesses the reverse proxy layer and forwards this request to the WSGI HTTP server layer according to the routes in the Nginx server. Then the WSGI server will parse the request based on the WSGI protocol and call the Flask framework in the worker layer to handle this request. The Gunicorn server in the WSGI layer is in fact a Python WSGI HTTP server for UNIX. It is broadly compatible with various web frameworks and has high scalability and performance so that it can handle multiple requests with high concurrency. Finally, the Flask framework in the work layer will instantiate multiple Flask instances to handle the request for error correction and return the final results to the clients.

4   Experiments

4.1   Experimental Setup

Data Set. We established a benchmark data set from a real-world intelligent speech interaction system for enterprise application scenarios, XiaoK Digital Speech Assistant, for error correction. The raw data set includes 960 Mandarin utterances recorded in 2018. To evaluate the accuracy of our method, we invite three well-trained human labelers to mark the correct sentence of each utterance. To address the inconsistency issue, if the labelers had different opinions, they would start a discussion about the inconsistent parts until reach an agreement.

Comparison Methods. We designed two machine learning methods to compare the performance with our proposed method: (1) character-level language model (language model); (2) our proposed method which is implemented only with the Flask framework (flask); (3) our proposed method which is implemented with the Flask + Gunicorn + Nginx framework (flask + gunicorn + nginx).

Evaluation Metrics. Like other NLP tasks, we evaluate the correction performance in terms of the accuracy with sentence level. For the whole data set, 700 utterances are used for constructing the model while 196 utterances for testing.

4.2 Experimental Results

Error Correction Performance with Different Methods. Table 1 shows the accuracy of error correction using different comparison methods. From the results, we can see that the performance of using our method is better than that of using other machine learning model. The reason might be that the method can better leverage the domain knowledge for error correction. By comparison the similarity between the segment and the candidates, the method can select the most suitable one effectively.

Table 1. Error correction performance with different methods.

Methods	Accuracy with sentence level
language model	0.49
flask	**0.95**
flask + gunicorn + nginx	**0.95**

Concurrency Performance with Different Methods. To demonstrate the usability of our method in real-world enterprise scenarios, we also compare the concurrency performance with different methods. For each method, 10 threads are used to start the error correction service and 100 simulated concurrent clients are started to send requests to the error correction service simultaneously. Table 2 lists the experimental results. As can be seen from this table, by using the Flask + Gunicorn + Nginx framework, our method can have much higher concurrency performance with other methods (almost 40 and 20 times faster than the language model and the method only with the flask framework, respectively).

Table 2. Concurrency performance with different methods.

Methods	Average response time (s)
language model	6.858
flask	3.324
flask + gunicorn + nginx	**0.178**

5 Conclusion and Future Work

This paper investigates implementing error correction as a service in intelligent speech interaction systems for enterprise scenarios. In this paper, we propose a domain knowledge enhanced error correction approach which first adopts improved phonetic editing distance to find the candidates which have the same or similar phonetics with the segment from the error text prompt, and then uses language model to further select the most suitable one as the final result. Besides, we also encapsulate the error correction task as a service with the Flask + Gunicorn + Nginx framework. Experimental results indicate that compared with other methods, our method can not only have much higher accuracy, the concurrency performance is also much higher.

Future work will be dedicated to reducing the ratio of the correct segments that are wrongly corrected.

Acknowledgements. This work is partially supported by the technical projects No. c1533411500138 and No. 2017YFB0802700. This work is also supported by NSFC (91646202). This work is also supported by NSFC (91646202), the 1000-Talent program and the China Postdoctoral Science Foundation (2019M652949).

References

1. Ning, Y.S., et al.: Multi-task deep learning for user intention understanding in speech interaction systems. In: Proceedings of AAAI Conference on Artificial Intelligence, San Francisco (2017)
2. Zhou, Z.Y., Meng, H., Lo, W.K.: A multi-pass error detection and correction framework for Mandarin LVCSR. In: Proceedings of the International Conference on Spoken Language Processing (ICSLP), pp. 1646–1649 (2006)
3. Mangu, L., Padmanabhan, M.: Error corrective mechanisms for speech recognition. In: Proceedings of the IEEE International Conference on Acoustics, Speech, and Signal Processing (ICASSP), pp. 29–32 (2001)
4. Che, J., Chen, H., Zeng, J., Zhang, L.J.: A Chinese text correction and intention identification method for speech interactive context. In: Proceedings of the 2018 International Conference on AI & Mobile Services (AIMS) (2018)
5. Flask Application Example 3 - Construct Web Services through Nginx+Gunicorn+Flask, 12 April 2018. https://www.jianshu.com/p/d71d6d-793aaa
6. Zhang, R., Wang, Z.: Chinese pinyin to text translation technique with error correction used for continuous speech recognition. Tsinghua University (1997)
7. Bertoldi, N., Zens, R., Federico, M.: Speech translation by confusion network decoding. In: Proceedings of IEEE International Conference on Acoustics, Speech and Signal Processing (ICASSP) (2007)
8. Frankel, A., Santisteban, A.: System and method for post processing speech recognition output. U.S. Patent 7,996,223 (2011)
9. Xu, Y., Du, J., Huang, Z., Dai, L.R., Lee, C.H.: Multi-objective learning and mask-based post-processing for deep neural network based speech enhancement. arXiv preprint arXiv:1703.07172 (2017)
10. Ringger, E.K., Allen, J.F.: Error correction via a post-processor for continuous speech recognition. In: Proceedings of IEEE International Conference on Acoustics, Speech and Signal Processing (ICASSP), pp. 427–430 (1996)
11. Bassil, Y., Alwani, M.: OCR post-processing error correction algorithm using Google online spelling suggestion. arXiv preprint arXiv:1204.0191 (2012)
12. Fujiwara, K.: Error correction of speech recognition by custom phonetic alphabet input for ultra-small devices. In: Proceedings of CHI Conference Extended Abstracts on Human Factors in Computing Systems, pp. 104–109 (2016)

13. Pucher, M., Türk, A., Ajmera, J., Fecher, N.: Phonetic distance measures for speech recognition vocabulary and grammar optimization. In: Proceedings of the 3rd Congress of the Alps Adria Acoustics Association, September 2007
14. Chen, X., Qiu, X., Zhu, C., Liu, P., Huang, X.: Long short-term memory neural networks for Chinese word segmentation. In: Proceedings of the 2015 Conference on Empirical Methods in Natural Language Processing, pp. 1197–1206 (2015)
15. Kim, Y., Jernite, Y., Sontag, D., Rush, A.M.: Character-aware neural language models. In: Proceedings of AAAI Conference on Artificial Intelligence (AAAI), March 2016
16. Ballinger, B.M., Schalkwyk, J., Cohen, M.H., Allauzen, C.G.L.: Language model selection for speech-to-text conversion. U.S. Patent 9,495,127 (2016)
17. Stewart, R., Ermon, S.: Label-free supervision of neural networks with physics and domain knowledge. In: Proceedings of AAAI Conference on Artificial Intelligence (AAAI) (2017)
18. Ye, Z.L., Zhao, H.X.: Syntactic word embedding based on dependency syntax and polysemous analysis. Front. Inf. Technol. Electr. Eng. **19**(4), 524–535 (2018)
19. Jieba Chinese Word Segmentation, 05 March 2018. https://github.com/fxsjy/jieba
20. Python Interface of Natural Language Processing Toolkit-HanLP, 05 March 2018. https://github.com/hankcs/pyhanlp
21. KenLM: Faster and Smaller Language Model Queries, 20 March 2018. https://github.com/kpu/kenlm

Author Index

Printed in the United States
by Bookmasters

Printed in the United States
By Bookmasters